"To Love the Wind and the Rain"

"To Love the Wind and the Rain"

AFRICAN AMERICANS AND
ENVIRONMENTAL HISTORY

EDITED BY

Dianne D. Glave and Mark Stoll

University of Pittsburgh Press

Published by the University of Pittsburgh Press, Pittsburgh, PA 15260

Copyright © 2006, University of Pittsburgh Press

All rights reserved

Manufactured in the United States of America

Printed on acid-free paper

10 9 8 7 6 5 4 3 2 1

Library of Congress Cataloging-in-Publication Data

To love the wind and the rain : African Americans and environmental history
/ edited by Dianne D. Glave and Mark Stoll.

    p.   cm.

   Includes bibliographical references and index.

   ISBN 0-8229-4275-5 (acid-free paper) — ISBN 0-8229-5899-6 (pbk. : acid-
free paper)

   1. African Americans—History. 2. African Americans—Social conditions.
3. African Americans—Civil rights. 4. Indigenous peoples—Ecology—
United States. 5. Human beings—Effect of environment on—United States.
6. Environmental justice—United States. 7. Social justice—United States. 8.
United States—Race relations. 9. United States—Environmental conditions.
I. Glave, Dianne D. II. Stoll, Mark, 1954-

  E185.T65 2006

  973'.0496073—dc22   2005020899

CONTENTS

FOREWORD

CAROLYN MERCHANT

President Theodore Roosevelt was on a ten-day bear hunt in the dense canebrakes of the Mississippi Delta in 1907. "I must see a live bear the first day," he told his guides. Holt Collier, African American hunter par excellence, and his trained dogs set out to track the quarry. In advance of the party, Collier trailed and drove a bear into the lake and, with his best dog, plunged into the water: "I slicked up the rope with the blue mud from the bottom. . . . I kicked the bear and he stuck his head up. While he was shaking the water from his eyes, I dropped the rope over his head, moved back about ten feet or so, and tied it to a tree." When Roosevelt reached the lake, he too ran into the water after the bear. "Don't shoot him while he's tied," Collier admonished the president. Despite the urging of the others to go for the kill, Roosevelt complied. The lives of the bear-hounds, who would have charged the dying, desperate bear, and the honor code of the sports hunter were at stake. Not until the last two days of the hunt did the guides corner a fleeing bear, and Roosevelt finally took his trophy.[1]

Roosevelt, in his own separate account of the hunt, describes Holt Collier as a former slave with "all the dignity of an African chief," who "for half a century . . . had been a bear-hunter, having killed or assisted in killing over three thousand bears." Together the two narratives—one oral, one written—form sources for a multistoried, multicultural environmental history. Collier the tracker and hunter knew intimately the wildlife of the impenetrable canebrakes, the formidable hanging vines and creepers of the bayous, and the habits of bears of all ages in all seasons. Roosevelt the wilderness writer and conservationist created the dramatic setting of the giant cypress swamp, filled with dangerous water moccasins, elusive wildcats, and striking ivory-billed woodpeckers. Together the two hunters paint a composite picture of nature in a local environment, its natural resources, and the relationships between blacks and whites.[2]

"*To Love the Wind and the Rain*" draws on such sources to craft an environmental history of African Americans and nature. Here blacks are the main actors in American development. Exploring responses to the natural world from slave subsistence to environmental justice and from urbanization to spirituality, the historians in this volume portray the ways that blacks lived and worked within larger forces of social oppression, racism, and activism. From slavery to Jim Crow segregation to the eras of civil rights and environmental justice, the authors guide us through a multitude of periods and places, skillfully blending theory with practice while building an environmental history of African America. They explore complex questions about African American access to and responses to a nature that is variously constructed as pristine and free, owned and segregated, or polluted and dangerous.

Along the way, we meet and share glimpses into the lives of unique and memorable individuals. Slave John Smith hunted rabbits, coons, and possums with his dog in North Carolina. Slave Jane Arrington and her sisters cooked the possums the men of the family brought home. Sally Moore, a Progressive-era women's club president, planted thirty-four different vegetables on her truck farm and exhibited a ten-pound cabbage in a home demonstration gardening contest. Ethylene Seastrunk, wife of a turpentine worker, wanted her family to leave the poverty of the backwoods camps, but was afraid she would miss the old trees and woods too much.

We also gain insights into the ways the environment affected the lives of blacks and shaped their actions toward it. Fourteen-year-old Eugene Williams, escaping the summer heat on a beach used by Chicago blacks, drowned in Lake Michigan when he was hit in the head by a white boy's rock, setting off the 1919 Chicago race riot and demands for black access to beaches and parks. Later in the century, civil rights leader Eugene Burnett was able to move out of Harlem to a Long Island suburb surrounded by woods and with a reputation for sending its children to good colleges. And in the 1990s, geologist Patrick Barnes, owner of an African American environmental consulting firm, provided expertise on the detoxification of the Warren County, North Carolina, landfill. Such individuals and their stories exemplify a spectrum of actions and reactions toward nature.

African American history exhibits a dialectical relationship between oppression and racism on one hand and resistance and activism on the other. The essays fall into three main periods: slavery, post–Civil War segregation, and the post–World War II civil rights and environmental justice movements.

The first Africans arrived at Jamestown, Virginia, in 1619. By 1640, the first black was sentenced to lifetime servitude. During the ensuing three centuries of development of the North American continent, slaves encountered brutal treatment at the hands of overseers and plantation masters. Yet within the slave system, in both the South and the North, blacks made substantial contributions to American history, not only by introducing foods and cuisine and transporting planting and production methods to the New World, but through their music, poetry, and science. The authors in this volume argue that the experiences and memories of blacks with slavery honed their abilities to defy authority while helping to establish a measure of control over their own livelihoods. Instead of receiving liberal, democratic values from emancipation and later from the civil rights movement, African Americans used their experiences and memories of slavery to create new values and identities for themselves.

After the Civil War (1861–1865), Jim Crow laws divided neighborhoods, schools, and businesses, and the Supreme Court's 1896 *Plessy v. Ferguson* decision established the "separate but equal" doctrine that reinforced segregation. During the ensuing decades of racial oppression, blacks aided other blacks in developing agriculture, documenting violence, and organizing exoduses to the North and West. In the urban North, many found jobs in industries and formed supportive communities, while also experiencing the effects of living in poor, segregated, redlined neighborhoods. The authors demonstrate that during the so-called "Progressive era"—in which Jim Crow segregation prevailed—African American women established their own identities and used their activism to improve the conditions of their lives and to garner respect for their race and gender. African American men who worked in nature, on the other hand, found it difficult to perceive of the woods as a place to spend leisure time, instead seeing it as both a home and a place from which they hoped to escape and leave their demeaning work. By contrast, middle-class blacks who sought out nature in parks or moved to suburbs had to overcome racism and sometimes violence, but the process of resistance strengthened racial identities that may ultimately have offered greater access to and appreciation of nature.

World War II and the postwar industrial buildup provided jobs for African Americans and opportunities to escape from slums and poor neighborhoods, but those very opportunities came with a toxic toll. Black communities often suffered the health effects of chemical discharges into waterways and the siting of landfills and dumps in minority communities. The civil rights movement of the 1960s challenged segregation and promoted school and workplace integration, while the environmental justice movement of the 1980s and 1990s carried those emancipatory struggles into communities and homes threatened by toxic pollution. Here the authors reveal complex connections between the civil rights and environmental justice movements. Not only did the experiences of the civil rights movement aid black and white activists to form coalitions to protest toxic landfills and demand environmental cleanups, they also led to stronger identity politics that sometimes worked to undermine those very coalitions. Both activists and decision makers had to deal with racial politics and hence with the long shadow of slavery and the legacy of segregation. Throughout these events, the shared religious experiences and the roles of churches in the struggles for freedom and justice contributed a deep moral sense to the movements for freedom and to the new history.

The stories of the African Americans in this volume must be read in the context of the enormity of this oppressive history and the struggles of individuals and communities to overcome its consequences. Set against this historical backdrop, the stories herein become more remarkable as the authors illuminate the vitality of their subjects' lives, the significance of their achievements, and the successes and failures of their work together. In so doing, the writers not only show us how to write a new kind of African American environmental history, but illustrate the ways that writing history can itself become a moral act.

ACKNOWLEDGMENTS

Three journals were kind enough to give us permission to reprint the following articles: Martin V. Melosi, "Equity, Eco-racism and Environmental History," *Environmental History Review* 19 (Fall, 1995): 1–16, 194–211; Dianne D. Glave, "'A Garden So Brilliant with Colors, So Original in Its Design': Rural African American Women, Gardening, Progressive Reform, and the Foundation of an African American Environmental Perspective," *Environmental History* vol. 8, no. 3, (2003) 395–411; and Dianne D. Glave, "Black Environmental Liberation Theology: The Historical and Theological Roots of Environmental Justice Activism by the African American Church," *Griot: The Journal of Black Heritage* 25 no. 2 (Fall 2004).

The Center for Bioenvironmental Research at Tulane and Xavier Universities, and the J. Aron Charitable Foundation deserve thanks for their support through an Aron Senior Research Fellowship awarded to Dianne D. Glave, which was critical for completing the final stages of publishing this collection.

"To Love the Wind and the Rain"

🌿1

African American Environmental History

AN INTRODUCTION

DIANNE D. GLAVE and MARK STOLL

> Southern trees bear a strange fruit
> Blood on the leaves and blood at the root
> Black bodies swinging in the Southern breeze
> Strange fruit hanging from the poplar trees
>
> Pastoral scene of the gallant South
> The bulging eyes and the twisted mouth
> Scent of magnolias sweet and fresh
> Then the sudden smell of burning flesh
>
> —"Strange Fruit," sung by Billie Holiday; music and
> lyrics by Abel Meeropol (better known as Lewis Allan)

"To Love the Wind and the Rain": African Americans and Environmental History evolved from a frustrating sense that African American perceptions of the environment—illustrated by metaphors of nature as lynching in "Strange Fruit"—remain invisible for the most part.[1] Critical elements in the development of American environmental history, particularly the complexities of race, ethnicity, gender, and class in which African Americans have had to live, work, and play, are revealed in the songs and stories of many lives.

One such story is that of Thomas Calhoun Walker, an African American who was the Advisor and Consultant of Negro Affairs for the Virginia Emergency Relief Administration in the Richmond office during World War I. Walker launched several environmental programs in the African American community, working to promote public recreation spaces, encourage cleanliness in homes, advocate gardening, and control rats on wharves. In each one of his endeavors, notions of race, ethnicity, gender, and class shaped his assumptions and his approach. For example, across the country throughout the first half of the twentieth century, segregation limited African Americans' access to parks and other public spaces. Walker's office responded locally by providing a model recreation center with plans to build similar facilities throughout the state. This project gave African American children admission to a swimming pool and a ball field, and, by extension, the outdoors.

Walker and his office also launched a visiting housekeepers program that employed African American women to teach hygiene. Yet it reinforced stereotypical gender and ethnic roles in an inequitable social hierarchy, since these women cleaned their own homes at night and whites' bathrooms and kitchens by day. Each woman visited six African American family cabins, promoted standards of sanitation and cleanliness prescribed according to middle-class standards, and put forward a model of housekeeping designed to reduce germs.

As part of a plan to raise more food for the war effort, Walker campaigned for rural gardening, but he found his work had to overcome racism institutionalized in a local government controlled by whites:

> I had always preached, year in and year out, that *if* the Negro was actually shown the advantage of a garden and *if* this idea was itself planted and made to take root by providing teachers who would cultivate it and show the owners how to make a success of it, the plan might work. . . . I went about talking gardens to individuals who were key people and those who were just keyhole owners of uncultivated tracts, to church groups and others wherever I went and whatever else I was doing. . . . So, in every case, it was the white people who were put in charge of the gardening movement for the Negroes.

Local governments did not think African Americans capable of supervising successful programs in their communities. Ultimately, however, Walker shifted the supervisory responsibilities to African Americans with gardening expertise, since he found that inexperienced whites impeded progress in the gardens.[2]

Walker's grimmest project, a rat-catching scheme on the wharves of Virginia, clearly illustrates how race, gender, and class discrimination worked against poor African American women. Walker and his office hired women with narrow employment options to trap rats consuming food on the wharves intended for American soldiers on the European front. The women flushed the rats out with sticks and led dogs to devour the pests. The fact that such work was not offered to a white man or woman, or to an African American man, reflects the prevailing racism and sexism that these rat catchers faced. Local, well-heeled African Americans rejected the proposal, arguing that the work would humiliate and demean their women—an unusual contention for the period. Yet Walker pushed his plan to publicize "a dangerous and disease-carrying plague that the public officials had too long taken for granted," reflecting the more prevalent chasm between a middle class comprised of men like Walker, who delegated work, and working-class rat catchers, who labored for others.[3] He declared the project a success, claiming that it had eliminated disease-ridden rats, saved food for the troops, and most importantly, at least to Walker, provided wages to African American women and heightened their self-esteem.

Like Walker's endeavors, the work of Mary L. Oberlin also served as an inspiration for this collection, specifically the title, *"To Love the Wind and the Rain."* Her article, "Learn to Live on the Farm," appeared in the April 8, 1916, *Negro Farmer and Messenger* and promoted Progressivism for African American farmers:

> Successful living in any place depends upon the spiritual and mental attitude. One must be in sympathy with the natural environment in which he finds himself. The family on the farm must have a feeling of permanency. They must believe that it is the best place for them to live, the ideal place for a home, the place where the children have the best opportunity to develop strong bodies, sound minds, and the characteristics that make for efficiency. They must be open minded and try to learn whatever they can that will improve farm conditions. . . . When they are convinced of these things and have learned to love the wind and the rain, the growing things, the birds, and all the rest, the dawn, the early morning ordor [sic], and to find each part of the day, each twilight, and each nightfall filled with wonders, they will know how to live on a farm and how to make a living on a farm will be less of a problem.

Through a relationship of body, mind, and nature, Oberlin promoted an agricultural evangelism of practical conservation, recommending a mixture of a farmer's conservation of the soil with a preservationist's appreciation of warbling birds, towering trees, and cool breezes.

This volume expands on the conservationist and preservationist ideas behind Walker's efforts and Oberlin's observations, drawing upon the racial, ethnic, gender, and class implications contributing to the fragmentary scholarship and new historiography of African American environmental history. Until recently, race in America has been defined according to such common physical attributes as skin phenotype. Historically, American social and cultural constructions of race used or distorted science to categorize and thereby oppress people because of their skin color and facial features—even though all humans were and are fundamentally and genetically the same, with only small variations. Many early-twentieth-century African Americans, ironically, identified themselves as "race" men and women, imbuing the word with meaning that empowered them and inverting the racist interpretation and manipulation of the term as used by many whites. The African Americans who did this, notably Ida B. Wells-Barnett and W. E. B. DuBois, transformed the language of inequality to equality and served as models for civil rights activists who dismantled segregation during the mid-twentieth century.

"Ethnicity," another complex word central to contemporary African American studies and African American history scholars, is a "consciousness of solidarity beyond real or fictitious kinship, based on shared symbols or images."[4] Individuals have, historically, chosen to identify with a particular ethnic group or been categorized by others based on many and sometimes muddied variables, including country of origin, history, and religion. As a result, ethnicity remains as problematic and contested as race. African Americans differed from others in the African diaspora because of assimilation into the American mainstream: most had roots in slavery, whereas others arrived in the twentieth-century wave of African and Caribbean immigrants; most were Protestant in the African Methodist Episcopal and black Baptist traditions, while some were members of the Nation of Islam and Seventh-day Adventist church. The contributors to this collection interpret race and ethnicity, and their expressions in racism, as fundamental categories by which to understand the control, uses, and abuses of the environment in agriculture, industry, urban parks, homes, and gardens. These categories reflect diversity among people of African descent, distinctiveness from the white mainstream, and syncretism of African and American influences.

The modern language of feminism and womanism lends tools for interpreting historical experiences of African American women. Such language helps scholars recount the stories of women both burdened by and defiant toward sexism and racism. Although such African American women as Fannie Lou Hamer and Rosa Parks acted as essential links in their communities and families, men often relegated women to invisible or diminished supporting roles that reinforced inequitable gender roles. Hamer lived in such a world—she spearheaded voter registration in Indianola, Mississippi, only to be beaten by African American prison guards directed by whites defending segregation. Marginalized in the male-dominated civil rights and black nationalism movements, and often barred from the ranks of the women's rights movement by its white and privileged architects, some African American women turned to black feminism as early as the 1960s. Black feminism became a politicized means for seeking sex/gender, race/ethnicity, and class equity in the public realm, particularly in the workplace, school, and politics.

Alice Walker coined the post–civil rights and postmodern term "womanism,"—depending on one's politics, a counterpart or alternative to black feminism—from the nineteenth-century word "womanish." As language-turned-into-practice, womanism expanded the meaning of feminism to embrace African American women, families, children, men, the church, and community. Walker defined a "womanist" this way: "A woman who loves other women, sexually and/or nonsexually. Appreciates and prefers women's culture, women's emotional flexibility (values tears as natural counterbalance of laughter), and women's strength. Sometimes loves individual men, sexually and/or nonsexually. Committed to survival and wholeness of entire people, male and female. Not a separatist, except periodically, for health." Long have such African American women as Sojourner Truth and Ida B. Wells-Barnett expressed a nascent feminism and womanism. As freedom fighters for women's rights and suffrage, Truth and Wells-Barnett were feminists. As caretakers, they were also womanists, serving "the African American church, the community, the family, and the larger society" of women, men, and children.[5] From an environmental perspective, African American women expressed feminism when they actively sought to clean up urban environments by promoting and improving sanitation through the black women's club movement in very public roles on behalf of the community.[6]

Class shaped the African American experience further, as African Americans labored for life, for food, for clothing, for housing, for leisure. Slaves were forced into unpaid labor in fields and kitchens. After the Civil War, former slaves worked in an environment of racism, violence, and segregation. In the late nineteenth and early twentieth centuries they were primarily rural, working-class sharecroppers and domestics living only somewhat better than their enslaved predecessors in the American South. During the Great Black Migration, many African Americans escaped a neo-slavery of southern peonage to work in northern industry, along with a small professional class of teachers, doctors, and lawyers.

"To Love the Wind and the Rain" builds upon the first wave of the historiography of African Americans and the environment, itself part of a broader American environmental historiography. Donald Worster defined environmental history in his widely cited comments, printed in "A Roundtable: Environmental History": "The field of environmental history began to take shape in the 1970s, as conferences on the global predicament were assembling and popular environmentalist movements were gathering momentum.... Its goal is to deepen our understanding of how humans have been affected by their natural environment through time, and conversely and perhaps more importantly in view of the present global predicament, how they have affected that environment and with what results."[7]

The nascent African American environmental historiography owes much to environmental historians Mart A. Stewart, Nicholas Proctor, and Andrew Hurley, who have documented under-, lower-, and working-class perspectives of slaves, sharecroppers, and industrial workers against the backdrop of fields, forests, and smokestacks. Stewart's *"What Nature Suffers to Groe": Life, Labor, and Landscape on the Georgia Coast, 1680–1920* explores how the cultivation of rice had distinct connotations for slaves and slaveholders. Stewart argues "that planters used the environment and appropriated knowledge about it to reinforce their own class interests, and that slaves created counterstrategies to promote their own class interests."[8] The daily experiences of slaves and share-croppers, slaveholders and landlords came together in an untidy tangle within a southern agricultural system in which whites exploited African American labor to work their land and plant their crops for their profit. Although caught within this inequitable system, African Americans skillfully refashioned Georgia's environment according to the culturally distinctive practices of planting and harvesting learned in Africa and preserved under slavery. Never passive or waiting, nature resisted human encroachment with pests, weeds, and creeping woods, always pressing to take back cultivated fields.

In *Bathed in Blood: Hunting and Mastery in the Old South,* Proctor, like Stewart, examines the meaning of labor and the environment in the South. Slaves and slaveholders did not hunt in "an atmosphere of egalitarian camara-derie," according to Proctor. The slave system kept African Americans virtually invisible as hunter-slave-workers, exploitable human resources that buttressed the masculine recreation of the antebellum slaveholder. In the tradition of the heroic narrative, slaveholders hunted at their leisure, pointing and shooting at wild game. Behind the heroic role of the hunter-slaveholder was hidden the backbreaking work of slaves, lasting long after the final gunshot. African Americans "hauled, tracked, cooked, cleaned, and chopped," and game almost magically appeared at the back door of the big house, or furs materialized to cloak the shoulders of the slaveholder and his family.[9] Such an inequitable re-lationship between the leisure of the slaveholder and the labor of the slave was of course an oppressive means of controlling the bodies and labors of African Americans. Yet slaves asserted their autonomy, snatching back some power by hunting independently to supplement the family's meager slave rations, sell meat and fur for profit, and present gifts to other slaves. All of these actions were means of cementing their status and role in slave communities.

Some descendants of these slaves and sharecroppers traveled north seek-ing better lives, only to face segregated industrial employment, as illustrated in Hurley's *Environmental Inequalities: Class, Race, and Industrial Pollution in Gary Indiana, 1945–1980.* Hurley explains that environmental "haves" and "have nots"—with the white middle class most favored, followed by European immigrants, and people of color such as African Americans bringing up the rear—vied for limited environmental resources and access to environmental amenities, essential elements of better standards of living in polluted postwar Gary, Indiana. Hurley measures the impact of social and racial status on each of these groups, testing "liberal capitalism's ability to reconcile competing environmental objectives and, indeed, its ability to balance the imperatives of industrial growth and social welfare." African Americans competed in an inequitably parceled urban environment for equal access to recreation in the green spaces of parks and on the waters of polluted Lake Michigan; for promotion and upward mobility to safer workplaces in industrial plants; and for decent housing some distance from industrial pollution that sullied curtains, walls, and clothing. Hurley notes that, historically, African Americans concerned themselves little with protecting endangered animal and plant species, unlike some middle- and upper-class whites. Instead, they worried about the poor quality of urban life, especially inadequate sanitation, inferior housing, and disease-ridden pests.[10]

Drawn from history, ecology, economics, geography, and other disciplines, environmental history has always been interdisciplinary. In keeping with this tradition, historians of African American environmental history can become more interdisciplinary still by looking to the sources and methodology of African American studies. In the chapter "Stranger," in her novel *Love*, Toni Morrison draws on different disciplines of African American studies as she interprets the environment as a naturalist, novelist, and historian. She describes The Settlement, an impoverished mountain village populated by beaten-down, underachieving African Americans during World War I in Anywhere, U.S.A. In one passage, in prose one might find in a nature writer's journal, Junior Vivian, a young African American girl, races through the woods to escape punishment by her uncles: "She found herself in the kind of wood lumbermen salivate over. Pecans the size of which had not been seen since the twenties. Maples boasting six and seven trunk-size arms. Locusts, butternut, white cedar, ash. Healthy trees mixed with sick ones. Huge black cauliflowers of disease grew on some. Others looked healthy until a wind, light and playful, ruffled their crown. Then they racked and fell like coronary victims, copper and gold meal poring from the break."[11] In this twisted paean to the woods—in the tradition of the African American novel, couched in history, chanted in spiritual tones, and pervaded by the disarray of nature—Morrison shows historians how they can expand environmental history through the interdisciplinary model of African American studies, which blends history, religious studies, and ecology. As just a few examples, the slave narratives of the Works Progress Administration, the writings of W. E. B. DuBois, and the art of Jacob

Lawrence—the historical, the literary, and the artistic, along with other disciplines—are sources that historians can integrate into African American environmental history, a subdiscipline with much to be written.

In this budding African American environmental historiography, *"To Love
the Wind and the Rain"* explores the relationship of African Americans to their
surroundings with essays on rural experiences, urban and suburban life, and
environmental justice. The final essay looks to the future at ways to expand
upon African American environmental history by exploring the African
diaspora and interdisciplinary perspectives. These contributions complement
well-known African American historiographical themes of race, ethnicity, and
gender with an environmental theme as a necessary component in the narratives of African American lives.

2

Slavery and the Origins of
African American Environmentalism

As the literature on environmental racism and justice continues to flourish, scholars need to look more closely at the deep history of the relationship of African Americans to the environment. The environmental values and political tactics and goals of African American environmentalism reconfigure themselves with each issue, but the core character of environmental values and tactics has a quality that can be illuminated by a study of the past experience of African Americans and the environment. Scholars now recognize that an understanding of African American political culture requires an understanding of the long history of slavery in the United States. African Americans did not simply receive democratic values from their liberators at the end of slavery. African American political culture was not created by the leadership of the civil rights movement, nor did it gain its credibility by the long-delayed assistance of the federal government in the destruction of apartheid in the American South. African Americans acquired a set of political values through their own efforts, not by way of the dispensation of others, in a process that has its roots in the experience of African Americans in slavery. An understanding of these values and this political culture must look from slavery outward.[1]

Environmental racism and African American environmentalism in the American South also have a long history, which is intricately bound up with and has some of its origins in the history of slavery. First of all, the history of slavery in North America shaped the history of the environment in North America in three ways: slavery made it possible for southern agriculturists to

9

wrest profit from an environment that was at first strange and continually challenging to them; slaves who were African or African American developed their own uses of the environment that were a hybrid of African traditions and practices produced by the condition of bondage and that sometimes produced a struggle for access to shared resources; and slavery shaped the environmental attitudes and values of both masters and slaves. The origins of conservation and environmental thought for both groups emerged from the experience of slavery and the kind of agriculture the labor of slaves supported.

The history of slavery in North America was from beginning to end deeply rooted in the environment in which it developed. By the mid-eighteenth century, colonists in British America had created a characteristic landscape of plantations, villages, small farms, and cowpens in Virginia, North Carolina, South Carolina, and Georgia. This landscape was lifted from the forests and swamps literally on the backs of slaves. They girdled and fired trees, removed stumps and cultivated land, herded cattle on the open range in South Carolina and Georgia, erected the hydraulic systems of banks, canals, and drains for tidewater rice plantations in the southeastern Atlantic tidewater, and planted, tended, harvested, and processed plantation crops throughout the colonies.

In 1793, Eli Whitney's invention of the cotton gin made it possible to accomplish by machine the difficult task of separating seeds from fiber in cotton bolls. This, in conjunction with the resilience of the plant itself and the expansion of a market for cotton among British and, later, American textile manufacturers, rapidly made short-strand cotton the most important staple crop in the South and assured the expansion of the cotton system—and along with it, slavery. The spread of row-crop monoculture etched the plantation landscape into a larger proportion of the region, and the Cotton South took shape. By the 1820s and 1830s, production had become significant west of the Appalachians—in the rich prairie lands of central Alabama and Mississippi, on alluvial river bottoms, and on uplands throughout the region—and this area became southern in character. In the South, the relationship between cultivation and culture—that is, between slavery, plantation agriculture, and environments that favored cotton and other plantation crops with long growing seasons and a regional culture—became tightly bound.

Slave owners who had labor to marshal dominated the making of southern landscapes and stood to gain from the riches these landscapes produced. Slaves lived closer to the ground and often understood southern crops and southern environments better than their masters. Though the South was not a neo-Africa, some southern environments had more in common with West African ones than anything European colonists knew or understood. Slaves who had cultivated rice in West African rivers brought knowledge about and skills for rice growing with them and then helped create the highly productive and profitable low-country rice industry. More generally, slaves' work accustomed them to a closer view of the cultivated environment than their masters. They were aware, from row to row, of the progress of the plants during the growing season. They put seeds in the ground and covered them with their feet, stirred and tilled the earth when hoeing, and bent down over rice stalks or moved slowly down rows of cotton during harvest. Their hands experienced crop cultures from dawn to dusk, from day to day, and from the ground up. Masters sometimes even depended on the firsthand—and often more tangible—perceptions of leading slaves to make decisions about crop regimens. At the same time, when a storm came up, slaves went in the fields or out on the levees or rice banks to do repairs and salvage crops. They endured suffocating heat—especially in the low-country rice swamps or in the damp thickets of Lower Mississippi sugar plantations—while doing the heavy labor of tending and harvesting the crops. Slaves were also sometimes responsible for cleaning out the small but destructive imperfections of the crops and for ridding the fields of the pests, weeds, and insects that periodically have population explosions in single-crop environments. Masters and overseers rode or strolled along the borders of the fields and sometimes down the rows, but the slaves who turned the soil, tended the plants, and harvested the crops acquired a firsthand knowledge of the cultivated landscape on the plantation. Some masters or overseers had direct experience with agricultural work themselves, and on smaller farms, masters and slaves sometimes had a kind of "sawbucks equality" that put them on opposite ends of the same understanding of agricultural work. But in general, slaves knew the ground under their feet on a day-to-day basis better than those who managed them.[2]

Slaves were essential to the expansion and profitability of the staple-crop economy. It rested upon their labor. But slaves were not simply passive participants in an economic relationship; neither did they commonly defy the domination of their masters by massive acts of resistance. Instead, they actively negotiated small portions of independence and autonomy from the master-slave relationship. Often, the small freedoms they acquired—the right to grow gardens, hunt in the surrounding woods, keep livestock, or market some of their own goods, for example—were achieved in part by way of their knowledge of the environment in which they worked. When they manipulated planters by manipulating the crops in ways that compromised productivity, they applied the precise knowledge that they had of the crop regimens in which they worked. Most of slaves' waking hours were spent in labor on the land, but this labor gave them knowledge of the land that was intimate and precise, and in turn had material, social, and political usefulness.

Many slaves translated this keen awareness and precise knowledge of the environment into a landscape of subsistence and small profit. They commonly planted small gardens near their cabins, on provision grounds allocated to them by masters, or even in "bottom places" in the swamps or woods surrounding the plantations. Here they raised small crops of corn, sweet potatoes, benne seed, sugarcane, red peppers, okra, groundnuts, guinea corn (sorghum), or rice. Some of these crops had special significance: benne, for example, was a plant of West African origin that was thought to bring good luck, and so slaves planted it at the ends of rows to elicit a good crop. Slaves in the rice districts in low-country Georgia and South Carolina also commonly owned a variety of barnyard fowl and ran cattle and hogs in the nearby woods and marshes.

Slaves also gathered, fished, hunted, or "layed out" in the swamps and woods beyond the borders of the plantations. Large areas of the South remained uncultivated in the plantation era—nearly 80 percent of the region in 1860—and forests, wetlands, and savannahs were part of every plantation district. Little of this land was unused, however, and slaves were often attentive visitors to this environment. The environment off the plantation was often as important to slave communities as were the fields, quarters, and garden patches on the plantation.

Hunting and fishing in the surrounding woods and waterways was an important source of food for slaves. On the Georgia and South Carolina coasts, for example, slaves may have procured nearly half the meat in their diets from wild sources—a crucial margin that added substantially to nutrition and sustenance. Not all slaves hunted—some plantation surroundings were not rich enough in game to yield much to hunters, and going off the plantation without a pass was too risky in some neighborhoods—but many did. They used guns they owned or had access to as hunters for their masters, an ingenious array of snares, set traps, and turkey pens, or whatever else was at their disposal. Georgian Aunt Harriet Miller reported to a WPA interviewer that when she was a slave, she and other slaves used blowguns made out of sugarcane and burned out at the joints to "kill squirrels and catch fish."[3] With sometimes nothing more than motivation, opportunity, and a good stick, slaves sought something of their own by way of hunting. Slaves hunted every kind of game, but the animals that most commonly found their way into pots in the quarters were rabbits, raccoons, and opossums. Rabbits were plentiful and had savory meat; roasted raccoon was rich, textured fare; and the meat of the opossum, when scalded, rubbed in hot ashes, and roasted, and then eaten with roasted sweet potatoes and coffee, was prized most of all by slaves who hunted.[4] Whatever the animal, slaves had to be doubly stealthy and more knowledgeable than other hunters: they had to avoid stepping into their masters' landscapes of control and domination at the same time that they had to be closely attentive to the nuances of the behavior and environment of their prey. Hunting was one more way that slaves acquired knowledge about the physical environment in their neighborhoods and annotated their surroundings with meanings that were both subversive of the totality of white power and positive expressions of an African American environmental ethos.

The food that slaves procured from the wild environment became imbued with cultural value when slaves developed a cuisine and tastes for certain wild foods and used gifts of meat and other foods to reinforce community bonds. Moreover, slaves wove the precise and detailed understanding they had of animal behavior into a binding cultural form: songs and animal tales in which the creatures they knew became the central characters. The behavior of rabbits, bears, alligators, deer, and other animals, which slaves had learned so well in order to hunt successfully, revealed itself in the accurate renderings of the idiosyncratic behaviors of characters such as Buh Alligator, Buh Bear, Buh Rabbit, Buh Cooter, and Buh Turkey Buzzard. These tales were also a vehicle for the portrayal of slaves' perceptions of natural social relations in two senses. African Americans saw themselves as part of a unified universe of all creatures and did not make a sharp distinction between humans and other creatures. At the same time, these tales, especially the trickster tales, were depictions of social relations as African Americans believed they were inscribed in nature. When a weak animal defeated a strong one by using its wits, this was a conquest with doubly meaningful social resonance for the slaves.[5]

Slaves also used what they raised and procured in the wild places to trade for goods and property of their own. For example, they collected sea grass or split strips of oak to make baskets, used parts of plants to dye cloth or as patterns for quilts, carved dugouts out of logs, collected Spanish moss to sell as mattress stuffing, and in general gathered wild foods to add to plantation rations. Cattle and hogs that ranged in the woods were, indeed, capital on the hoof, which increased by way of the browse that could be found there. Like their masters, slaves extracted commodities from the environment in which they lived and worked. Indeed, masters often encouraged some property ownership by slaves—they believed it would make them less likely to run away, and recognized that it was often an important supplement to the rations they supplied to slaves. For slaves, however, who existed in a relationship with other humans and larger institutions that defined them as human property, subject to the almost absolute domination of their masters, possession of small pieces of land represented considerable increments of independence and autonomy, even when they also served the goals of masters. Property was not simply wealth, but represented a measure of security and something that was their own, and more slaves than not had some.[6]

Wild resources and the property obtained from them were used not merely to strengthen individual positions of power, but were important in consolidating family bonds. Cooperative arrangements that freed some slaves to cultivate their own plots, fish, hunt, or gather, and then trade or sell, were usually kin arrangements. Slaves worked with relatives to extract resources, relatives took care of property when the owner was absent, and some slaves got their start—a few chickens or a shoat or a calf—by way of a gift or a loan from a relative. When slaves disputed ownership of something, they negotiated a resolution by way of kinship networks—relatives or reliable neighbors were witnesses and trusted ones were arbiters. When slaves died, their children inherited what they had. Property ownership was so interrelated with kinship for slaves that the making of property and the making of family often went hand in hand. Slaves metabolized resources from the fields, forests, and swamps of plantation neighborhoods in their social arrangements as well as adding to their food supply and nutrition—they crafted expressions of culture and values, and also quite literally claimed family ties with what they extracted—both in the process and the product—from the environment.[7]

The social and sacred meanings of the things African Americans procured in the wild were just as important as whatever practical and nutritional values they had. Some plants, indeed, saved both body and soul; others were powerful weapons of resistance. For example, in spite of the efforts of masters to impose their own kind of medicine on the slaves they owned—to achieve mastery even over the bodies of slaves—slaves held fast to their own traditions of doctoring. Sharla Fett, in her study of healing and slave culture on the plantations of the Old South, explains that medicine made of herbs and roots, both by whites and by blacks, were "characterized by a high degree of exchange across lines of race, ethnicity, class, and region."[8] In colonial America, settlers, African slaves, and Native Americans sought and exchanged herbal remedies with each other in a dynamic process that proceeded informally and actively whenever people were sick. Even though racial lines were clearly drawn in the antebellum South, masters and slaves—and more often, mistresses and women slaves—continued to exchange plant remedies in a pragmatic response to illness. Even southern medical practitioners, at the same time that they decried slave medicine as superstition, were attentive to the herbal knowledge of slaves. When Charleston surgeon and plant specialist Francis Peyre Porcher compiled the single most comprehensive guide to the plant use and knowledge of nineteenth-century southerners—the massive

Resources of the Southern Fields and Forests, published in 1863—he gathered information from enslaved South Carolinians as well as his white neighbors.[9]

Though information about herbal medicine was shared across class and racial lines, whites and blacks communicated and understood this kind of medical knowledge in different ways. Slave knowledge of herbal medicine was akin to their knowledge of everything else in the plantation environment—discrete, detailed, and close to the ground. It was also conditioned by experience; slave women, especially, went out into the woods and wetlands to find supplies for household manufacturing and healing. They also cultivated common medicinal herbs in their garden patches. In turn, they taught others what they learned, both by practice and by storytelling.[10]

Plant knowledge also provided slaves with another weapon of resistance. Slaves used plant-derived substances to poison slave owners. When they used them on each other, plants and plant knowledge also became the means to gain power in the quarters. Just how often this occurred is impossible to discern, because fantasy and reality were blended in the perceptions masters had of slaves in this capacity, as well as in the perceptions slaves had of other slaves. Accounts of slow deaths by poisoning are especially difficult to unravel, because the climate of paranoia that surrounded master-slave relationships often caused masters to credit human agency for lingering illnesses and slow deaths that in fact may have had other causes. But this fear also recognized indirectly the extensive knowledge some slaves had of natural pharmacopoeia and the skill with which they were able to wield it.[11]

What is also significant about African American plant knowledge in the Old South is that it was amplified by a worldview that acknowledged the spiritual significance of plants—not just in terms of their usefulness for restoring health and providing energy, but also because of indwelling vital forces and the potential power of those forces. Slave herbalists saw their ability to use plants well as a God-given talent, and their ability to find them in the woods as an exercise in revelation. The uncultivated landscape where slaves gathered the plants they used for sustenance, dyeing cloth, making baskets and other household items, and especially for healing was, for them, alive with spirit and spiritual meaning. Wilderness was a place where the health of individual bodies as well as communities could be restored and strengthened.

Nature uncultivated also provided both highway and sanctuary to African Americans who were slaves on the farms and plantations of the South. Few were able to follow the route Toni Morrison imagines so eloquently in *Beloved*, when she envisions Paul D. escaping slavery and following the path of spring "tree flowers" through space and time to a latitude of freedom in the North.

Most slaves ran away or were "truant" for just awhile. *Grand marronage*, as the French called it in Louisiana, was not common in the South, but also not unknown. More common was the *petit marronage* engaged in by slaves who sought either to briefly escape a particularly repressive master or overseer or who wanted to visit with family on other plantations. Slaves made their way from plantation to plantation, usually at night and with both short and extended periods of truancy, to visit kinfolks and to improve the quality of their family relations. When the Civil War came, knowledge of local environments not only gave slaves the means to achieve *marronage* but also to accomplish liberation. Some slaves later used their understanding of the geography of their neighborhoods to help Union troops liberate them, as well as to liberate themselves by running away for the last time to Union lines. Slaves also assisted Union troops and escaped Yankees find their way through a terrain that was strange to them. One prominent Georgia planter explained: "They know every road and swamp and creek and plantation in the country, and are the worst of spies . . . They are traitors who may pilot an enemy into your *bedchamber!*"[12] The physical environment off the plantation, then, was an intricate part of the elaborate geography of kinship in the antebellum South, and the wilderness was not a place where African Americans went to find themselves, but a place of potential deliverance as well as a site where family and community values could be affirmed.

The connection between social relations and environmental ones deepened the sense of place among many African Americans and produced a loyalty to locale. The relatively stable African American populations in the low-country South developed strong kin networks that were defined by areas of residence. These social ties, sometimes developed over generations, connected the blacks with others in the area and sometimes had a more powerful influence than the intrusions of the master and the enforced relationships of slavery. The identification between the social network and the locale of residence has been so strong on St. Helena Island in South Carolina, for example, that the old plantations, albeit with modified geographical boundaries, continued into the recent past to be the units of communal identity for kin networks on the island. African Americans in other parts of the South also developed a strong sense of place that webbed networks of family, friends, and environmental practices together with locale and what freedmen called their "old homes" or the "old range." Union officers and Freedmen's Bureau officials who worked in the plantation districts of the South after emancipation and the Civil War often remarked on this tendency: J. W. Alvord, a Freedmen's Bureau official who worked throughout the South in 1865 observed that African Americans were "a remarkably permanent people. They love to stay in one place, where they have always lived, where they were born and where their children are buried."[13]

African Americans developed what in modern terms might be regarded an environmental ethos long before the environmental justice movement, before the civil rights movement, and before they were emancipated and had citizenship rights conferred upon them. They transformed the experience that they were forced into by slavery into a positive expression of freedom—in small measure, to be sure, and one that was seriously circumscribed by the harsh realities of bondage—that marked out a different landscape of interactions with the natural environment than the one forced upon them by those for whom they were forced to labor. Nearly every aspect of their experience put them into contact with the natural environment, and gave them a knowledge that was both detailed and practical. They did not, at the same time, make clear distinctions between the spirits and forms of the natural world and those of the human world, and found it easier to move from the latter to the former when they sought animals and plants in the wild, when they called upon natural pharmacopoeia to heal, conjure, or poison, and in the stories and songs they performed to enact in code important social meanings. All aspects of their relationship with the environment were furthermore mediated by the ties of kinship, and environmental relationships were also political and social ones.

African Americans, when they were slaves, also participated in what may be regarded as an active conservation or environmental ethic. First of all, they participated—usually invisibly, as planters had it—in the conservation movement that emerged among leading planters in the antebellum South. Conservation in the plantation South emerged out of concerns about the declining fertility of southern soils and the competitiveness and self-sufficiency of the southern economy in a nation where southerners had begun to feel embattled. Conservation in the antebellum South, quite simply, was agricultural improvement. Planters were especially concerned about declining soil fertility in the older regions of the South. Many of the most educated planters in Virginia, South Carolina, and Georgia began to argue for changes in farming methods that would preserve or restore fertility, rather than mine it to death and then escape to fresh lands in the West. They "assumed that they had to be what one called, 'good stewards,' because the land was vulnerable and human beings had to work carefully within its limitations," explains Joan Cashin.[14] Improving planters developed elaborate methods for manuring, crop and land rotations, and most famously, excavating and amending soils with marl. These efforts did not really accomplish reform, and in the end the rhetoric of agricultural reform in the South produced a good deal more air than improve-

ment. But at the heart of the efforts to recover the fertility of the older agricultural regions of the South was an ecological sensibility. "Long before the
science of ecology," Steven Stoll explains, "they came closer than anyone before them to a full (if sometimes inaccurate) sense of interdependence among
organisms and interconnectedness in nature generally."[15]

Much of the history of these early conservation efforts in the South remains to be written, and needs to be more fully connected to the efforts to
improve the productivity of slaves and, at the same time, make the institution
of slavery more palatable to critics in both regions. The agricultural improvement movement in the South cannot be separated from the social context in
which it took place, nor extracted from the political economy that shaped it.
While planters sought to introduce methods that would restore vitality to the
sagging fortunes of their neighborhoods, they also sought to improve slave
management techniques. In doing so, they were paternalists all. They advocated a more respectful attitude toward the land that gave them their livelihoods and also argued for the humanity of slaves and a more humane treatment of the slaves who sustained them. The shifting perceptions of slaves by
their owners—who often considered the master-slave relationship as pat-
terned after the firm but understanding father toward his children, yet regarded slaves more as working pets than as humans—should also be studied
more closely as part of a larger effort to discern the sources of conservation
values in the South. Ideas about conserving nature were intricately connected
to ideas about improving the management of slaves.[16]

Slave owners talked about modes of agricultural improvement with the
same intensive detachment with which they talked about labor in the fields—
as if they themselves accomplished it. This labor had an ecological function: it
contributed energy into agricultural ecosystems, which were, in turn, transformed into improved productivity. Moving mud, marl, or manure from
highly productive salt marshes, from the stored energy of marl deposits, or
from plantation compost piles used energy to transfer energy, and slave owners became invested in the improved ecological health of agricultural lands.
But accounts of planter conservation presented the process of improvement as
if mudding and marling got done by itself. The enormous labors contributed
by slaves and the ecological function these labors constituted—in the work of
marling and manuring as well as in the traditional tasks of southern agriculture—were simply invisible. Planters who sought to improve the lots of both
land and slaves were green paternalists, not husbandmen.[17]

Black southerners who knew how to extract resources discretely and who
occupied a natural landscape that was infused with spirit had the makings of
a different environmental ethos. It was this very experience with green pater-

nalism and the coercive management regiments of elite southerners—those who extracted the labor of slaves but to whom slaves were partly invisible—that contributed the crucial element to African American environmentalism. Slaves had to negotiate for everything, either directly or indirectly, with masters and with the systems of control masters devised. They had to bargain with both words and behavior for access to resources, to move around on the plantation and beyond the bounds of the cultivated fields, to manipulate adjustments to the burden of labor that was placed upon them, and to do anything in the interest of kin and community. Anything they did for themselves was potentially and sometime quite overtly an act of resistance, and had to be negotiated carefully. Even the medicines they sought to apply to treat illness, even if it brought back a slave's health and his or her capacity to be a productive worker, was usually regarded by planters, who wanted to control the bodies of slaves as well as what those bodies could do, as an act of subversion. Reformers and Freedmen's Bureau officials who worked with freedmen in the South just after emancipation were often surprised—stunned, even—by the speed, deftness, and collective force with which freedmen laborers negotiated with landowners or managers to secure better terms for themselves. What these officials were witnessing and experiencing was not something new, but a political behavior with deep roots in the conditions of slavery.

This history left twentieth-century black southerners with a double-edged inheritance. Those who lived in the old plantation districts were more likely, at the end of the century, to live in poverty than their urban African American counterparts. Poor, underdeveloped counties in the South with large black populations have been more likely to be locations or proposed locations of hazardous waste sites or factories that spew noxious pollutants. But slavery and emancipation and the political culture that came out of them—both in the countryside and in the urban places to which rural southern blacks migrated—have produced a positive response to injustices, including environmental injustices. Relationships with the environment have always been social and collective for African Americans, and always in the process of negotiation.[18]

Nature provided resources not just for profit but often to consolidate the community—moving into nature and through nature was usually a collective matter, as was negotiating either individual or group spaces from masters using environmental knowledge or by way of spaces in the fields and the surrounding forests and swamps. For African Americans, "wilderness" was not a place in which the preservation of the world could be found, but a site of healing, a highway to kinship, a place where a decisive edge of resources could be added to meager plantation rations, and a place where salvation could be gained, either through worship in the holler, through the strengthening of kin connections, or through stealing oneself away permanently. Slave experiences with the environment were profoundly social ones: slaves moved into nature to enact social meanings, although they did not make the sharp distinction between the human and nonhuman worlds that were common for whites. For African Americans, nature was negotiated, it was kin, and it was community. African American environmentalism comes out of this history, and the responses of current African American environmentalists, especially in the South, are shaped by it. Even if it cannot be demonstrated that race is the prominent factor in an environmental justice problem, African Americans' perceptions of the issues, how they respond to them, the tactics they employ, and the goals they seek have been conditioned by their historical experiences with injustice and by the political culture and environmental ethos that comes from their long history first as an enslaved and then as a marginalized minority in America. The environmental justice movement in the South is not the consummate expression of an invariable heritage of values, ideals, and strategies that were forged by African Americans during slavery; African Americans made and remade their relationship to the environment and the politics with which they expressed those relationships. This politics has been again remade during the course of specific struggles. But certain general qualities of African American environmental politics—the pursuit of collective rights, the tendency to see community in broad terms that include both humans and nonhumans, the connection of environmental concerns to the world of work and production rather than to lifestyle choices and consumption, and versatile gifts for political negotiation, for example—are rooted in the experience of African Americans as slaves. More importantly, these qualities and practices are part of a politics that African Americans deeply made, and not one that was thrust upon them or that was learned or assimilated from other traditions of grassroots activism. To recognize this history of African American environmental justice is to recover the depth, richness, and even grandeur of African American environmental values and politics.

3

Slave Hunting and Fishing
in the Antebellum South

SCOTT GILTNER

What yo' gwine do when de meat give out?

—Slave song, from *The WPA Oklahoma Slave Narratives*

Throughout the nineteenth century, the fields, forests, and streams of the American South were important economic and cultural battlegrounds in the wider conflict between white and black southerners. In both the antebellum and post-emancipation periods, hunting and fishing were bound to this larger conflict.[1] Southern elites used hunting and fishing to set themselves apart from slaves and freed people and to reinforce their legal, economic, and cultural control over African Americans. For their part, slaves and freed people protected their customary reliance on hunting and fishing in order to challenge that control and resist efforts to define such activities as inherently elite, white, and exclusionary.

In the antebellum South, hunting and fishing were critically important to slave communities. These activities strengthened slaves' nutritional and material condition, providing food, money, and material goods, and giving slaves time for asserted familial and community camaraderie. These benefits created and augmented feelings of independence among slaves and turned what masters viewed as privileges to be granted into customs to be expected. Once such privileges became established, slaves regarded them as a sort of contract— informal, of course, yet important and worth defending. Just as some masters hoped to use the slave economy to solidify their hold on slave labor, slaves themselves used it to expand their rights and privileges, make further claims to their own time and productive labor and cultivate rare opportunities to resist, subtly and overtly, the conditions of bondage. Thus masters used hunting and fishing to discipline their labor force while slaves used it to create additional space between themselves and slave owners and to develop additional privileges that, as the *Southern Planter and Farmer* noted in 1852, "plants the germ of rebellion in the contract for obedience."[2]

Studies of hunting and fishing are rare among histories of the United States. With few exceptions, such as the classic general plantation studies, which discuss them only briefly, analyses of hunting and fishing in the United States have given scant attention to the intersection of those activities and race relations. Most barely mention race or the evolution of conflicts arising over the different uses of and cultural meanings derived from the sporting field.[3] Studies of hunting and fishing in the United States between the eighteenth and twentieth centuries have typically focused on such topics as the elite's use of field sports to reinforce class distinction, the confluence between the sporting field and changing conceptions of American masculinity, and the ways hunting and fishing have fit into the ebbs and flows of American evangelicalism.[4]

Studies of southern hunting and fishing fit this general pattern, giving little more than passing notice to the ways that such utilization of the South's environmental resources reflected larger and long-lasting racial conflict.[5] Aside from Nicholas Proctor's study of hunting in the antebellum South, few scholars have addressed the importance of hunting and fishing to slaveholders and slaves or placed hunting and fishing within the larger context of the slave regime. If the broader economic and cultural meaning of hunting and fishing by African Americans in the nineteenth-century South is explored, then hunting and fishing may reveal more about race in the antebellum South than just subsistence habits.[6] The impact of hunting and fishing on slaves and slavery—through the production of food and money, the creation of physical and psychological distance between master and slave, and the cultivation of opportunities to resist the conditions of slavery—demonstrates that southern fields, forests, and streams were contested arenas wherein key tensions in antebellum southern life were played out. Examining the importance of and varied meanings behind nineteenth-century African Americans' "larger landscapes of subsistence," to use Mart A. Stewart's phrase, can reveal as much about race and race relations as about class conflict, crises in masculinities, and American religiosity.[7] Hunting and fishing served as challenges to the racial hierarchy, causing post-emancipation, multigenerational attacks on African American activities.[8]

Hunting and Fishing and Control

Although a slave's life and labor was not entirely dominated by the master, the majority of a slave's time was spent laboring in the service of the plantation or under the master's watchful eye. In order to maintain efficient operations, masters struggled to keep their slaves laboring for as long as possible, employing systems of routines, incentives, and brutal discipline. Each slaveholder coerced labor in different ways but with a common goal—increased profitability. Thus, any independent economic activity sanctioned by slave owners was believed to be a tool for maximizing efficiency, either through refreshing slaves for labor or making slaves beholden to the benevolent master who indulged them with such privileges. Hunting and fishing, from the slave owners' perspective, were tools of maintaining authority that primarily served the interests of the plantation. By employing slave huntsmen to procure meat for their tables and storehouses, slave owners found yet another way to profit from their slaves, in this case by reducing provision costs. In Mississippi, according to Charlie Davenport, "mos' ever plantation kep' a man busy huntin' an' fishin' all de time." Former North Carolina slave Alex Woods remembered that "Dey 'lowed my father to hunt wid a gun. He wus a good hunter an' he brought a lot o' game to de plantation."[9] Because fishing was often a simpler activity than hunting, which typically required special skills and entailed the use of dogs or guns, masters could employ a greater number of slaves. Employing slaves to fish was also theoretically safer, because, unlike many kinds of hunting, fishing did not have to be performed at night—when masters preferred slaves to be resting for the day's labor. As Susan Dabney Smedes recalled in her memorial of antebellum plantation life, food was often acquired by "one of the colored fishermen whose sole occupation was to catch fish for the table at the great house."[10]

Removing harmful pests, especially the opossum and raccoon, and other animals, was another benefit of hunting. These scavengers destroyed crops and cost plantation owners much money each season. Planters thus encouraged their eradication, "because every marauding coon that is killed is so much saved from the standing corn."[11] In his recollections of antebellum North Carolina, former planter and cavalry officer James Battle Avirett described one plantation huntsman: "Uncle Amos, who did nothing but hunt and 'stroy varmits from year's end to year's end (making the best wages of any servant on the estate, because he killed so many eagles, coons and an occasional bear, with untold numbers of squirrels, black and red fox and the gray or cat squirrel)."[12]

Masters also drew on slave skills to enhance their own sporting interests. Hunting and fishing, since the initial settlement of Virginia, was a favored pastime of southern elites. During many expeditions, slaves accompanied their masters for the purposes of performing the variety of laborious tasks required. This tradition did not diminish in the antebellum period, as slaveholders—ever seeking to cultivate mastery over both nature and the slave population—made forced labor a key symbol of that mastery.[13] Charley Williams, a slave in Louisiana, recalled that his "young master used to do his fishing in White River, and take a nigger or two along to do the work at his camp." British zoologist Philip Henry Gosse, who lived in Alabama for a year in the 1830s, described the many tasks performed by slaves in preparation for a hunt, noting that it was a time of great amusement: ". . . for Sambo likes the wild excitement of a hunt, especially by night, as well as his betters, and enters into it with as much zeal and zest. One or two were sent to saddle the horses, others to collect the dogs of the establishment, and others to search up axes for felling trees, knives for clearing away tangled briers in the woods, and a few other small implements, while another was sent into the swamp to procure a dozen pine-knots for torches."[14] For slaveholders, having slave subordinates on hand to perform required tasks, especially those that were menial or degrading, was important for maintaining both accepted sporting behavior and the racial order.

Slaves frequently performed tasks for their sporting masters that were no more than simple drudgery. Former slave John Finnely recalled that "Massa use me for huntin' and use me for de gun rest. When him have de long shot I bends over . . . and Massa puts his gun on my back for to get de good aim. What him kills I runs and fetches and carries de game for him." W. Solomon Debnam, often included in his master's son's hunting excursions, recalled that slaves were used both to retrieve game and as a source of amusement. "He let us go huntin' squirrels with him," he remembered. "When he shot and killed a squirrel he let us race to see which could get him first, while he laughed at us."[15]

Subsistence and Control

Hunting and fishing for and with the master were ways slave owners sought to control slaves' time; however, it was not necessary for the master to be directly involved in such hunting and fishing for those endeavors to be classified as attempts at control. It is likely that most slave hunting and fishing was done away from the master's supervision, with his approval. During such times, slaves made full use of their owners' desires to reduce provision costs. Slaves worked to provide additional food to buttress the precarious subsistence of the slave quarters, while masters granted that privilege to create good order and docile labor. Thus food procured from slave hunting and fishing was both a cost-saving device and a tool of labor control.

Extra food from hunting and fishing may have supported some paternalist vision, but it was much more valuable to slaves, particularly since normal rations were typically inadequate. "The food [the master] allowed them per week was one peck of corn for each grown person, one pound of pork, and sometimes a quart of molasses. This was all that they were allowed," recalled Henry Bibb. Likewise, former Virginia slave William Grimes wrote of his master, a Colonel Thornton, that he "made his slaves work harder than anyone about there, and kept them poorer. Sometimes we had a little meat, or fish, but not often anything more than our peck of meal."[16] Despite laws mandating minimum food allotments and claims by some ex-slaves that their diet was more than adequate under slavery, it is clear that many needed and wanted more.[17] As former Texas slave Mary Reynolds put it, "We prays for the end of Trib'lation and the end of beatin's and for shoes that fit our feet. We prayed that us niggers could have all we wanted to eat and special for fresh meat." Two ways to obtain such meat were hunting and fishing. Solomon Northup recalled that this was often the only way that slaves on the Bayou Boeuf, Louisiana, plantation got by: "The weekly allowance of meal scarcely sufficed to satisfy us. It was customary with us . . . where the allowance is exhausted before Saturday night, or is in such a state as to render it nauseous and disgusting, to hunt in the swamps for coon and opossum. . . . There are planters whose slaves, for months at a time, have no other meat than such that is attained in this manner.[18]

Archaeological studies of slave living quarters demonstrate that hunting and fishing were fruitful activities. Excavations have shown that slaves enjoyed a wide array of fish and game, including numerous varieties of fish, opossum, squirrels, rabbits, raccoon, deer, turkeys, pheasant, and other animals. Of course, the availability of specific prey depended upon the region, as some parts of the South were richer in certain kinds of fish and game than others. However, narrative evidence drawn from accounts of ex-slaves, both anecdotal and empirical, suggests that, despite regional variations, some game was available to slaves everywhere, particularly small game such as opossum and squirrels.[19] The availability of game to hunt is a running theme in slave narratives. "De smart nigger," noted Julius Nelson, "et a heap o' possums an' coons, dar bein' plenty o' dem an' rabbits an' squirrels in abundance." Louisa Adams recalled, "My old daddy partly raised his chilluns on game. He caught rabbits, coons, an' possums. He would work all day and hunt at night."[20]

Since most slaves were not permitted firearms, they were forced to hunt by wit and skill, using various traps, snares and other, often homemade, devices. Former slave Peggy Grigsby described one such trap. "Sometimes dey [male slaves] caught rabbits in wooden boxes, called 'rabbit,'" she recalled. "It had a trap in the middle, which was set at night with food in it, and when the rabbit bite at night, trap sprung, and the opening at the front was closed so he couldn't get out." "Aunt" Esther Green recalled, "old Ben, a nigger who had turkey traps, was always bringin' in lots of dem big fat birds."[21] Frederick Law Olmsted, while traveling in Mississippi, saw another creative method of pro- curing game: "The stock-tender, an old negro . . . had an ingenious way of sup- plying himself with venison. He lashed a scythe blade or butcher's knife to the end of a pole so that it formed a lance; this he set near a fence or fallen tree which obstructed a path in which deer habitually ran, and the deer in leaping over the obstacle would leap directly on the knife. In this manner, he had killed two deer the week before my visit." Such trapping displayed not only slaves' ingenuity, but also their need to hunt efficiently. Traps and snares re- quired little attention; once set, slaves need only return to them at regular in- tervals to collect catches, and reset or fix their devices.[22]

Fire proved another effective hunting tool for slaves. As W. Solomon Debnam described, using firelight to paralyze prey, known as "bird blinding," went a long way toward making up for a lack of guns. "I remember killin' birds at night with thorn brush," he wrote. "When bird blindin' we hunt at night wid lights from big splinters. We went to grass patches, briers, and vines along the creeks and low groun's where they roosted, an' blinded 'em an' killed 'em when they come out." Robert Hinton also remembered this practice: "Yes sir, I went blindin'. I 'members gittin' a big light an' jumpin' 'round de brush heaps an' when a bird come out we frailed him down."[23] This method, effective for locating and paralyzing (by illuminating the eyes) birds and game, was one of the most effective ways slaves hunted, although it angered the elite white sportsmen who viewed such methods as unsportsmanlike. The practice was also seen as a source of intentional and unintentional fires, as evidenced by the many statutes enacted by southern general assemblies limiting the practice.[24]

Dogs were another valuable tool—indeed perhaps the most valuable tool in lieu of firearms—used by slaves in their hunting excursions. Former North Carolina slave John Smith recalled that he and his dog always fared well. "I caught rabbits, coon, an' possums wid dogs. Dey fared but middlin' pore chance wid us. We caught rabbits in hollers an' caves; an' possums in trees. . . .We caught all dese wid dogs."[25] Dogs helped slaves drastically improve their chances of supporting themselves and their families. Moreover, the hunting dog represented a rare part of slave life that was controlled and cared for al- most exclusively by the slave. J. Vance Lewis, born a slave in Louisiana, noted this dual importance. "The slave loves his dog," he wrote. "They are constant companions. He talks with him by day and hunts with him by night. . . . His dog is the only thing under the sun that he can call his own; for the master claims the woman that is called his wife, his offspring, his hut, his pig, his own body—his very soul."[26]

Although there were statutes restricting or forbidding slaves' gun use in all southern states, masters, who in the end had more control over slaves than did legislatures, frequently allowed the privilege. Charles Ball's master, for example, greatly aided Ball's weekend hunts by giving him an old, broken musket. After taking it to a local blacksmith to be fixed, the weapon proved invaluable. "I now began to live well," Ball recalled, "and to feel myself, in some measure, an independent man." Obviously only trusted slaves were given this opportunity, but the fact that some were allowed demonstrates how far some masters were willing to go to permit slaves to supplement their diets. It also demonstrates that many slaveholders were confident that hunting, even with dangerous weapons, was a minimal threat to their personal or financial security.[27]

Fishing posed a less obvious threat to the plantation's smooth operation. Slaves caught fish in a variety of different ways: with poles, nets, traps and any other device that worked. "Fishin' was good too," remembered George Dorsey. "We cut our poles in the woods an' used the flax thread for lines."[28] Fishing could be effective with a simple pole such as the one used by George Dorsey, or through use of more complicated methods, including complex traps and weirs. In his autobiography, Solomon Northup recalled the first fish trap on his Louisiana plantation, noting that "a mine was opened—a new resource was developed, hitherto unthought of by the enslaved children of Africa, who toil and hunger along the shores of that sluggish but prolific stream."[29]

Some slaves utilized canoes or other small craft, which they often built themselves, in fishing. Charles Ball became a much more effective fisherman using such craft. "I had no canoe, but made a raft of dry logs, upon which I went to a suitable place in the river and set my weir," he remembered. "I took as many fish from my weir as filled half bushel measure."[30] Such vessels were particularly common in low-country regions with abundant creeks and rivers, such as areas of South Carolina, Georgia, and Louisiana, where employing slaves in the transport of goods on waterways was an economic necessity. Of the slaves on the Georgia seaboard plantation of his youth, Edward J. Thomas noted: "having their own boats, they [slaves] could always have fish and oysters."[31] Allowing slaves the use of such craft was inherently dangerous due to the risk of flight, but many owners permitted the practice, particularly when slaves fished in their service.

"Der was a ribber nearby de plantation," Midge Burnett remembered of her days as a slave in Georgia, "an' we fished dar a heap too. We ketched a big mess of fish ever' week an' dese come in good an' helped ter save rations ter boot."[32] The fish she caught, like the game slaves acquired through hunting, was essential for the slave community's subsistence. From the slave's point of view, such nourishment was a way to enable them to better endure daily labor; from the master's perspective, it enabled them to better perform that labor. Moreover, granting permission to slaves to provide for themselves in this fashion was a way, slave owners hoped, to increase good feelings between master and slave and make slaves more dependent. Thus from the master's point of view, slaves hunting and fishing with the master's permission, like doing so explicitly with or for the slave owner, was another way for planters to benefit from the power they wielded. However, slave hunting and fishing was not always about control, since slaves cultivated benefits that did not always serve, and were not always foreseen by, their masters.

Beyond Control

In addition to providing needed food, hunting and fishing were also important components of an internal slave economy whose benefits extended beyond planters' interests. Slaves often engaged in trade, exchanging what they had acquired from gardens, odd jobs, and hunting and fishing for other goods, including foodstuffs, tools, clothes, and toys for children. George Rogers, a former slave in North Carolina, recalled how he and other slaves traded fish to the folks in the Big House. "We fished a lot in Briar Creek. We caught a lot o' fish. . . . We would trade our fish to missus for molasses to make candy out uv."[33] Surpluses were sold to people on the plantation, including the "massa" and "missus," and to other people in the area. South Carolina rice planter J. Motte Alston recalled that his slaves marketed the coot [a small game bird] they caught during evening excursions: "Hundreds would be killed in a short time by those dusky pot-hunters, and numbers sold to the planters."[34] The Reverend Squire Dowd found such arrangements an ideal way to obtain currency for purchasing extra goods: "We hunted a lot, and the fur of the animals we caught we sold and had the money."[35]

Former slave John Evans recalled that selling his catches saw him through the tough parts of the year. "When I growed up, my job was fishin'. I made enough sellin' fish to the summer folks all along Wrightville and Greenville Sounds to keep me all winter."[36] Slave fishermen on the Maryland plantation to which Charles Ball was bound "caught and sold as many fish and oysters, as enabled them to buy coffee, sugar, and other luxuries for their wives besides keeping themselves and their families in Sunday clothes."[37] It appears that slave owners widely accepted, even directly aided, such slave activities. Sam T. Stewart remembered, "We caught birds and game, sent it to town, and sold it for money. We caught birds and partridges in traps. Our master would bring them to town, sell them for us, and give us the money."[38]

The money and goods acquired from hunting and fishing went a long way in providing subsistence, even a degree of material comfort, for slaves and their families. Such activities also helped to establish and expand larger networks of labor and exchange through which slaves created still more distance between themselves and their owners. By using hunting and fishing to develop commercial ties with neighboring planters, merchants, poor whites and free men, slaves cultivated opportunities to engage in other substantial economic endeavors.[39] William Hayden, once a slave in Kentucky, used time away from regular labor to catch fish in the Kentucky River. "These fish I conveyed to market," he recalled, "and obtained a considerable sum of spending money, without, in the least, encroaching on my master's time, as I had in a short time become acquainted with all the inn-keepers, who did not hesitate to purchase my 'FINNY TRIBE.'" The contacts Hayden created were perhaps just as important as the income, because these contacts turned into other opportunities: "Having become intimate in my fish speculation with the principal inn-keeper in Frankfort, I made arrangements with him to work for him on holidays and Sundays, cleaning boots, washing dishes, & c.; and in this capacity was my leisure moments employed, during my whole sojourn at Frankfort."[40] For slaves like Hayden, commercial ties created by activities like fishing could be expanded into other valuable chances to both improve the material and financial condition of the quarter and counteract slave owners' efforts at completely controlling their economic lives.

In addition to securing the commercial and economic interests of some slaves, hunting and fishing also benefited the slave family, which, under bondage, was never completely secure. Fathers, mothers, and children could be, and often were, sold at any moment, and many families were torn apart by separation and distance. The slave family acted as a buffer against the system of chattel labor, serving as a refuge from it, ameliorating the wounds brought by it, and socializing young slaves into its rigors. Thus the protection and maintenance of the family was vitally important to slaves. In addition to living with the knowledge that family members could be taken away or otherwise abused at any time, adult slaves faced considerable difficulty in maintaining the position of parents and role models. Since laboring in the master's service constituted the bulk of a slave's existence, having the time to be with children, to teach and nurture them, and perform the normal functions of parenthood was often a challenge.[41] Assuming a role of provider was also difficult. With limited time, energy, and freedom of movement, slaves were forced to live with the painful reality that the family's primary care was often the slave owner's responsibility.

Slaves' inability to assume total control over their families' care was a built-in part of bondage, but through activities like hunting and fishing, slaves created opportunities to maintain their status within the family and reassert their role of providers. By supplementing the family economy with extra food, material goods, and money, slaves provided for their families and gained a measure of autonomy from the slaveholder. Such traits were sometimes so valuable that they earmarked family memory. John Glover's most lasting memories of his grandfather were tied to his ability as a huntsman. "Uncle Ben (father's father) was a great possum hunter," he recalled, "but he died fore I got big enough to go huntin' wid him. He went possum huntin' every night." Former Maryland slave George Jones recounted: "When hunting came. . . . I have often heard my father speak of rabbit, opossum, and coon hunting, and his dogs."[42] Such remembrances illustrate the centrality of hunting and fishing in the family economy and shed light on the importance of a slave's ability to employ them.[43]

Hunting and fishing also helped slaves reassert their roles as teachers and role models by creating time to spend with their children. Because time away from regular labor was limited, such activities were valuable moments for children to be with their parents, relatives, and other adults. These were excellent opportunities both for establishing bonds and for transmitting survival skills from generation to generation.[44] Former Kentucky slave George Henderson fondly recalled hunting with his father: "My daddy used to hunt rabbits and possums," he remembered. "I went with him and would ride on his back with my feet in his pockets." Aaron Ford, a slave in South Carolina, spent similar time with his grandfather: "I remember my grandfather allright," Ford noted. "He de one told me how to catch otters. Told me how to set traps."[45] Through such immensely valuable experiences, children learned the talents and tactics necessary to augment the family's provisions and possessions through hunting and fishing. This time of asserted family and kinship, away from the normal rigors of the plantation system, strengthened adults' roles of teacher, provider, and role model within slave communities. Reverend J. W. Loguen illustrated this point well with a story of a day when his father, Dave, took him out into the woods to hunt:

"Jump on my back, Jarm," half whispered Dave, as rifle in hand, he stepped lightly down the bank of the creek where little Jarm was playing with the pebbles, suiting his bulky frame to the body of a child three or four years old.

Well did the child understand the accustomed ceremony, and he clasped his little arms upon his father's shoulders.

"Be still now—say not a word and you shall see me shoot a deer."[46]

The Subversive Potential of Hunting and Fishing

Since many slaveholders allowed hunting and fishing, it is logical to conclude that they did not view those activities as potential threats. Evidence suggests that those who did not explicitly permit it were either unable or unwilling to completely stop the practice. Slaveholders attempted to exploit slaves' independent economic activities for their own benefit. Yet despite any increased profitability that hunting and fishing may have created, allowing slaves to provide for themselves did not always produce the desired effect. As Betty Wood has argued, expansion of slaves' independent economic activities opened new areas of negotiation as material and financial gains motivated slaves to expand productive activities and see them respected as custom.[47] Thus, while hunting and fishing as a privilege may have allowed for stability and order, these activities as a custom gave slaves important benefits which prompted them to seek greater freedom.

In a popular slave folktale, entitled "Old Marster Eats Crow," a slave named John is caught somewhere he does not belong:

John was hunting on old Marster's place, shooting squirrels, and old Marster caught him and told him not to shoot there anymore. "You can keep two squirrels you got but don't be caught down here no more." John goes out the next morning and shoots a crow. Old Marster went down that morning and caught him, and asked John to let him see the gun. John gave him the gun, and then old Marster told him to let him see the shell. And old Marster put the shell in the gun. Then he backed off from John, pointing the gun, and told John to pick the feathers off the crow, halfway down. "Now start at his head, John, and eat the crow up to where you stopped picking feathers at." When John finished eating, Marster gave him the gun back and throwed him the crow. Then he told John to go on and not let him be caught there no more.

John turned around and started off, and got a little piece away. Then he stopped and turned and called old Marster. Old Marster said, "What you want, John?" John pointed the gun and says, "Lookee here, old

Marster," and throwed old Marster the half a crow. "I want you to start at his ass and eat all the way, and don't let a feather fly from your mouth."[48]

This fictional tale demonstrates both the cruelty of slavery and the potential for resistance to it. In the folktale, John's hunting against his master's wishes resulted in a challenge to authority and a blow against his servitude. His ability to hunt with a gun gave John the chance to make the master "eat crow."

Although masters often encouraged slaves to use time away from plantation labor to improve life in the quarter, not all masters allowed them to hunt and fish. Slaves nevertheless frequently defied the rules, demonstrating that the benefits of hunting and fishing often outweighed prohibitions against them. Jenny Proctor remembered: "our master, he wouldn't 'low us to go fishing—he say that too easy on a nigger and wouldn't low us to hunt neither."[49] Sometimes a master's attitude changed, as William Wells Brown remembered. "While I was with Captain Reynolds, my master 'got religion,' and new laws were made on the plantation. Formerly, we had the privilege of hunting, fishing, making splint brooms, baskets, &c. on Sunday; but this was all stopped."[50] So opposed to hunting and fishing was the driver on John Andrew Jackson's South Carolina plantation home that when Jackson's father was found to have turkey pens and fish traps hidden in the woods, the driver ordered them found and destroyed because they were "too good for niggers."[51]

Despite such prohibitions, slaves refused to give up hunting and fishing. The supplemental food, money, material goods, recreation, and increased family solidarity brought by those endeavors were worth the risking the consequences of disobedience. Whippings, beatings, and the wrath of slave patrols might be evaded, but slaves' basic nutritional and material needs could not. Uncle Wes Woods recalled that "my mistus would not let me go fishing on Sunday, but I would slip off and go anyhow."[52] Former Virginia slave James L. Smith recalled that he and friends hunted and gathered oysters and crabs at night against orders. Once they stayed out all night. The next day James fell asleep while working. Not wanting to get into trouble, he lied to his mistress. "She asked me what was the matter; I told her I felt sick. (I was a great hand at feigning sickness.)"[53] It was a dangerous prospect to defy authority but slaves learned to do it covertly. "Slaves weren't supposed to go hunting at night," recalled James Bolton. "Just the same we had plenty possums and nobody asked how we caught them."[54]

George Rogers provides perhaps the best example of the lengths to which slaves went to procure game in defiance of the master's will: "We used to kill squirrels, turkeys, an' game wid guns. When Marster went off some o' us boys stole de guns, an' away we went to de woods huntin'. Marster would come back drunk. He would not know, an' he did not care nuther, about we huntin' game."[55] This blatant defiance of authority, made more dangerous because of the implications southern whites would draw from firearm theft, demonstrates slaves' attachment to hunting and the great chances they took to take to engage in it.

Hunting or fishing despite prohibitions—itself a form of subversion that stretched the bounds of what slaves could and could not do—was only one antiauthoritarian element of those activities. A slave who hunted or fished, even with permission, could defy the slaveholder's will. For example, slaves used sanctioned hunting and fishing to defy authority by using them to mask participation in other forbidden endeavors. One story about former slave Allen Allensworth recounts a time when he and his fellow slaves used hunting to hold an illegal, multiplantation dance:

> The Slaves on the Ficklin farm, among whom Allen was a leader, would . . . receive permission from Mr. Ficklin to go coon or 'possum hunting; and oh the noise they would make calling the dogs preparatory to starting; the object being to mislead Ficklin. They had already brought one or two coons and 'possums from the city market, as it would never do for them to go hunting and fail to bring back game, it might furnish a good excuse for denying them the privilege again. After the dance the slaves would return to their home plantation, hang out their bought game, so that Ficklin could see it, and retire.[56]

Another activity usually forbidden slaves was the opportunity to learn to read and write. Literate slaves were dangerous slaves, believed southern whites, and strict regulations were placed on slave education and possession of learning materials. Such prohibitions did not stop slaves such as Allensworth, who, after emancipation, became a noted minister. In his biography of Allensworth, Charles Alexander described how one of the slave's favorite activities away from the daily routine—fishing at a nearby creek—provided time for self-education: "During the fishing season Allen would obtain permission to go to the creek and fish. It was while fishing that he had a better opportunity to study his book. He advanced from b-a ba, b-e be and b-i bi to p-r-a pra, p-r-e pre and p-r-i pri. This lesson he would study between bites. . . . The boy was very fond of fishing; later he became a fisher of men."[57]

Slave hunting and fishing excursions also created opportunities for exchanging information. In 1840, according to former slaves Peter Still and his wife Vina, debates about manumission overheard at a Tuscumbia, Alabama, convention for that year's presidential election created rumors of freedom among slaves. These rumors quickly spread throughout the region because:

"On Sundays, the slaves from 'town' met their plantation friends at their fishtraps on the river, and there the joyful news was communicated—in whispers at first—but as they became more certain that their hopes were well-grounded, they gradually grew bolder, till at length they dared to discuss the subject in their religious meetings." As word spread, slaveholders in the area were forced to order a severe reduction of slave privileges and mobility as "a panic pervaded the whole community."[58] Calm did eventually return to Colbert County, but not before whispers of liberation, first spread by town and country slaves meeting at their fish traps, brought a measure of disorder and the possibility of subversion to northwestern Alabama.

Slaves also subverted the master's authority by employing a different kind of hunting. There was plenty of available "game" right on the plantation in the form of the master's livestock. Gus Feaster recalled that slaves usually only had meat at midday, but sometimes "'sharpers' 'ud eat meat when marster didn't know. Dey go out and git 'em a hog from a drove of seventy-five er a hund'ed; dat one never be missed."[59] In some instances, this hunting was disguised. "When a turkey or fowls were wanted," remembered former Kentucky slave Andrew Jackson, "we used to catch them—dress them and eat them up in the night taking care to leave the feathers so scattered around as to indicate the havoc of foxes, and were always ready to follow our master's wishes in hunting for the foxes after a night of their depredations."[60] Augustus Ladson remembered slaves killing the master's livestock and passing the meat off as fish: "De driber use to shoot cows an' in do night de slaves go an' skin em an' isue um 'round to all the slaves, 'speciall w'en cows come frum nudder plantation. He go 'round an' tell the slaves dey better go an' git some fish 'fore it all go. Any time any one say e hab fish it wus understood a mean cow-meat. Our boss ain't nebber catch 'em nor did e ebber miss any cow . . ."[61] This type of "hunting" was another way slaves met their needs, but it was dangerous and could result in punishment. Annie Young recalled a slave who stole and killed a shoat [a young pig] and was subsequently caught. "What's that you got there?" asked his master. "A possum," replied the slave. The master looked in the bag and saw it was a shoat. "Master," the slave responded, "it may be a shoat now, but it sure was a possum while ago when I put 'im in this sack."[62] Such defiance was a direct challenge to slaveholder authority. By engaging in this "hunting," slaves stretched the bonds of slavery, showing that they would not behave as the master intended if vital needs were not met.

Hunting and fishing also carried other possibilities for attacking the master's property. For example, one of the great fears of southern elites was property loss from accidental fire and, especially frightening, arson. In her memoir of life on her father's plantations in King William County and

Gloucester County, Virginia, Susan Dabney Smedes noted that some fires happened accidentally. "When the fields were burned, in preparation for another
crop," she wrote, "the fires, unless well managed, sometimes did mischief. Not
infrequently, too, the Negroes in their coon-hunts left their half-extinguished
torches about, with no thought of the dangerous proximity of valuable property."[63] One wonders, however, if all such fires were accidental. Former Kentucky slave Harry Smith, for example, recalled: "Some colored person who had
received a severe whipping from the patrollers would wreak his vengeance by
firing the grain in the field." He also recalled a time when John Montgomery—
head of the slave patrols for Nelson and Spencer—lost all of his grain in an
apparently intentional fire. According to Smith as many as three hundred local slaves were examined or whipped to find out who committed the arson.
Eventually, it was assumed that George Willis and Soloman, two local slaves,
were guilty: "The way it happened to be fixed on them they were out possum
and coon hunting the night of the fire. They had to go with a large company
of men and show them tracks and cut trees, and also the routes where they
climbed over the fences and where they came home that night. They caught
eight possums and five coons. After proving their innocence they still insisted
on whipping them, but George Wills [their owner] would not permit it." [64]

It is unknown if George Willis and Soloman were actually involved with
the fire, but the fact that two slaves known to be hunting at night were immediately presumed guilty of arson suggests a connection between slave hunting
and fears of that most dreaded assault on a master's property. Whether the
connection between slave hunting and arson was explicit or merely a possibility in the minds of slaveholders, the fact that such an association existed demonstrates that hunting and fishing could, at least, provide opportunities for
such direct subversion.

When possible, slaves used hunting and fishing to facilitate the most obvious form of resistance—running away. Opportunities for flight and hunting
and fishing complemented each other well. From hunting and fishing, slaves
acquired knowledge of a region's woods, fields, and waterways, as well as contacts with nearby slaves, free men, and money—all useful for escape. In addition, these activities gave slaves tools for the journey, including the ability to
provision a flight and the chance to own dogs or weapons to catch game and
protect themselves from patrols. Planter Edward J. Thomas noted of runaways
on Georgia plantations, "Being accustomed to the use of boats and firearms,
and knowing every little inlet through the marshes, which furnished all the
fish and oysters they needed, these runaways could keep up their frolic of idle-
ness and theft almost indefinitely."[65]

James Smith, a slave in Virginia and Georgia, used his hunting skills to escape slavery. Having long employed a dog to catch small game, when he decided to flee to Canada, he took the dog along. Catching food and fighting off pursuers, the dog helped him survive the arduous journey north.[66] Belmont, Missouri, slave William Nelson found freedom in turtle eggs: "How'd I cum North? Well, one day I run 'way from plantashun and hunted 'till I filled a bucket full turtl' eggs den I take dem ovah on river what I hears der's sum Yankee soljers and de soljers buyed my eggs and hepped me on board de boat."[67] Thomas Cole of Alabama also employed such skills to escape. Aware that his master frequently employed slave huntsmen to restock supplies, Cole repeatedly asked for the privilege over a period of months. Finally, his master assented: "This is the chance I been wanting, so when we gits to the hunting ground, the leader says to scatter out, and I tells him me and 'nother man goes north and makes circles round the river and meet 'bout sundown. I crosses the river and goes north. I's gwine to the free country, where there ain't no slaves."[68]

So important were hunting and fishing to slave communities that they became a cherished custom that could not easily be taken back. By granting slaves that privilege or turning a blind eye to it, slave owners unwittingly created an expectation among slaves for additional opportunities and more control over their own time and labor. The ceaseless process of negotiations, made possible by the slave's centrality to the master's prosperity, was intensified and expanded by slave hunting and fishing. This heightened bargaining position, along with the increased freedom of provision and labor won through hunting and fishing, allowed slaves to improve their lives and gave some the means and opportunity to break rules, defy authority, and even escape from slavery entirely. Hunting and fishing were thus two potent weapons in the battle of wills between master and slave that ultimately served to stretch the slave system as a whole.

Rural African American Women, Gardening, and Progressive Reform in the South

DIANNE D. GLAVE

> Guided by my heritage of a love of beauty and a respect
> for strength—in search of my mother's garden, I found
> my own.
>
> —Alice Walker, *In Search of Our Mothers' Gardens*

To plant their flower and vegetable gardens, African American women used their hands—darkly creviced or smoothly freckled; their arms—some wiry, others muscled; and their shoulders and backs—one broad and another thin. They dropped small seeds into the soil with their veined hands. They wrapped their arms around freshly cut flowers to decorate tables in their homes. They bent their shoulders and backs to compost hay, manure, and field stubble, and transplanted plants from the woods into their own yards. These women developed a unique set of perspectives on the environment by way of the gardens they grew as slaves and then as freedwomen. They continued these practices and exercised these perspectives into the early twentieth century. Rural African American women then joined these traditional ways of gardening with horticultural practices they learned from Home Demonstration Service agents and from the special programs developed in African American schools in the South.

An examination of these traditions and practices of gardening changes the reading scholars have had of African American participation in Progressive-era agricultural reform and also reveals the outlines of a rural African American environmental perspective of the time. Progressives envisioned national agricultural reforms that subjugated the discrete and nuanced expertise of local actors to models of bureaucratic efficiency and skill. Yet African American women developed an expertise from community knowledge, from their own interpretations of agricultural reform, and from the training they received in horticulture in the Cooperative Extension Service, African American schools, and other places. Scholars have missed the critical role of African American women gardeners in Progressive reform efforts, or at least have not viewed the participation of African Americans in these efforts through the critical lens of gender.

These women cultivated with simple tools: a hoe, trowel, or shovel in one hand and seeds or fertilizer in the other. But they gardened within a gendered and racial milieu that gave the application of these simple instruments of skill a complex social potency. Rural African American women and men often supported one another in complementary roles and with strategies that were designed to support the family unit. Some women met their own and their families' needs by harvesting vegetables for meals and by planting shrubs and cultivating flowers to create more appealing homes.

The value of these women's contributions to household productivity was often invisible to Progressive reformers, who practiced enormous condescension in their efforts to uplift the poor. Many African American reformers shared this condescension, making women special objects of disdain. Thomas Monroe Campbell, an agent for the Negro Cooperative Service, was haughtily dismissive of rural women, characterizing them as "too careless as to the loud manner in which they act in the streets and in public places . . . and unduly familiar with men."[1] But ultimately, African American women in the rural South controlled how and where they gardened, and, by implication, why they gardened.

Scholars of environmental history have yet to say much specifically about African American gardening practices. While southern environmental history, a scholarship in its infancy, provides some useful context for understanding the experiences of these African American women, lacunae about gardening also exists in this scholarship. Useful works in developing a context for understanding southern gardening traditions include Albert Cowdrey's comprehensive environmental history of the American South, Mart Stewart's work on the landscapes of slaves and masters in the tidewater South, and Pete Daniel's agricultural study of the evolution of the sharecropping system in the post-emancipation South. These provide important insights into the relationship between African Americans and the environment in the nineteenth- and early-twentieth-century South. But except for an analysis of the landscapes that emerged from the creative subsistence practices of slaves and a section on the gardening practices of plantation mistresses in Stewart's book, these studies say little about the relationship of gender, ethnicity, and gardening practices.[2]

Other scholars have traced the geography of significant spaces, including gardens, for southern African Americans. John Michael Vlach explores slave spaces in his architectural interpretation of antebellum slavery in *The Back of the Big House: The Architecture of Plantation Slavery*. Slaves recontoured the landscape, more than whites understood, by the very placement and types of slave buildings. Though Vlach only intimates this, yards as well as cabins were significant spaces of meaning for slaves. Richard Westmacott looks more carefully at the living spaces proximate to African Americans' cabins in *African American Gardens and Yards in the Rural South*. He describes gardens as vital places and spaces of survival, spirituality, subsistence, ornamentation, work, and leisure. Vlach and Westmacott offer tantalizing glimpses of environmental perspectives critical to this study.

At the cross section of gender and labor in African American women's history, Jacqueline Jones argues that African American women and society defined their roles in the gendered and separate spheres that were social commonplaces in Victorian America. The African American community valued the productivity of women, which reinforced their commitment to work in the home and garden. Deborah Gray White, in *Ar'n't I a Woman: Female Slaves in the Plantation South*, counters by saying that slave women and perhaps freed women were not passive and proper Victorian women at home and work. Whether accepting or rejecting Victorian mores, African American men and women worked together in complementary roles that must be seen as viable family economic strategies within the context of racism in the segregated South.

The African American Garden

African American and white gardens possessed distinctive characteristics, which reflected in many ways the roles of the women in each group. Though Vera Norwood argues that both were "responsible for designing and maintaining the yard and its ornamental garden" according to gender, ethnicity was as important as gender in shaping the unique gardens of African Americans.[3] These gardens featured flowers, shrubs, trees, and plants that were purchased individually, accepted as gifts, or cultivated from cuttings. African Americans created colorful motifs from gifts and cast-offs. Whites could more readily buy several plants and group and organize them. African Americans relied on an oral tradition, unlike whites, whose expertise came from magazines and books.

African American women manipulated and controlled their yards for multiple functions in slavery and then in freedom. Free-range pens, extended kitchens, cleaning and leisure spaces, swept areas, pathways to the fields, woods, slaveholders' homes, and fenced flower and vegetable gardens comprised overlapping spaces in the yards. Each space, and thus, each function, was often fluid with few or no boundaries. Unlike most slaves, renters and owner-operators had some income and could purchase livestock, including chickens and hogs that were allowed to roam the yard. The women sought the shade and protection of trees from the sun and heat to prepare meals, feed and entertain family and friends, scrape pots, scrub dishes, wipe tables, beat rugs, and launder clothing. Children played and adults sought recreation throughout the yard, particularly in the shade. Outside the green spaces, women carefully swept clean any foliage, including weeds, creating a bare and austere yard. The pathways took the women beyond their homes and yards to the environs of the woods, fields, the big house, neighbors, and town.

In these gardens, African American women planted vegetables, fruit trees, flowers, shrubs, trees, and plants in red clay, sandy, and dark loamy soils. They generally cultivated vegetable gardens on a side or to the back of the cabin for easy access. To keep out livestock, their partners probably built enclosures of tied stakes for gardens. Most women grew vegetable gardens primarily to sustain their families. They planted okra, milo, eggplant, collards, watermelon, white yams, peas, tomatoes, beans, squash, red peppers, onions, cabbage, potatoes, and sweet potatoes. Others planted truck gardens and sold corn, cotton, peanuts, sweet potatoes, tobacco, indigo, watermelons, and gourds at the market for profit. African Americans also displayed flowers for everyone's viewing and pleasure, beckoning neighbors to take a closer look or visitors to chat in the yard's fragrance and color. The women looked out upon exquisite flowers including petunias, buttercups, verbenas, day lilies, cannas, chrysanthemums, iris, and phlox planted not only in the ground, but in old tires, bottles, planters, and tubs as well. Women placed shrubs—roses, azaleas, altheas, forsythia, crepe myrtle, spirea, camellias, nandina, and wild honeysuckle—throughout the yard. Azaleas and roses were most commonly planted. The dogwood, oak, chestnut, pine, red maple, black locust, sassafras, hickory, willow, cottonwood, and redbud dotted the landscape. African American women chose ornamental plants that were self-propagating, along with annuals that were generally self-seeding. Colorful combinations of blues, reds, pinks, oranges, whites, and yellows often clashed with little or no sequencing. A mix of color and placement, depending on where the gardeners could find space, resulted in a lack of symmetry and formal design. African Americans simply could not afford to buy several shrubs, plants, or flowers at the same time to create such symmetry.

Women's roles were transformed as the lives of African Americans moved from the era of slavery to that of sharecropping. Jacqueline Jones observed that

African American men reinforced gender roles by hunting large game during slavery. Men were primarily responsible for cultivating the tiny household garden plots allotted to families by the slaveholder. They practiced conservation, tilling their own vegetable plots when time off from the slaveholder's tasks allowed. Dating back to the antebellum period, slaves used organic farm methods such as composting, when they took or were given the opportunity to grow their own gardens. A Louisiana slave gardener also built birdhouses from hollowed gourds to attract nesting birds that protected vegetables from insects and other pests. Though some slave women did hunt and fish, they certainly must have assisted the men with the vegetable gardens planted primarily for family consumption. Some women tended flowers—feminine work in which they aesthetically enhanced and embellished their quarters with limited leisure time. One slave vividly remembered the leafy plants and bright blossoms encircling the family cabin: "Us live in a log house wid a little porch in front and de mornin' glory vines use to climb 'bout it. When they bloom, de bees would come hummin' 'round and suck the honey out de blue bells on the vines. I members dat well 'nough, dat was a pleasant memory.'" Many women probably "dressed up" the exterior of their homes with blossoms.[4]

After slavery, Glenda Gilmore has argued, educated African American women sought to establish partnerships with men "that maximized the potential and efficiency of both members, and they tended to do that by avoiding hierarchical ideas of male dominance and female subordination. Men and women were different, but they had complementary work to do; once trained for that work, women were anxious to establish domestic relationships that allowed them to get on with the job."[5] Similarly, rural African American women and men cooperated with one another, cultivating loosely along gender lines: Men tended fields and women kept gardens. African American men produced cash crops to support their families after slavery was dismantled, while women expanded their roles by cultivating family vegetable patches and continuing to plant ornamental and flower gardens.

Gardening and Home Demonstration

These gardening traditions and the values of the women who practiced them were illuminated by their contact with Progressive reform. Rural African American women were both reformers and the objects of reform as part of the national Progressive movement. Though fragmented, Progressives shared core themes: opposing abuses by private and government organizations, promoting social reform or justice, and promulgating the gospel of scientific efficiency. Of the three, scientific efficiency or the gospel of safe farming most influenced African American women who gardened. Using agricultural and conservation methods, they applied Progressive "principles of efficiency, scientific management, centralized control, and organized economic development" in rural housekeeping.[6] Across the country, upper- and middle-class African American women formed their own Progressive organizations like the National Association of Colored Women in 1896, along with other local clubs. African American women served the community by pressuring dairies to supply pasteurized milk for infants, building libraries, and supporting homes for the elderly and orphans. In the South, Margaret Murray Washington called the first Tuskegee Woman's Club meeting in 1895, and club members crossed social barriers to assist their poor sisters. Well-heeled women sought upward mobility and entrée into exclusive social events. Club members also visited local women to teach them to care for their homes, children, and ultimately the community. Affluent African American women combined elitism and service and were often condescending to their poor rural counterparts.

Rural African American women who were agents, teachers, students, and housewives also gardened under the auspices of a broader Progressive agricultural reform. The 1914 Smith-Lever Act created the Cooperative Extension Work in Agriculture and Home Economics, a branch of the Federal Extension Service, to promote the wise use of natural resources in forestry as well as in farming and to offer rural families training and information on topics from beekeeping to women's canning to boys' pig clubs. The Extension Service persuaded farmers and their families across the country to implement scientific conservation methods such as applying fertilizers and planting cover crops, such as crimson clover, in the off-season to protect the soil. The Extension Service directed money and resources to white colleges catering to white farmers and creating centralized, racially tiered administrations, classes, and services. The agency assigned Cooperative Extension agents from the colleges to other groups such as African Americans; some agents traveled from farm to farm, while others worked in experiment stations.[7]

Booker T. Washington launched the prototype of the Negro Cooperative Extension Service at Tuskegee Institute. He reinforced the racial hierarchy of the Progressive period by promoting separate education and unequal employment in the trades and agriculture for African Americans. Sharing his vision with rural farmers in Alabama, Washington encouraged them to improve their farming methods. The Tuskegee Institute Movable School, which carted the latest farm and household implements around the countryside on a horse-drawn carriage, was used to demonstrate conservation techniques to local African American farmers. On November 12, 1905, Tuskegee appointed Thomas Monroe Campbell as the first Cooperative Extension agent. Working with African American farmers, he traveled in the Movable School truck, loaned farm implements, set up displays for safe farming, and attempted to improve the health and homes of local sharecroppers and owner-operators. In ensuing years, agents like Campbell expanded the program throughout the country.[8]

Women both represented and were served by the Home Demonstration Service of the Negro Cooperative Extension Service. One hundred women worked as agents for Home Demonstration in the South in 1923. These salaried employees were selected as demonstrators to train local women to improve their homes and yards. African American women worked in one hundred counties in eleven states, with approximately half in Georgia, Mississippi, Texas, and Arkansas. The agents modeled household and family healthcare to local African American women and girls in demonstration and club work. Agent Campbell undervalued some of the women's duties: "During certain months of the year there is little or no work for women. We urge upon every woman the raising of poultry and consequently, the production of eggs, the making of butter, the pickling, drying and canning of fruits, such as berries, plums, peaches, and apples, the cultivating of a garden and raising of bees. Let her sell her produce to the best advantage, reserving a portion for home use." Campbell failed to acknowledge that rural women's work was labor intensive throughout the year.[9]

The vigor of their activity was demonstrated in other ways as well. African American women completed 17,311 demonstrations in home beautification of lawns and flower gardens in 1920. The Cooperative Extension Service also documented that African American women cultivated 20,494 home vegetable gardens across the country in that same year. They grew personal vegetable and truck gardens, planted fruit trees and vines, and beautified their yards with flowers and ornamental plants. Agents also performed some rural engineering by building and remodeling homes and other buildings. Their engineering responsibilities probably extended to terracing and horizontal plowing in larger gardens. The women first developed an expertise in gardening in the community, and then applied the Progressive scientific housekeeping principles of cleanliness, thriftiness, and management of Home Demonstration work. The government trained African American women to cultivate flowers, vegetables, trees, and shrubs. Agents sponsored yard contests, provided training, and evaluated soil conservation and aesthetics under the aegis of Negro Beautification of Grounds. They sought to uplift lower-class African Americans by modeling home improvement, particularly the exteriors of homes. One agent said, "practically every home has put forth some effort to have flowers around the place and much beauty has been added in the country-side by these patches of color."[10]

African Americans practiced two types of gardening that conflicted with and paralleled Progressive agricultural techniques: mimicking nature and cultivating the row system. Some gardeners reinforced African and African American traditions in cosmology, an interpretation of the natural ordering of the universe of wilderness, settled spaces, and crossroads. Slaves, sharecroppers, and even members of the gardening clubs created distinctively African American spaces that simultaneously mimicked nature and rejected white control. Though the gardens appeared chaotic, the disarray of plants also created diversity that reduced opportunities for weeds and pests to take hold. Some gardeners sought ethical, moral, and spiritual enlightenment in these chaotic or wilderness spaces in a way much like their African ancestors.

Zora Neale Hurston fictionalized just such an early-twentieth-century yard cared for by her character Missy May in the short story "The Gilded Six Bits": "The front yard was parted in the middle by a sidewalk from gate to door-step, a sidewalk edged on either side by quart bottles driven neck down into the ground on a slant. A mess of homey flowers planted without a plan but blooming cheerily from their helter-skelter place." Effie Graham, a white novelist, also fictionalized an urban African American woman in turn-of-the-twentieth-century Kansas who kept "a half-pleasing, half-offending jumble of greenery and gleaming color, of bush and vine; of vegetable and blooming flower, of kitchen ware, crockery, and defunct household furniture." This novelist disparagingly compared the yard to an African jungle, park, and dump. In Beaufort and Wayne Counties, North Carolina, an agent similarly critiqued African American women's yards in a garden contest, concluding that the women kept their yards in disarray out of poverty. Though not overtly racist, the agent's conclusions probably were based upon the racism of the period. Some observers, including Progressive Home Demonstration agents, did not know or care that African and African American experience influenced some African American gardeners.[11]

Yet other African Americans planted symmetrical gardens that met the goals of Progressive agricultural reform but likely were rooted in older row-crop traditions. African Americans applied their own understandings, though, in their community appreciation of the best method for gardening. African Americans valued doing things properly by applying the "'right way' of arranging poles of beans, a 'right way' of building a potato bank." Neighbors often competed in a friendly fashion, using a uniform design, aesthetics, and old-fashioned labor. The North Carolina "Richmond County Yard Improvement Contest" agents reinforced this approach: "Instead of trying to judge all of the yards before and after they are planted, we decided to offer one point for every shrubbery plant planted in a permanent place by next fall, but to encourage their planting them in the right places. I have had demonstration in

planting all over the county and have particularly stressed foundation planting. All of the women who are on the committee are interested in flowers and
the majority of them have well planted lawns. . . . This contest includes white
and colored homes as the colored yards detract from the view as much as the
others. This will enable every home to feel that they can make some effort to
beautify their yard and community."[12] Gardeners integrated Progressive gardening ideas with older traditions within a context of community expecta-
tions about what was right and what was not in the garden.

Jacqueline Jones documented an early-twentieth-century community tradition practiced by African American women who dug up woodland flowers
to permanently improve their cabins. They transplanted azaleas, wild roses,
honeysuckle, and dogwoods in their yards. A Beaufort County agent praised
poor African American women who practiced frugality by collecting roots in
the woods as part of Home Demonstration. The agent also criticized the
women's homes before they "borrowed" plants from local woods, imitating
nature, to cover "unsightly porches." Similarly, agents in Wake County, North
Carolina, sponsored a contest for thirty African American and white participants who transplanted local shrubs and small trees from the swamps to their
yards, creating beautiful exteriors. Some planted long-leaf pines, including
Lob Lolly, along with holly. They cultivated inexpensive native shrubs, making
their yards more attractive. Smaller plants included wax myrtle, yucca, cedar,
laurel, sumac, and poinsettia. According to another agent, women doggedly
scouted out plants, trees, shrubs, and flowers: "In some places I may have
made beggars of the women, in other places I have sent them into swamps in
crowds, but for it all I am sure, we will have a more beautiful county and a
more satisfied home-loving people."[13]

African Americans also developed a garden aesthetic based on traditional
and Progressive influences. According to Richard Westmacott, women gardeners cultivated flower patches for visual appeal: "The flower yard results from
some inner conviction to create something beautiful. . . . The impression was
that these yards were gestures of graciousness in otherwise desperately hard
lives." Home Demonstration agents contributed to this aesthetic by evaluating
segregated neighborhood yard improvements, with a focus on aesthetics, in
the North Carolina Forsythe Improvement Contest. The judges reviewed aesthetics, emphasizing borders and foundations, and recommended that the
women use native shrubs, probably borrowed from the local woods. An agent
observed that, "Many walks were re-arranged, flower beds moved from lawns,
lawns sowed in grass, unsightly buildings removed, houses painted, steps re-
paired, shrubbery grouped on corners and at entrances to grounds, and some
terracing done." The agents encouraged African American women to make

their homes and yards beautiful by starting or continuing to plant flowers.[14]

The advances Progressive reformers believed they were introducing into African American households also were integrated into long-practiced traditions of conservation. Slaves composted oak leaves with fire ash and applied barnyard manure and human waste to fertilize their gardens. African Americans continued to use conservation techniques in the early twentieth century. In Alabama, Onnie Lee Logan, an African American midwife, reminisced about her mother's garden: "We had three big gardens. String beans, butter beans, turnip greens, English peas, sweet potatoes, Irish potatoes, okra, ever'thing. Tomatoes, three or four different kinds of squash . . . love, care, and share, that's what we did. We had it and my daddy and mother they shared with the ones that didn't have it. Mother would send a piece and share." Her mother's resourceful diversification of vegetables made good gardening sense, and translated also into a sense of community and social responsibility that was common among rural African Americans. Lacey Gray from Longleaf, Louisiana, said her mother fed her healthy food from the garden: "Mother never used pesticides or chemical fertilizers and we never had problems with insects either. Used cow manure on big crops and chicken manure on the kitchen garden." Mary Lee from Shreveport, Louisiana, reminisced about her mother who used laundry water to fertilize the vegetables and herbs in her yard.[15]

Progressive reform efforts, conscious or not, joined or built on these traditions, which included numerous examples of applications of conservation and agricultural techniques in Home Demonstration gardening. In the Richmond County Yard Improvement Contest, ten women's and seven girls' clubs competed in home garden contests and continued to practice such techniques. One contestant, Sally Moore, an African American woman and club president in the Hilly Branch, North Carolina, community, practiced diversification and planted thirty-four different vegetables in what might have been a truck farm garden, and produced a ten-pound head of cabbage. She probably fertilized her garden with compost and manure. In demonstrations on how to root plants, agents suggested the women ask one another for cuttings from plants, a gardening method borrowed from agriculture. In addition, they evaluated the efforts by the women in conservation and agricultural techniques in terracing for drainage and maximizing space for planting, along with planting and maintaining plants. They recommended that women use native grasses to protect against wind and water erosion. Two other women of unknown ethnicity competed for prizes. Mrs. Roscoe Johnson of Wake County won a fifteen-dollar second prize for a garden made with "good soil." Mrs. Bryan Bizzell, a third-place, ten-dollar winner, resurrected the beauty of her old homestead by using grass, flowers, shrubs, and other improvements to create "a lovely scene." Other improvements might have included water and erosion control, along with fertilizing techniques using nitrate and manure, leaving fields fallow, and rotating crops, all based upon Progressive scientific conservation and agricultural techniques—some already based on traditional practices in the community.[16]

Participants in Home Demonstration took the initiative in planting their own gardens and practicing conservation and agricultural methods outside these competitions. Mrs. Clarence Vincent of Winterville diversified her North Carolina vegetable garden in a way typical of African Americans and whites. She planted Irish and sweet potatoes, beans, and peas, which were stored and consumed in winter. During the rest of the year she cultivated lettuce, radishes, celery, carrots, cabbage, spinach, turnip greens, kale, collards, mustard, turnips, rutabagas, and parsnips. She further diversified her garden, mixing vegetables and fruits by planting strawberries, blackberries, and figs. Women in North Carolina's Home Gardens Work of Beaufort County also planted hotbeds and cold frames and prepared the soil for "early and successive planting and frequent cultivation of the tried and true vegetables along with the introduction of a few new ones." Mrs. W. H. Shavender, another North Carolina woman, diversified and fertilized two plots: "I tried beans, tomatoes, corn, beets, spinach, turnips, onions, pimentos, pepper and kale both with and without nitrate of soda. My ground was prepared exactly the same for both, same amount of stable manure, everything except the side dressing of Nitrate of Soda on one and not on the other. The yield was more than double with the soda and the plants and corn were not affected by the weather. The rows that had soda application stayed green and kept bearing even after the other was gone, especially so with beans. . . . I never intended to plant anything in my garden again without Nitrate of Soda. Last year I had lovely celery but this year it was killed completely by drought. Nitrate of Soda gives such a wonderful start while plants are young." She also may have applied barnyard manure to restore soil fertility. The women continued a tradition in gardening, influenced by the community and the government.[17]

Gardening in African American Schools

African American gardening traditions were bolstered and reinforced by the education efforts initiated by the schools for African Americans that were founded after the emancipation of slaves. Education was of premier importance for freedmen and freedwomen, and they went to great lengths to encourage opportunities for learning. African American women had their own interests, and sought out more knowledge in gardening. They opened, supported, and attended their own segregated schools to reduce high illiteracy among African Americans in the South. To promote and develop southern education after slavery, African American women struggled against a substandard education system of inadequate facilities, supplies, and teachers compared with white schools across the nation. The teachers taught in one-room buildings, which often had been built for other purposes like sheltering livestock. A typical room was drafty and chilly in winter and humid and sweltering in summer. Schools paid African American teachers far less than their white counterparts, giving them salaries as low as $1.60 a month. Women, the primary pool for secondary teachers, generally lived on these subsistence wages, supplemented by room and board with a local family. In addition, teachers foraged for school supplies including chalkboards, books, pencils, and paper. W. E. B. DuBois described his own rural teaching experience in *The Souls of Black Folk* (1903): "There was an entrance where a door once was, and within, a massive rickety fireplace; great chinks between the logs served as windows. Furniture was scarce. A pale blackboard crouched in the corner. My desk was made of three boards, reinforced at critical points, and my chair, borrowed from the land-lady, had to be returned every night. Seats for the children—these puzzled me much. I was haunted by a New England vision of neat little desks and chairs, but, alas! The reality was rough plank benches without backs, and at times without legs."[18]

Education for southern African Americans came from a number of outside sources, including northern philanthropists and societies, the Freedmen's Bureau, and state governments. For example, northern reformers were eager to work in partnership with southern freedmen and founded many of the first schools. Yearning for autonomy and self-improvement, African Americans also practiced self-help, hired and paid teachers, purchased building materials, and constructed their own schools and campus facilities. When Reconstruction ended, African Americans continued to improve and support education. State agricultural and mechanical colleges, along with private institutions, also served the community, offering longer and more extensive agricultural and home economics courses. The schools offered full-time agricultural school programs—which translated into education in the rural community—planned yard competitions, and home demonstrations.

African American schools offered classes with practical and aesthetic applications and involvement with model yards, on school grounds, for teaching and profit. The model yards featured traditional elements found in a rural African American culture, including gardens, livestock, and laundering. Schools like Tuskegee and Hampton Institute also offered home economics classes, which included gardening training for women and an agricultural curriculum for men. Most significantly, African American women teachers taught other women to cultivate aesthetically pleasing gardens. Some applied their training to teach at secondary schools. In 1937, the African American Elizabeth City State Normal Summer School in North Carolina offered a class in housing titled, "The Rural Community Background and Rural School Organization and Management," which emphasized home and yard aesthetics in the curriculum, and suggested "ways and means of making rural life more attractive and joyous to those who live in the open country." Students sketched "attractive lawns and backyards and [gave] suggestions of what native shrubbery to use and when to transplant it" in this class. They created images of nature in their art and searched the woods for plants to dig up, carry home, and replant.[19]

Progressive influences continued at Hampton Institute, which offered African American women courses with aesthetics in mind, ranging from "Flower Arrangement" to "Landscape Design" in the "Curriculum for the Division of Agriculture." These courses nurtured creativity through symmetry and beauty. Hampton also offered "Flower Arrangement" and "Flower Growing for Amateurs"—classes focusing on aesthetics and scientific housekeeping already practiced in the community and Home Demonstration. In the flower arranging class, teachers taught "the fascinating art of flower arrangement [that] provides a medium of expression universal in appeal. Students in all divisions of the Institute will find value in learning to utilize plant materials in home, store, school, or office decoration." Instructors demonstrated "the necessary methods involved in knowing and growing ornamental plants commonly used about the home can well be learned with study and practice" in "Flower Growing." As teachers, Home Demonstration agents, or homemakers, women applied scientific housekeeping to gardening.[20]

Hampton also offered classes in advanced gardening. Teachers there taught "Ornamental Horticulture," a course general enough in scope for the layperson and the horticulturist. Students, both men and women, learned to arrange and enhance "the homes and grounds and larger properties in order to make them more useful as well as attractive" while "growing and caring for trees, shrubs, and flowers as a commercial enterprise or as a hobby." One of the courses, "Landscape Design of Small Properties," was more advanced than basic flower planting and arranging, and taught vegetable gardening with an emphasis on aesthetics: "Landscaping one's own home or school grounds is an economy and a pleasure as well as an art. Teachers, community workers, and home owners alike will find it much to their advantage to be able to improve their surroundings in their respective communities." In the "Landscape Gardening" class, students learned "the practical methods of beautifying grounds around the buildings, the construction of wind breaks, placing ornamental flower beds, laying out walks, planting trees and shrubs, arranging and planting window boxes." Once again, African Americans had the opportunity to layer Progressive horticultural education upon community experiences.[21]

By using yards in different ways, African American women took possession of them. They manipulated and interpreted the spaces for sustenance, comfort, joy, and sometimes profit. African American wives, mothers, agents, community volunteers, and students created gardens that were both new and old, with practices that integrated tradition with Progressive practice.

Alice Walker reminisces about her mother, who planted a flower garden in the 1930s and 1940s, just after this Progressive period: "I remember people coming to my mother's yard to be given cuttings from flowers; I hear again the praise showered on her because whatever rocky soil she landed on, she turned into a garden. A garden so brilliant with colors, so original in its design, so magnificent with life and creativity, that to this day people drive by our house in Georgia—perfect strangers and imperfect strangers—and ask to stand or walk among my mother's art. I notice that it is only when my mother is working in her flowers that she is radiant, almost to the point of being invisible—except as Creator: hand and eye. She is involved in work her soul must have. Ordering the universe in the image of her personal conception of Beauty."[22]

Other stories are waiting in the hands, arms, shoulders, and backs of these rural African American women like Walker's mother. More remains to be written about African American women in gardening, and indeed, about the history of rural African American interactions with the environment. How did African traditions in gardening cross the Atlantic into the yards of slaves and then sharecroppers? Did African American and white women differ in their gardening traditions and techniques? Did wealthier African American women tend more ornamental flower gardens and poorer women plant more food and vegetable gardens? Was there any evidence of "lifting as we climb" in gardening work, so pivotal in the African American women's club movement? Were southern gardening traditions transformed when African Americans migrated to cities like Los Angeles and Detroit? How did African Americans create their communal and personal urban and suburban gardens? Do any of those practices continue today, and in what context do things grow for African Americans who engage in gardening—this most fundamental interaction with nature?

❦5

Turpentine Negro

CASSANDRA Y. JOHNSON and JOSH MCDANIEL

> In the pines, in the pines, where the sun never shines
> And I shiver when the cold wind blows.
> I asked my captain for the time of day, said he throwed
> His watch away. . . .
>
> —From the folksong "In the Pines"

Studies have documented the gap between African American and white interaction with the natural environment: generally, African Americans are less likely than whites to visit wildland recreation areas or to participate in forest-based outdoor recreation.[1] Other studies also indicate that African Americans show less environmental concern, although more recent work indicates similar concern levels. These differences have been found even when place of residence and access to wildland resources are controlled. Various explanations have been given to account for these differences, including ethnicity and marginality.[2] This chapter examines an aspect of marginality theory by examining African American labor in relationship to the land, specifically African American experiences working in southern forests in naval stores or turpentine operations.

It is important to explore the relationship African Americans had with the land through labor because woods work such as turpentine extraction may have historical importance for how contemporary African Americans interact with and view forested wildlands.[3] Southern, rural African Americans have a legacy of working and living in close proximity to forested wildlands. While this historical connection to forests through turpentining and other woods work provided African Americans with an intimate lay knowledge of plants, animals, and a general environmental understanding, the exploitation, abuse, and racism that accompanied the industry, and which persist in the contemporary southern forest industry, have resulted in a dramatic decrease in the numbers of African Americans working in the forest. Just as important, we believe that African Americans' collective memory of land-based labor—particularly woods work involving turpentine extraction and other timber products—has contributed to reluctance among African Americans to engage in many forms of forest-based leisure time activities. Collective memory is knowledge held in common by a group of people. The memory is salient to the group and may be "known" by individuals with no firsthand experience of the event or events. In this sense it is a vicarious remembering that is handed down to successive generations through both public and private means.

These associations are not entirely linear because of mitigating factors that may counteract collective recollections. Despite the drudgery associated with woods work, African Americans have always gone to the woods to fish and to a lesser extent to hunt. As Elizabeth Blum maintains, though slaves were frightened of the woods, they also saw the woods as a safe hideaway from plantation overseers. Mart Stewart's scholarship on the agricultural transformation of coastal Georgia by European settlers and African slaves examines the environmental knowledge possessed by African Americans in the postbellum era and how African Americans used this social capital as a leverage to command better wages and working conditions. In terms of domesticated outdoor spaces, Dianne Glave and Richard Westmacott both describe how rural African American women applied their knowledge of nature to gardening and how these practices contributed to traditional, sustainable lifestyles.[4]

Contemporarily, however, there is a continuing chasm between African American and white engagement with the woods, despite substantial socioeconomic gains for the African American middle class in recent decades. The disparity seems to relate more to differences in acceptance of core American values rooted in the frontier ethic. The frontier ethic espouses ideals of American individualism and expansion, the individual (principally white male) constrained by neither law nor land to explore supposedly uncharted and uninhabited territories. White Americans were urged by early conservationists to venture to the frontier and remain there because this geography, the wild and semi-wild, is what made the unique American character.

The wilderness ideal and encouragement to settle the frontier were extended to African Americans begrudgingly. Although African Americans contributed considerably to the settlement of the western frontier (as fur traders, miners, agricultural workers, soldiers, cowboys), they nevertheless experienced anti–African American sentiment and hostility in these regions. Eugene Berwanger comments: "From the beginnings of their settlement the western free states and territories enacted stringent restrictions against free Negroes. . . . In fact, the illiberal racial attitudes in the Old Northwest caused Alexis de

Tocqueville to comment in the 1830's that prejudice against Negroes was more extreme in 'those states where slavery has never been known.'[5] Both pro- and antislavery forces campaigned against African American settlement in the West because of the idea that the western territories were the manifest destiny of whites.

African Americans and other oppressed groups formed a somewhat different relationship to the land based on their relative lack of access to it. For many African Americans, this relationship was severely restricted by racism and a resulting lack of economic, social, or political rights to land, including forested wildlands. The American ideal of wilderness exploration and engagement contributed less to African American identity formation than to that of most European groups. Again, this is not to gainsay the achievements of countless African American pioneers, who like their white counterparts, managed to thrive on the frontier. Still, the African American relationship to the woods, and most other natural lands, emerged from a context of exploitation that presently informs the African American relationship to wildlands.

The Turpentine Industry

Numerous accounts exist of African American work in the plantation economy, both before and after the Civil War, but comparatively little scholarship documents African American labor in naval stores operations. Post–Civil War turpentining, however, contributed significantly to African American southern labor history. Turpentine employment trailed only cotton and timber production in the number of wage earners employed between 1880 and 1930 and accounted for 6 percent of all wage earners in the South in 1900.

The descriptor "naval stores" originates from the colonial era when the British Navy used pine-derived resources such as tar, pitch, gum, turpentine, and rosin in shipbuilding and repair. The British made extensive use of virgin pine forests in the New England and Carolina colonies when their European supply was either depleted or threatened by war with other nations. Similar depletion of pines occurred in the northern American colonies, and the industry was forced to move steadily southward in search of new pine forests. During the antebellum period, mostly small farmers in North Carolina were involved in naval stores production. As demand for these products increased, the planter class moved into the industry in the 1830s and 1840s, and naval stores operations became part of the plantation economy. By the mid-nineteenth century, naval stores products ranked third in exports from the South behind cotton and tobacco. By 1860, roughly fifteen thousand slaves labored in the naval stores industry.

The majority of turpentine workers were African American, both before and after the Civil War. Tegeder notes that in the postbellum period, naval stores operations employed the greatest percentage of African Americans. Most employers considered African Americans as particularly fit for the grueling tasks associated with the work.[6] In both 1910 and 1920, African Americans accounted for at least 80 percent of turpentine laborers in twelve southern states; in 1930, at least 80 percent of turpentiners in Florida, Georgia, and Mississippi were African American, and at least 70 percent were African American in South Carolina and Alabama. This type of labor market stratification continued well into the twentieth century with the establishment of turpentine camps throughout the South.

The monikers "Turpentine Negro" or "Turpentine Nigger" were common because African Americans were so closely identified with the work. One turpentine operator went so far as to develop a grading system for rosin, a turpentine by-product, that assigned value to rosin based on skin tones of African American turpentine workers and their families. The lighter, clearer rosin was considered to be of superior quality and commanded higher prices. The darker rosin brought lower prices. Robert Schultz describes the taxonomy: "The originator of the system picked out a very light skinned negress [sic] named Nance whose color matched his best rosin grade. Mary was next— slightly darker. Then Kate, Isaac, Harry, Frank, Edward, Dolly down to Betsy who was almost black."[7]

After the Civil War, naval stores operations moved from plantations to camps established by producers who secured financing for the operations. The industry also moved steadily southward as pine forests in the Carolinas became depleted. Turpentining took place in remote pine forests. The extraction of gum, or oleoresin, occurred from March or April until November. Workers used a set of specialized tools to debark trees and to "chip" or streak the face of the tree to stimulate gum flow. Chippers maintained a "drift" of trees (usually about five thousand), which they visited and streaked about once a week with a hack. The gum flowed into a receptacle that changed over time from simple boxes cut in the base of the tree to aluminum and clay cups that were hung on the tree beneath a system of metal gutters.

In later years, chippers also applied acid to the tree to stimulate flow.[8] Following the chippers were dippers who emptied the cups and boxes and filled barrels for transportation to the stills. Most turpentine operations divided labor between chippers, dippers, drivers, supervisors (or woods riders), and distillery workers. At the beginning and end of the work cycle, workers hung cups and gutters and raked around the trees to prevent destructive fires from killing the trees through their exposed faces.

Until the 1930s, turpentining was a purely extractive operation. The longleaf and slash pine forests were viewed like minerals to be extracted rather than as renewable resources. Turpentining often preceded logging operations, and the trees were worked for three to six years before they were cut for timber.

Debt Peonage

Like many extractive industries throughout the world, the postbellum and twentieth-century turpentine industry relied heavily on cheap labor. In the late nineteenth century, demand for turpentine and other naval stores products increased significantly, but turpentine workers were scarce. To ensure a cheap and ready labor supply, turpentine agents recruited African Americans from the Carolinas who were familiar with turpentine operations to travel with the camps when the operations moved into the lower southeastern states. Labor shortages continued to be a problem around the turn of the century, and as noted above, foreign workers were recruited to help fill the demand. Repressive contract labor laws were also enacted in several southern states. These laws broadly defined vagrancy and essentially made it illegal for males over eighteen to be unemployed. Any man caught "idling" on the streets could be arrested and sentenced to a turpentine camp.

Turpentine workers and their families lived in camps established by operators or producers. These camps were reminiscent of the antebellum plantation system in which African Americans were absolutely dependent upon white operators for their livelihood. Producers provided for every aspect of the workers' existence in the camp, including housing, food, equipment, and supplies. In many instances, turpentine camps operated on a cashless basis. Employees were paid in company script that could be used only at company stores. Workers paid in actual money were still required to purchase all food and other necessities from the company store or commissary. New arrivals to the camps were often advanced food and other supplies with the expectation that the costs for the goods would be subtracted from subsequent salaries. Because of extremely low wages (either on a piecemeal basis or $1.00 to $1.50 per day) and the inability to pay cash for supplies, turpentiners had to purchase on credit and thus became deeper in debt. Various taxes and penalties were also subtracted from wages, so that workers invariably found themselves indebted to their employers.

Wayne Flynt, a historian of the rural South, has described how debt peonage was backed by state laws and local law enforcement.[9] The state of Alabama had a law until the early 1930s that allowed plantation owners to have laborers arrested for failure to repay debts. If a worker was arrested, the state would lease the prisoner back to the owner for wages less than the worker was originally being paid. Laborers who tried to leave a plantation to which they were indebted were treated as escaped criminals and hunted down, just as their slave ancestors had been pursued after escaping cotton plantations.

Turpentine Camps

"How did you get into turpentining?" I asked a ragged, half-toothless old man in one of the surviving camps.

"Sugar," he grinned back, "you is *born* into the teppentime. Ain't nothing you *go into*. Something you get *out of*."[10]

The wilderness is benign; however, in the case of turpentine workers, it provided the backdrop or context for oppression. Turpentine camps were located in isolated woodlands far removed from regular society. This remote environment facilitated a social and economic order based on exploitation and, in many cases, brutality. The early turpentine camps had a reputation for being hard, inbred places where there were few religious, educational, social, or recreational outlets save gambling or other illicit activity.

In the postbellum era and early twentieth century, workers were compelled to labor in the camps without any rights recognized by owners or camp bosses. The operators set the conditions and rules for camp life and any infractions were punished severely. Camp bosses and woods riders (a position analogous to an overseer) commonly whipped workers to keep order and instill fear and obedience. It was also not uncommon for laborers to be locked in their quarters after work to prevent them from leaving the camp. As indicated above, in cases where a worker escaped, he was hunted down by the turpentine owner or his agent and returned to camp with the justification that the worker owed the producer money for goods advanced. Early turpentine producers reasoned that they owned African Americans' labor and felt justified working him until injury or death.

Like white pioneers venturing into the western territories, turpentine workers around the turn of the twentieth century lived, literally, on southern frontiers; yet their experience seemed the inverse of that predicted by Frederick Jackson Turner. Turner argued that wilderness promoted democracy, while civilized society, by contrast, fertilized tyranny because the very process of civilization compelled one to conform.[11] Turner's "frontier thesis" is challenged by the experience of turpentine workers. The managers and the workers in some sense may have developed a rugged individualism from being in the wild; but instead of this evolving into a unique individualism and independence that challenged authoritarian rule, workers were subjugated by the worst kind of despotism.

The microsociety that supported turpentine operations was an extension and intensification of the oppression existent in everyday southern society. After Martin Tabert, a young, white worker from a middle-class South Dakota family, was murdered by an infamous camp boss in 1921, the Florida legislature investigated turpentine camps throughout the South and surmised: "conditions—not limited to the single camp but existing throughout the turpentine belt . . . were revolting to the most hardened person."[12]

Tegeder has described typical conditions in the work camps: "Rural employers on remote plantations or isolated turpentine and railroad construction camps, for example, routinely regulated, prohibited, and punished African American behavior—however removed from the process of production—without assistance from the state. Local authorities simply considered African-American misbehavior, according to sociologist Arthur Raper, as 'a labor matter to be handled by the white landlord or his overseer.' With the approval of local law enforcement officials and white public opinion, southern employers could rule their workforce with a ruthlessness, even cruel, discipline that rivaled the legendary abuses of Simon Legree."[13]

Over time, many turpentine camps consisted of multiple generations of turpentine workers. People were born in the camps, grew up there, and when the males came of age, they learned how to harvest gum like their fathers before them. Children grew up with little opportunity for education because they lived so far from local schools, and also because the camps moved every few years.

Industry Decline

After World War II, the gum naval stores industry in the United States began to decline. This decline was precipitated by a number of factors, the most important of which was the lack of manpower.[14] Turpentining was very labor intensive, with labor accounting for more than 60 percent of production costs. The arduous nature of the work and the expanding economy and industrial development after the war lured many workers from the South to more amenable northern industries. This labor shortage made it increasingly difficult for turpentine farmers to operate, given foreign competitors who could produce at lower costs.

In a study of the turpentine industry's decline by Chiang, Burrows, Howard, and Woodard, the authors list several factors that contributed to the labor shortage. Among these are: an unflattering industry image, the paternalism of producers, low wage and job status, competition from other industries, poor living conditions in the turpentine camps, bad working conditions, employment instability, and poor employer-employee relations. Turpentine operators interviewed in that study also stressed that welfare programs lured workers away from turpentine camps. The low salaries earned by workers qualified them for federal financial assistance programs that provided competitive incomes without the difficult working conditions.[15] Owners believed that these programs removed the incentive for turpentine work.

Due in large part to the rough terrain and difficulty in navigating dense forests, technological innovations did not replace the loss of human workers. The actual work of harvesting gum was virtually the same in 1940 as it had been in the antebellum era.[16] Declining production of turpentine continued through the 1960s and 1970s, and had virtually disappeared by the 1980s, except for a few remnant operations. The last remaining working crop in Georgia was harvested in 2001, but this last crop represented only a tiny fraction of pre–World War II output.

Turpentine in the African American Collective Memory

Turpentining has been held in the African American collective memory and passed down to successive generations orally. The principal means of this transference has come through folktale and song. Zora Neale Hurston's compelling documentation of turpentine workers' songs in the early Florida camps provides a vivid and "lived" account of the conditions that accompanied the work.[17] These recollections are not cemented in the academy but comprise an important part of African American folk tradition.

Though turpentine workers lived separately from other African Americans, knowledge of the harshness and meanness of their rustic existence was pervasive in the larger African American society. Not only turpentine laborers but other African Americans as well considered turpentining to be demeaning, and the latter sought to distance themselves from those who worked turpentine. Turpentiners were considered to be among the most uncouth and ignorant of African Americans. This attitude suggests a disdain for not only the workers but also the environment in which they labored, the woods. This viewpoint is consistent with Eldridge Cleaver's proclamation: "In terms of seeking status in America, blacks—principally the black bourgeoisie—have come to measure their own value according to the number of degrees they are away from the soil."[18]

Despite their hardships, turpentine workers exercised agency by developing an awareness and appreciation for the world in which they found themselves. Like other groups living close to nature, they aligned themselves with it. They learned to tell time by the sun's position, to forecast rain by watching insects congregate, and to "read" the signs and omens proffered by nature. The ambivalence these workers and their families exhibited towards the woods was expressed by Ethylene Seastrunk, the wife of a turpentine worker in north Florida in the 1960s. She commented that she desperately wanted her sons to find work outside the turpentine camps. But she also says that it would be difficult for her to leave her wooded home because of her attachment to it: "Surely, surely, I think about livin' in the city sometimes. But, you know, I fraid I miss the woods too much. I love them old trees and the shade. And then, you can't hardly do no fishing in the city."[19]

Most of the early turpentine workers have died, and with them, firsthand accounts of life in the camps. Josh McDaniel located several turpentiners in south Alabama and talked to them about their lives working in the turpentine industry. These workers generally reference the turpentine camps of the post–World War II era, a time when camp conditions had improved, but the desire to leave the backwoods cabins and isolation remained.

Leander Showers is a retired turpentine worker. He was born in 1933 in Wallace, Alabama, and lived most of his life in turpentine camps throughout Alabama and Florida. He is named after the owner of the camp in which his father worked for most his life in McKinnonville, Florida. Showers started in turpentine when he was young: "My daddy started me off when I was five years old. I had a little ole syrup bucket and I'd be putting about two or three cups in there. They had the clay cups, the galvanized, and the aluminum. Sometimes it takes about three to fill my little bucket up, and I would carry it to the barrel." When Showers turned eighteen, he left the camp in McKinnonville and traveled from one camp to the next starting in north Florida and working his way down to central Florida over the course of fifteen years. He worked for different companies that leased land and continually moved turpentine camps further south as each lease ran out. He says that most of the abuses that have been written about in turpentine did not exist by the time he started working in the industry. It was hard work, and he didn't make much money, but he mainly has fond memories of the work and takes pride in his skill and knowledge of the woods. According to Showers, a good turpentine worker could look at a tree—the number of branches and cones, the lushness of the needles, and tell what quality and quantity of gum it would produce.

> You could tell how well a tree was going to run by looking at the canopy. If it was top-heavy you could count on more sap than one that hardly had any limbs on it—lots of needles—a good heavy straw. That meant it was going to be pulling a lot of sap and you was going to catch your share of it. When they had a heavy pinecone crop you could figure that there was going to be a light turpentine year. It was going to feed that pinecone, you know. I've seen good running trees with a big, heavy top and all. After I

tacked up a cup, I would throw down a couple underneath because I knew it would fill it up before I got back to collect it.

Turpentiners also developed complex understandings of the ecological properties and interaction of forests and climate, as evidenced by this comment from Showers: "As soon as the sap started running, we started streaking. Your turpentine runs when the sap goes up in a tree, when it comes down it quits running. I've seen these creeks be plum dry and sap start coming down and they would go back to running. That is moisture going back into the ground from them trees."

Showers learned to hunt and fish in the woods while he was working, and he would often bring back small game like rabbits and squirrels from a day in the woods. He knew the behavior of animals well and developed a respect for rattlesnakes: "You had to be careful because you had to be watching for them rattlers. If you change your route you are sure to run up on them. So if you are supposed to go up along there Wednesday, you better try to that same day. If you go another day earlier or a day late you going to meet him. But if you don't ever change your route you are all right."

In the 1960s, Showers moved back to McKinnonville where he had grown up. He wanted to settle down and raise a family. When his children were born he decided that he did not want them to be raised in a turpentine camp. He moved out of the camp in McKinnonville and purchased a house for his family nearby. Showers drove a truck into the camp everyday after that and joined the rest of the workers. He said that his children never worked a day in the woods. By the 1970s and 1980s, when Showers's sons were old enough to work, there were not many jobs left in the turpentine industry. Many of the former turpentiners were going into the timber business and working on shortwood logging crews. Like Seastrunk, Showers encouraged his children to get out of any work that would keep them in the forest. When asked why, he said: "There just ain't no money in it. The owners and the companies make all the money and the working man is stuck down at the bottom with nothing left over. It is a hard life, and I thought they could do better in something else. A lot of the people I knew who worked in turpentine went into the lumber business, but all of them are done now. There ain't no life in that neither." Both of Showers's sons now work in construction.[20]

In the 1940s and 1950s, as sharecropping and turpentine production were declining, some turpentiners shifted into pulpwooding—supplying wood to the mills that were beginning to dot the southern landscape. The pulp and paper industry developed a wood-supply system consistent with the social structure of the region. The relationship between the mill owners, wood dealers, producers, and workers typified the hierarchical social organization under slavery, sharecropping, and turpentine camps. Poor whites and African Americans did the work in the woods while landowners and merchants collected the profits. However, as the industry has moved toward highly mechanized, sophisticated wood-harvesting systems, employment opportunities dried up for those at the bottom of the job hierarchy. In a recent study of Alabama pulpwood producers, a woods worker and wood producer expressed it this way: "You can't find no wood now, you just can't find it. I can't. . . . They turned it to the big man, you see the big man got it all, see. These big haulers, these ones that got, the big companies are the ones that got it now. Boy, these trailer trucks, they haul everywhere, they go everywhere. They go for one hundred fifty miles, day and night too, I know some that does. So, the little man can't find no wood now, he can't do it. I can't."[21]

Poverty and unemployment are endemic in the rural counties of the South dominated by forest industries. Landownership and income from timber sales are concentrated in the hands of a few white owners, mirroring patterns established during the antebellum period. Relatively few African Americans have gained access to employment opportunities in the pulp and paper mills, and with the disappearance of shortwood logging and the increased mechanization of woods work, few are able to continue making a living in the forests. Migrant workers from Mexico and Central America, willing to work at reduced wages and under horrible working conditions, now supply the primary labor at the bottom of the work hierarchy. In many areas of the rural South, little has changed since the turpentine quarters were occupied by impoverished workers who provided labor for a vast industry with global connections.

"The thousand faces of the piney woods" as Zora Neale Hurston described the turpentine forests, elicit echoes of labor, suffering, and abuse. Scars remain in the trunks, built through years of "pulling streaks" to capture the once valuable resins as they rose and fell through the woody veins of the pines. Scars also remain in the communities consumed by turpentine. This remote industry once dominated the economy, and culturally it shaped the relationship between whites and African Americans and landowners and laborers in many parts of the South. That influence can be still be sensed in conversations with those who worked in the industry.

Turpentine evokes some of what has made southern society what it is today, and it is an essential part of the way in which the landscape has been transformed so completely and dramatically. In some ways, the story of turpentine tells of a time when people depended on their knowledge of the forest for sustenance, health, and livelihood. Such intimacy with trees and forests speaks to a period when seasons were measured by the rising and falling of resins in stately pines, fire dominated the landscape, and the forests were filled with the songs of workers singing to the tallyman.

This romanticized description of the turpentine era, however, should be weighed against the larger reality of poverty and African American longing for that elusive, other, modernized and popularized America—the soda pop and hot dog world that Seastrunk's children found in town schools away from the camp.[22] Though the woods provided a livelihood and a knowledge base for turpentine workers and their families, this meager subsistence was not sufficient to keep most turpentiners in the woods. The hardships outweighed the benefits. Like other Americans, turpentiners longed for more for both themselves and their offspring.

After Jim Crow was abolished in the southern states by the 1960s, many African Americans fled the rural backcountry in search of the modern amenities available in the larger southern cities and in the North. The very idea of going back to the forest for recreation would be to abandon the African American quest for modernization. For as many years as African Americans have been in North America, they have striven to debunk negative stereotypes and categorizations of themselves as primal, natural, simple, and uncivilized. If African Americans are to return to the woods en masse as nature enthusiasts, they must first reconcile with the past and then move forward to reclaim and reacquaint themselves with the forests and woodlands in which their forebears both learned and survived.

✿6

African Americans, Outdoor Recreation, and the 1919 Chicago Race Riot

COLIN FISHER

Since the late 1960s, practitioners in the field of environmental history have labored to make nature a critical category of historical analysis, and over the past three decades, their insights have altered the ways in which historians, environmentalists, and even the larger public understand the relationship between nature and culture. But in exploring this relationship, environmental historians have often downplayed differences within human cultures, especially along lines of race, class, and gender. As historian Alan Taylor points out, when it comes to human history, environmental historians tend to "lump" rather than "split."[1]

More recently, though, the field is paying far more attention to divisions within human societies. Motivated in part by the environmental justice movement, many environmental historians are examining the inequitable distribution of scarce natural resources, such as water, and the disproportionate impact of environmental hazards, such as pollution and "natural" disasters, on disadvantaged people.

One subject largely untouched by environmental historians who "split" is disadvantaged Americans' use of nature for leisure. It is commonly assumed that people of color and working-class European Americans were simply too preoccupied struggling for the necessities of life to concern themselves with a "luxury" such as leisure in nature or in the wilderness. Only those who had satisfied basic needs—middle- and upper-class European Americans—made the retreat back to nature.[2]

63

Yet in the early twentieth century, many black Chicagoans saw recreation in nature not as a luxury but as an essential escape from unhealthy urban conditions. Despite forced exclusion from parks, playgrounds, and beaches, blacks struggled for access to open space. Indeed, this struggle for nature and accompanying white resistance played a major but unacknowledged role in one of the most violent racial altercations in twentieth-century American history: the 1919 Chicago race riot.

The riot began on a hot Sunday afternoon in July. As the mercury rose, thousands of working-class Chicago residents, both black and white, escaped the heat of the city by seeking out nature, particularly the Lake Michigan shore. Five African American boys from the South Side joined in this exodus. They met at an industrial area on the shore called "Hot and Cold," so named because of the temperature of the effluent coming from a nearby ice company and brewery. The informally segregated "black beach" at Twenty-fifth Street lay just to the north. Directly south lay Twenty-ninth Street Beach, a lakeside swimming area that working-class whites had claimed for themselves. At Hot and Cold, the boys boarded a raft made of railroad ties and pushed off into the water of Lake Michigan.

As the five moved out into the cool lake, a white man on the jetty off Twenty-sixth Street spotted their approaching raft and began throwing rocks. One of these hit fourteen-year-old Eugene Williams in the head. Williams, who had been treading water alongside the raft, slipped beneath the surface of the lake and drowned. Horrified, the other four boys raced back to the black beach at Twenty-fifth Street, where they alerted a black lifeguard and police officer. After a futile rescue effort, the black officer took the boys to the white beach to look for the rock thrower. The boys identified the perpetrator, but Daniel Callahan, the white policeman in charge at the beach, refused to apprehend him. Callahan also forbade the black officer from making an arrest. As often-exaggerated stories of the drowning and Officer Callahan's dereliction of duty spread, an angry crowd of African Americans began to congregate by the railroad tracks next to the white beach. Callahan arrested one man in the unruly crowd, but others responded by hurling bricks and rocks. Then a black man named James Crawford stepped forward and fired a revolver at the police. A black officer returned fire and killed Crawford.

These events on the Lake Michigan shore sparked the worst race riot in Chicago's history. Four days of upheaval left 38 people dead, 537 injured, and 1,000 homeless.[3]

Historians of the race riot have treated the drowning of Eugene Williams and the immediate altercation on the Twenty-ninth Street Beach as symptoms of far deeper issues. In particular, they have identified struggle between ethnic whites and blacks over housing, politics, and labor, with greater or lesser emphasis, as the causes of the ensuing riot.[4]

Large-scale black migration to Chicago began during World War I. War orders to city factories and plants increased at precisely the moment that the flow of cheap immigrant labor from Europe dried up. When America entered the war, thousands of existing industrial workers in Chicago left to fight in Europe, further depleting the workforce. African Americans headed north to take the newly available positions, leaving debt peonage and southern racism behind.

New arrivals from the South moved into the largest existing African American neighborhood, the South Side's Black Belt, a narrow strip just a few blocks wide that ran along State Street from Twenty-second to Fifty-fifth Streets. During the war, population increase led to greater density, higher rents, and a perceived decline in quality of life for established black Chicagoans. To escape these conditions, some relatively affluent African Americans began to venture beyond the confines of the Black Belt into nearby "white" neighborhoods. Fearing a decrease in property values, Irish and Anglo Americans responded to the "invaders" with violence, repeatedly bombing the homes of African Americans and the realtors who had facilitated their move out of the ghetto. Clearly, this battle over housing created an enormous amount of racial tension and fueled the riot to come.

While growth in population created cramped conditions in the Black Belt, it also brought greater political power. During the war years, African Americans elected their first representatives to the city council. Even more importantly, the Republican mayor, William "Big Bill" Thompson, won his 1915 election by catering to the black community, much to the chagrin of Irish Democrats and middle-class white reformers. Resentment of these African American political gains generated further ill feelings that led to violence between the races.

While acknowledging the importance of politics and housing, some historians identify conflict over labor as the single most compelling explanation for the 1919 riot. Since the beginning of the century, Chicago industrialists had relied on black labor during strikes. In turn, white workers often reacted with violence toward the strikebreakers who took their jobs. Just after World War I, the Stockyards Labor Council, a confederation of craft unions, began another effort to organize the stockyards. The council leadership realized that its success depended on recruiting African Americans, who had taken many stockyard jobs during the war. But blacks were not easy converts. Last hired and first fired, blacks recognized that they occupied a far more precarious position in industrial America than the average white worker. Moreover, many of the new migrants from the South simply had no experience with unions. Lastly and most significantly, white organized labor still had not overcome its history of formal and informal racism against blacks. As whites in a variety of industries struck against their employers, many blacks, including those in the stockyards, cast their lot with management.

Tension between blacks and whites over housing, politics, and labor certainly played a major role in the resulting race riot, but it is a mistake to interpret Eugene Williams's drowning and the immediate conflict on the Lake Michigan shore as a mere symptom of deeper underlying issues. We need to take the supposed symptom—conflict over access to nature—seriously as a significant cause of racial tension.

Many Chicagoans, as the historian William Cronon points out, contrasted the supposed artifice of Chicago with a seemingly natural countryside stretching just beyond the boundaries of their city. If one asked early twentieth-century Chicago residents which section of the city seemed most unnatural, many would no doubt point to the European-immigrant and black neighborhoods on the South Side, a place where the original prairie ecosystem had been nearly obliterated by one of the most grim residential and industrial landscapes anywhere in America. Packinghouses, steel mills, and factories emitted noxious odors and oily smoke that blocked the sun and choked the lungs. Industry also dumped waste products into open sewers, such as Bubbly Creek, known for enormous gas bubbles produced by the slow decay of organic waste in the slimy depths. One could find enormous open-air dumps, which children combed looking for rags, metal, or a meal. Residents of the Back of the Yards neighborhood and the Black Belt just to the east confronted a built landscape of railroad tracks and yards, factories, and a grid of dirty, garbage-lined streets. Many lived in dilapidated, dangerous, and congested wooden-frame tenements, sometimes with collapsed roofs and porches and garbage-filled backyards and alleys.[5]

There were occasional opportunities to escape this harsh, gray cityscape. After a streetcar ride, visitors could hike old Pottawatomie Indian trails into one of the Cook County Forest Preserves surrounding the city to the south, west, and north. These wilderness parks, which the county began to administer in 1916, contained an "Indian paradise" of Illinois meadows, native wildlife, seemingly untouched forests along the banks of scenic prairie rivers, and rugged terrain of ravines and hills left by ancient glaciers.[6] And to the east of the city lay Lake Michigan, an untamed and seemingly limitless expanse of water every bit as wild as Yosemite or Yellowstone National Parks, if not more so. Along the shore one found developed beaches, but also informal lakefront spots, such as Hot and Cold, where Eugene Williams and his friends left industrial Chicago behind and entered the lake's chilly waters.

Black and white working-class residents could also visit a few oases of green closer to home. South Side inhabitants made regular use of commercial beer gardens and private parks that offered an escape from the urban environment, and children and young adults escaped to weedy abandoned lots and the unused margins alongside canals and railroad tracks. Residents also frequented public parks. The South Side was home to Washington and Jackson Parks, 1,055 acres of rolling greensward, irregular groves of trees, winding paths, and lagoons for boating designed in the English style by the landscape architects Frederick Law Olmsted and Calvert Vaux. There were also dozens of smaller block-sized neighborhood parks or playgrounds. Buildings and athletic fields often dominated these small parks, but they also contained natural amenities, such as stretches of lawn, groups of trees, shrubs, flowers, and ponds. By World War I, the blighted South Side contained over a dozen of these small islands of green.

For years prior to the race riot, whites restricted black access to this green space. White youth gangs or social athletic clubs, composed of American-born ethnic and especially Irish youth, who were sometimes closely aligned with local Democratic politicians, played the biggest role in driving blacks away from parks. The Chicago Commission on Race Relations, which was organized in 1919 to study the causes of the riot, reported racial tension in Beutner Playground as early as 1903, when a young black man had been run out of the park. In 1913, a gang of white boys attacked nineteen black boys and a YMCA official as they left Armour Square Park. The black children fled into nearby saloons and houses until police rescued them a half hour later. In 1915, white youths attacked a group led by a black priest from St. Thomas Episcopal Church that had come to Armour Square to play basketball. At Ogden Park, white gangs routinely attacked black visitors. During one such encounter in 1914, a white youth with brass knuckles hit a black park director. White gangs also frequently attacked blacks in Washington Park, especially at the baseball diamonds and boathouse. In June of 1918, the *Chicago Defender,* the city's pre-eminent black newspaper, reported that for the last two weeks, a "gang of white hoodlums, a modern Ku-Klux-Klan" had ambushed black visitors, regardless of age or sex. Fifty of these "white rodents" had attacked a couple in the park, beating the boy nearly unconscious and then throwing his girlfriend in the lagoon. The gang then gave chase to two girls, ages fourteen and sixteen, who were "almost outraged, right under the shining arc lights of the boathouse."[7]

Long before the "red summer" of 1919, blacks also faced intimidation and violence on the Lake Michigan shore. "Even the waters of Lake Michigan are not available to colored children," reported the Juvenile Protective Association in 1913, noting that a little boy's efforts to enter the water at Thirty-ninth Street Beach had resulted in mob action by white bathers and a riot call. Starting in 1913, projectile-throwing white gangs made it impossible for the black YMCA to escort children to the lake. At the Jackson Park Beach, a white crowd dunked and nearly drowned a black boy whom they accused of "polluting the water." During the summer of 1918, the *Defender* reported that "a gang of white ruffians" was patrolling the shore between Twenty-ninth and Thirty-third Streets, trying to "prevent Race people from bathing in the lake."[8]

White youth gangs played a significant role in barring blacks from access to nature in the years prior to the race riot, but it would be a mistake to lay exclusive blame on white ethnic youth for racial tension in the parks. There is also good evidence that the park district itself pursued a policy of segregation. When, despite white resistance, black visitation increased at Beutner Playground, the park district hired a black park director and instructed him to "turn over the playground particularly to Negroes" and "to give them more use of the facilities than whites." In similar fashion, the city hired black lifeguards at the unattractive Twenty-fifth Street Beach and informally designated the spot as the black beach. The creation of exclusive black parks and beaches ought not to be seen as an example of "discrimination in favor of the Negroes," as the Chicago Commission on Race Relations put it in 1922. Rather, white officials no doubt hoped that the creation of a few black parks and beaches would serve as a device to limit black encroachment on "white" outdoor recreational amenities.[9]

White park directors, park police, and lifeguards all played a significant role in blocking full black access to nature. Before Beutner Playground became a black recreation facility, for instance, the white park director, at the behest of the surrounding community, "showed by his actions to the colored people that they were not fully accepted." A similar pattern appears to have occurred at Armour Square, Fuller Park, and Hardin Square, all of which had very low black attendance despite close proximity to black neighborhoods. White lifeguards also limited black use of the lake. When a crowd of whites assaulted a black boy at the Jackson Park Beach, the white lifeguard on duty reacted by helping the other bathers dunk the black boy. Two black aldermen investigating racism along the Lake Michigan shore in 1918 reported that white lifeguards "were largely responsible for the assaults on Race people seeking the privileges of bathing there." The aldermen also blamed the lifeguards for encouraging gang violence against blacks. White police officers, such as Officer

Callahan, also turned black children away from parks and beaches and failed to protect black visitors. When a white gang tried to attack two girls in Washington Park, the *Defender* reported that a white park policeman at the scene simply looked on.[10]

Many nonprofit organizations that used the Chicago parks, playgrounds, beaches, and forest preserves also practiced discrimination against blacks. Starting in 1910, the Cook County Baseball League tried to force the African American teams sponsored by Grace Presbyterian, Quinn Chapel, Bethel AME, and Olivet Baptist churches into a separate segregated league. In 1913, the YMCA set up a separate "colored branch," and the YWCA followed two years later. The Boy Scouts also established separate troops. White ethnic Chicagoans could form their own ethnic Boy Scout troops (such as the Italian Garibaldi Troop or the Polish Boy Scouts), but they also could freely join more ethnically mixed troops if they desired. According to historian Thomas Philpott, this was not the case for African Americans, who were barred from white troops. Even the Prairie Club, the Midwest's answer to the Sierra Club, drew the color line. As late as 1939, the club baldly stated that its wilderness activities were "open to white people of any nationality or creed."[11]

African Americans did not stand passively in the face of white efforts to limit access to parks and the regenerative nature they provided. As the Black Belt grew increasingly crowded during the war, African Americans began making more use of park space. Blacks challenged informal segregation at Chicago parks and beaches because they saw these restrictions as racist and unfair. But demand for equal access to city parks and beaches was far more than simply a civil rights issue. It was also an issue of health. Like their Euro-American counterparts, many African Americans maintained that contact with nature renewed the human body from the ill effects of urban life.

In the years prior to the riot, Dr. A. Wilberforce Williams, the weekly health columnist for the *Defender*, urged readers to seek out nature during their leisure. He stressed the importance of summer vacations away from the city, either at resorts or camps in the wilderness. "There is an ever increasing demand," he wrote, "for us to get out, and away from the city—to get close to nature—to commune with the running brooks, trees, and singing birds, and all growing vegetation—to get far away from the heat, the dust, the hurry, the bustling marts, and streets of the overcrowded, jostling municipality and find some cool, shady spot to camp where one may find rest for mind and body with nature's purest food, water, and air." Echoing the views of many white writers on the value of outdoor recreation in nature, Williams explained that a vacation in the countryside "conserved" human health and energy, which led to greater physical efficiency once back at work in the city.[12]

Affluent black readers took Williams's advice to escape the city and return
to nature during summer vacation. A few well-off African Americans visited
national parks in the western United States and Canada and places of natural
beauty in the South and East; many more trekked into the Illinois, Michigan,
Indiana, and Wisconsin countryside to hunt, fish, camp, swim, ride, hike, and
relax. At the black-owned West Michigan Resort, the most popular vacation
spot before and during the war, Chicago visitors stayed in cottages and in tents
along a beach and enjoyed a whole variety of outdoor recreational activities.
Here, a *Defender* writer reported, visitors could find beautiful scenery and
country life, a place run with the "sole purpose of giving a breathing spot to
our people."[13]

For those without the means to travel to the woods and lakes of Michigan,
the *Defender* urged frequent visits to nearby parks, beaches, and forest preserves. In articles and editorials, the newspaper told readers of the benefits
that came from frequent experiences with nature and reminded them that
they paid taxes, that the parks were theirs, and that they should not be intimidated. Pay the ten-cent fare, the paper urged in August 1913, and take your
children by trolley out to the forest and fields surrounding the city. If that is
too expensive, then resort to the city parks, "beautiful bits of God's country
brought right into the city for the benefit of those who dwell in sections where
air, sun, and elbow room are hard to get." Work and urban life, the paper edi-
torialized in May 1914, make the individual into an "automaton, performing
his duties in a methodical, perfunctory manner amid the smoke grim[e] and
roar of city life." In nature, the editorial continued, the individual can find renewal and a new life and realize that he is but an insignificant atom in the
universe. "It is spring and to those who are not financially able to answer the
call of the wild, the parks afford at least a breathing space, a place to dream."[14]

Like their white counterparts, reform-minded black Chicagoans saw active
leisure in nature as a healthy alternative to passive commercialized amusement and vice, which they believed led to juvenile delinquency, degeneration,
and ill health. As many African American and some white reformers lamented,
black children grew up in an artificial, unhealthy environment of pool halls,
cabarets, cheap theatres, liquor stores, policy outlets, and houses of prostitu-
tion. "The predominating recreational facilities available to the colored people
are commercialized and the colored youth are left to develop as best they may
in a hazy moral atmosphere," complained the black park advocate Ernest
Attwell. The lack of wholesome recreation in parks and the overabundance of
unhealthy commercialized amusement, Attwell concluded, resulted in the disproportionately high rate of black juvenile delinquency in Chicago.[15]

To fight the lure of demoralizing and enervating commercialized amusement and vice, African American churches, women's clubs, and settlement houses pushed sports and outdoor recreation. Having been "Jim Crowed" from the Cook County Baseball League, the major churches in the community banded together and created the Sunday School League, which played throughout the summer in Washington Park. The churches also sponsored picnics and other outings to Chicago's public and private parks. The leaders at the Frederick Douglass Center, the Clotee Scott Settlement, the Negro Fellowship League, the Wendell Phillips Settlement, and the Emanuel Settlement pushed physical culture and outdoor recreation, which they saw as critical for the health of black children confined to the city. The Urban League, which had successfully campaigned for playgrounds in Harlem during the early teens, continued this work in Chicago, fighting not only for better relations between the races, but for more and better parks. The all-black YMCA organized sports teams and took Chicago youth on outings, as did all-black Boy Scout troops, some of the first in the country.[16]

It would be a mistake to see nature as simply something that black reformers, church leaders, and settlement house workers pushed on the black masses. On their own initiative, thousands of southern-migrant and working-class African Americans used Chicago parks and beaches to temporarily escape the noise, confinement, and congestion of the South Side and make contact with the natural world. Most rank-and-file blacks went to the parks and to the Lake Michigan shore to picnic, swim, play baseball, stroll, and unwind, but some used natural spaces in ways that dismayed and even outraged their "social betters." Like their white ethnic counterparts, black youth used the parks to shoot dice, bet on baseball games, fight, drink, sleep, and pick up members of the opposite sex. The behavior of Eugene Williams and his friends (who hitched a ride on the back of a produce truck to get to Lake Michigan, probably trespassed to get to their secret beach, and most likely created their raft out of stolen railroad ties from the Illinois Central Railroad) would have surely alarmed middle-class African Americans, who saw structured outdoor recreation as an alternative to juvenile delinquency.[17]

While tension between blacks and whites over access to nature had existed for years prior to 1919, it is also true that such tension increased dramatically just before the race riot. White gangs stepped up their attacks in Washington Park, and fights at the baseball diamonds and the boathouse became a weekly occurrence. At Carter Playground, a fight between a white and black child turned into a mini–race riot, as spectators divided along racial lines and began fighting in the adjoining street. On July 12, 1919, just two weeks before the race riot, the *Defender,* in an editorial entitled "Ruffianism in the Parks," complained that "young savages" had been attacking black people of all ages and that "no citizen of color, even when accompanied by women members of his family, is safe." The *Defender* urged white judges and park officials to enforce the law and protect blacks in parks. "The attention of the park boards," the *Defender* concluded, "has been repeatedly called to this situation, and the blame for whatever happens under their jurisdiction rests with them alone."[18]

African Americans refused to be intimidated by mounting threats and continued to make use of the parks during the weeks just before the race riot. Despite the appearance of signs near Washington Park warning blacks that they would be run out of the neighborhood on July 4, African Americans picnicked there and at other parks on Independence Day, although they brought weapons along with their food. African Americans also did not shrink from intimidation at the beaches. Just before the raft of Eugene Williams and his friends drifted within range of the white rock thrower, a group of African American men and women tested informal segregation at the white Twenty-ninth Street Beach by trying to walk into the water. Whites responded to the group with rocks and taunts, but instead of retreating, the African Americans regrouped, called reinforcements, and threw rocks back. It was during this melee that the white man on the jetty spotted the boys and their raft and threw the rock that drowned Eugene Williams.[19]

More than a mere manifestation of deeper underlying issues, the drowning of Eugene Williams and the conflict on the Lake Michigan shore was the culmination of years of conflict between white ethnic youth and African Americans over access to precious natural space on the crowded South Side. The Chicago Commission on Race Relations, which, in the early 1920s, investigated the origins of the race riot, identified struggles over limited park space as one of the causes of the riot. The commission recommended that more recreational facilities be built in the Black Belt, that the city hire more African American recreation leaders, that park police protect all citizens regardless of race, and that the city end the "gross discrimination by white persons which practically bars Negroes out of certain recreation centers near their own congested residence area."[20] The 1919 race riot is not simply a story about politics, labor, and housing. It is importantly also a story about nature, and as such, the race riot is a significant and unexplored event in American environmental history.

❧

The race riot certainly frightened some African Americans away from nature. In his autobiographical history of black Chicago, the African American businessman and writer Dempsey Travis blamed the race riot for the fact that as a child he never learned to swim. He recalled: "the tragedy forever affected my parents' attitude toward Lake Michigan. . . . To Dad and Mama, the blue lake always had a tinge of red from the blood of that young black boy."[21]

Black Chicagoans, such as the parents of Dempsey Travis, were no doubt frightened away from nature not only by the riot, but also by ongoing racial intimidation. After the riot, blacks continued to face hostility and violence at nearby recreation parks, such as Armour Square, Fuller Park, and Hardin Square, and white directors at these parks continued to advocate segregation. According to the director of Fuller Park, "separate parks and playgrounds for colored people are advisable . . . not because one group is any better than the other, but because they are different. Human nature will have to be remodeled before racial antipathy is overcome." Armour Square's director told interviewers from the Chicago Race Riot Commission that her park had traditionally been reserved for whites and that the city should build blacks their own park and field house so they would not use Armour Square. At Hardin Square, Officer Daniel Callahan, the white officer who failed to arrest the rock thrower at the Twenty-ninth Street Beach, explained that you "can't make the two colors mix" and that if "a Negro should say one word back to me or should say a word to a white woman" a group of young men from the district would fight shoulder to shoulder with him and that they would make a "complete clean up this time."[22]

Some of the greatest hostility during the interwar period occurred when African Americans tried to use Jackson Park, the lakeside site of the 1893 Columbian Exposition. The middle-class Anglo and Irish American residents of Hyde Park resented African American use of the grounds, especially Jackson Park Beach. In the mid-1930s, Spencer Castle, the editor of the *Hyde Park Gazette,* called for official segregation of the lakefront, and Republican Joseph M. Artman promised his constituents that if elected alderman he would maintain Jackson Park Beach "for WHITE PEOPLE." During the summer of 1933, a mysterious fence appeared on the sand, which many blacks saw as a subtle effort by the park district to separate the races. When a group of white communist students from the University of Chicago invited some blacks to the white side of the fence, the park police arrested the group. The police explained that they had acted to break up an effort to "mix niggers and whites" and "prevent a race riot."[23]

The continuation of white resistance, informal segregation, and racism meant that black Chicago remained underserved by the city park system. After the riot, black leaders such as Ida B. Wells campaigned for the creation of more parks accessible to African Americans, but with mixed success. As black migration to Chicago continued, park space remained a scarce commodity, and in 1927, the Chicago Health Survey reported that the Second Ward, inhabited primarily by African Americans, had less park space per citizen than any other ward in the city. In addition, the park district failed to properly maintain the few parks available to African Americans. In 1927, the *Defender* complained bitterly of this injustice, noting that while the city spent taxpayer money on parks and parkways in other parts of the city, tired black workers had no place to "sit in the sunshine and rest and breathe the clean fresh air, as nature meant them to do." The situation, the *Defender* continued, forced black men, women, and children to use the filthy and polluted streets for their recreation. Maxwell Bond, a black playground supervisor, noted in 1926 that despite some playgrounds filled with "moving, playing colored life," African Americans lacked adequate opportunities for restorative outdoor recreation. "The remaining masses," he lamented," are left to frequent pool rooms and other questionable places of warmth and immorality."[24]

While the race riot and the ongoing threat of violence did keep some African Americans away from Chicago parks, black enthusiasm for nature continued to grow during the 1920s and 1930s. Despite Indiana gas stations that posted "we cater to white trade" signs, segregated state parks (such as the Indiana Dunes), and racist wilderness organizations (such as the Prairie Club), African Americans continued to make excursions out of Chicago and into the country. During the interwar period, Idlewild, Michigan, eclipsed the West Michigan Resort as the most popular vacation destination for Chicago's black elite. Visitors to Idlewild enjoyed hiking, canoeing, swimming, fishing, and stargazing. Idlewild was "rugged, natural and beautiful with dirt roads, trails, and very few modern conveniences," reminisced one patron who visited the resort as a twelve-year-old boy in 1928. He continued, "I saw for the first time in my life snakes, porcupine, deer, bear, rabbit, and a variety of birds." W. E. B. DuBois wrote, "For sheer physical beauty, for sheen of water and golden air, for nobleness of tree and shrub, for shining river . . . and all the wide leisure of rest and play—can you imagine a more marvelous thing than Idlewild?"[25]

As before the riot, many affluent and middle-class African Americans not only sought the country and the wilderness, but also supported organizations that made nature available to less privileged children and young adults. Reform-minded African Americans continued to believe that outdoor recreation in parks and wilderness served as a much-needed antidote to unhealthy life in the ghetto, especially the enervating vice and artificial commercialized leisure to which African American youths were disproportionately exposed. Unlike commercialized amusements, which led to dissipation, recreation in nature would conserve the health of the race.

While the rationale for leaving the city may have stayed the same, the

scope of black efforts to get children out of the city and back to nature expanded dramatically. By the late 1930s, the predominantly African American
neighborhoods on the South Side boasted twenty-five Boy Scout, five Cub
Scout, two Sea Scout, six Girl Scout, five Campfire Girl, and three Blue Birds
troops, most of which were sponsored by the numerous African American
churches in the area. Black organizations brought city children to the Cook
County Forest Preserves and to the Indiana Dunes, an ecologically unique
area on the southern tip of Lake Michigan that many in Chicago hoped to
permanently set aside as a national park. "Hike along out to the dunes once in
a while," urged the writer of the *Defender*'s "Boy Scout News Column": "Nothing surpasses a hike to the dunes any day. Now that the leaves are falling and
nature is coloring up a little. Nothing will give you more of a thrill than an
over-night hike to the dunes." Organizations brought black children even farther afield—to Sturgeon Bay, Wisconsin, for cherry picking; to Hammond,
Indiana, for "pure country air, swimming, wienie roasts, and hikes"; and to
Camp Wabash in Benton Harbor, Michigan, where newsboys could swim in
"crystal lake water, fish, go canoeing and boating, make overnight hikes, go
hunting, and [do] many other things which you cannot do in the city."[26]

In 1941, a group of African Americans, working with the Chicago Area
Project, formed the South Side Community Committee (SSCC), a black organization aimed at combating juvenile delinquency and improving the community. The SSCC immediately set about to send as many disadvantaged
children to Camp Pottawatomie in Indiana as possible. African Americans
contributed checks and sometimes nickels and dimes to the drive, which
raised $3,200, and local people organized, directed, and staffed the camp.
Throughout the 1940s, thousands of poor African American boys and girls
left the city and traveled to black-run camps where they hiked, swam, canoed,
and learned archery, nature study, and Negro history.[27]

After the riot, churches, settlement houses, scout troops, and the black
YMCA and YWCA continued to sponsor recreation programs in accessible
Chicago playgrounds, beaches, and parks. Moseley, Doolittle, Beutner, Carter,
and Madden Parks and run-down black beaches served as the sites of picnics,
beach outings, baseball games, track meets, swimming matches, and Egyptian
pageants organized by neighborhood groups. In the early 1940s, the SSCC
not only continued the call for more public park space, but also organized volunteer labor from the community to clear out vacant lots and to create parks
for local children. African American volunteers also built a seven-thousand-
square-foot community garden.

For black organizations, Washington Park stood as the single most important oasis of nature on the South Side. After the 1919 riot, Irish Americans

who lived to the north and west of Washington Park fled to Hyde Park, South Shore, and the Bungalow Belt, leaving Washington Park to African Americans, a transition recounted in the fiction of the Irish American writer James T. Farrell. Washington Park became the front yard of the black metropolis. The park, which some whites and blacks referred to as Booker T. Washington Park, became the site of countless baseball games, church barbecues, ice-skating parties, and settlement outings. Starting in 1929, the *Defender* made the park the site of the annual Bud Billiken parade and picnic, the single most important event in black Chicago. The 1933 picnic, for instance, attracted tens of thousands of people to Washington Park. After a parade, which included floats built by local businesses, hundreds of uniformed Boy Scouts, Campfire Girls, and Girl Scouts, local luminaries, and the boxer Joe Louis, black Chicago regrouped in the park. There, participants played sports, welcomed a visiting Nigerian prince, and listened to the jazz of Duke Ellington and his band, who played under the trees.[28]

As before the riot, the impetus to make contact with nature came not only from above, but also from below. "To this park in the summer," the sociologists St. Clair Drake and Horace R. Cayton reported of Washington Park, "Bronzeville's teeming thousands swarm, lounging on the grass, fishing and rowing in the lagoon, playing softball, tennis, or baseball." Southern, unemployed, and working-class black Chicagoans slept and played musical instruments in the park, while unsupervised children and young adults danced, wore inappropriate attire, and climbed trees, much to the dismay of the *Defender*. The northwest corner of Washington Park served as a speaker's corner, where blacks could go listen to communists, preachers, and the followers of the black nationalist Marcus Garvey express their views. Tens of thousands used this and other natural spaces to temporarily escape life in the ghetto.[29]

≫

The story of the 1919 race riot reminds us that nature and wilderness did not exist as the unique passion of privileged European Americans. Many blacks recognized outdoor recreation as a vital antidote to the ill effects of the modern urban environment. Thousands of black men and women from a number of class positions drew a line between country and city—between nature and culture—and sought to cross that line during their leisure. But unlike their white neighbors, African Americans who sought nature frequently had to overcome racism, de facto segregation, and sometimes violence. As we have seen, Eugene Williams and many other black Chicagoans did not shrink from these formidable challenges.

☙7

Women, Environmental Rationale, and Activism during the Progressive Era

ELIZABETH D. BLUM

Reformers who emerged during the Progressive Era to challenge some of the growing problems of urbanization and industrialization generally shared several characteristics. They each reflected: "a desire to bring order out of the chaos induced by the economic revolution of the nineteenth century. They shared a faith in humankind and an environmental determinism, which led them to expect that the good in people would prevail if the evils produced by imperfect social, political, and physical circumstances were eliminated. They also placed their faith in an expert elite and in the scientific method to solve society's problems."[1] In addition to this basic belief in the social power of the environment, reformers generally failed to connect the various problems faced by the city or to critique the nature of industrialization and capitalism. Smoke pollution reformers, for example, rather than critique industrialization directly, frequently focused on smoke as an inefficient and wasteful use of resources. The elimination of smoke through more efficient burning of coal, reformers argued, would allow businesses to produce more energy for the same cost and therefore operate more efficiently.

Both middle-class African American and white women formed an integral and most visible component of these reformers during the Progressive Era. The rationale and justification for involvement, which often used "maternalistic" language, stands as the most prominent common theme for both groups. At a time when American society discouraged female participation in the public sphere, women lobbied for legislation, changed public perceptions, and influenced the path of the nation. They accomplished these forbidden activities while stressing their traditional and nonthreatening roles as wife, mother, and housekeeper.[2] In addition to maternalism, middle-class African American and white women shared a similar view of the city and nature. Women saw nature, or at least a rural environment, as an antidote to the pervasive evil and filth of the city. These views led middle-class women into a great variety of reforms, including public health issues, the development of parks and retreats, animal protection, and pollution issues. Finally, the middle-class women who dominated the period's reforms also shared a highly condescending view of their lower-class sisters—the very group at whom they aimed their reforms. Both white and African American women attempted to enforce a middle-class culture through their benevolence in an effort to raise all to a desired standard. These similarities, and particularly the ever-present use of maternalism, reflect concerns and attributes of middle-class women's activism during the period that stretched across lines of ethnicity or skin color.

The role of racially gendered stereotypes, on the other hand, certainly differentiates the activism of African American and white women by demonstrating the importance of considering the connections and implications of race, class, and gender. During the Progressive Era, white women worked *with* their gender stereotypes to gain access to the public sphere. Stressing their roles as guardians of the home, children, and morality, they found a safe, acceptable avenue for public involvement. The societal perceptions that had, for decades, limited white women's involvement in public life and "elevated" them to a pedestal now provided a release from gender boundaries.

African American women's stereotypical image, however, failed to provide the same safe path. Whites identified African Americans as culturally, intellectually, and socially inferior. To many, African American men existed as composites of various racial stereotypes, either the submissive Sambo, the affable Jack, or the rebellious Nat.[3] Stereotypical images of African American women also surfaced to present a specific view. Whites developed two distinct images of African American women, the overtly sexual "Jezebel" and the motherly kind "Mammy."[4]

African American women could hardly argue for greater acceptance in a white world by stressing the wantonness of the Jezebel image or the complacent, obedient Mammy image. The women's justification for environmental activism, therefore, tied them more closely to the white stereotype of woman as moral leader of the home. Their Progressive Era literature focused on the safety and comfort of the home, as well as the African American woman's power in society through her ability to rear children. They attempted to alter radically the gender stereotype of African American women by driving it closer to the idealized image of white women.

This strategy of emphasizing a maternalistic role may be interpreted as inherently conservative: African American women could be seen as simply trying to apply white gender roles. These women, however, were not merely parroting white attitudes. Although they used similar rhetoric as their white counterparts, African American women incorporated a far more dangerous critique of society in at least one way. Cognizant of the rabid system of Jim Crow segregation leveled against them in the South and equally pervasive racism in the North, they linked every element of their activism directly to their efforts to improve the conditions of their race and the image of their gender. Through a language stressing their roles as homemakers in environmental activism, many middle-class African American women sought to transform race relations and American society.

Beginning with its formation in 1895, the National Association of Colored Women (NACW) actively campaigned for many of the same urban environmental issues as white female Progressive reformers. The NACW operated as an umbrella organization for local African American women's groups across the country. Although educated, highly literate, middle-class African American women formed the leadership corps at the national and local levels, geographic dispersal of NACW clubs was far less limited. Reports in the national newsletter flowed from clubs in Alabama, South Carolina, Tennessee, and Georgia, as well as New York, Rhode Island, Indiana, and California. Clubs were spread equally over the country. In 1899, for example, Alabama and Massachusetts tied for the most number of clubs per state at ten each.[5]

Although the leadership of the NACW fell solidly to the middle class, women of other class levels also joined the NACW during the period. Indeed the organization's motto of "lifting as we climb" inspired middle-class women not only to improve the lives of those below them, but also to include them in NACW clubs. C. M. Wells and M. L. Lenard, both of the NACW's Women's Uplifting Club of Eufaula, Alabama, reported that after their visits to "the lowly," "we take them into our club as soon as they are willing to come, for it is by close contact that we can impress our character upon them."[6] Although lower-class women joined local NACW clubs, their voices faded into obscurity at the national level.

Local groups remained largely autonomous, choosing projects important to the neighborhood membership. Their activities included political topics, both racial and reform oriented, as well as educational, social, moral, public health, charitable, pacifist, and international issues, all falling under their "lifting as we climb" rubric. Perhaps because of this freedom to define goals at the local level, membership grew quickly. At its formation in 1896, the NACW listed twenty-five clubs as members. Only two and a half years later, in January 1899, they had eighty-five clubs in twenty-six states. In less than twenty years, the NACW "represented 50,000 women in 28 federations and over 1,000 clubs."[7]

To justify activism in their selected causes, the NACW's rhetoric at both the national and local levels contained significant elements of maternalism. In the organization's 1895 constitution, the women agreed to develop the clubs to yield the "upbuilding, ennobling, and advancement of the race," through "homes in which purity can be taught."[8] Some of the women in the organization held a very optimistic view of the results maternalistic reforms would produce. Selina Butler of Georgia stated that she had "studied the question socially, physically and spiritually, and was convinced that the foundation of race prejudice, lynching, bloodshed and strife had its origin at the fireside. She believed that if mothers were more careful to teach their children properly, much of these would disappear."[9]

Middle-class white female reformers also reflected this use of maternalism as justification for environmental reform. Many of the white women involved in conservation and preservation issues justified their activism through family-centered rhetoric just as African American women did. Some white women noted that women's conservation efforts complemented women's role in the home. Mrs. Overton Ellis stated, "Conservation in the material and ethical sense is the basic principle in the life of woman."[10] In 1908, Lydia Adams-Williams criticized male tendencies to exploit and overuse resources, stating in addition that "it [will] fall to woman in her power to educate public sentiment to save from rapacious waste and complete exhaustion the resources upon which depend the welfare of the home, the children, and the children's children."[11] Adams-Williams assisted in the conservation movement to prevent the complete loss of necessary resources to future generations.

Female settlement house workers, including Jane Addams in Chicago and Lillian Wald in New York, frequently used language stressing women's "traditional" roles as justification for involvement. Women, according to Addams, had a historic role in keeping the city clean. "From the beginning of tribal life," she wrote, "they [women] have been responsible for the health of the community. . . . From the days of the cave dwellers, so far as the home was clean and wholesome, it was due to their efforts. . . . From the period of the primitive village, the only public sweeping which was performed was what they undertook in their diverse dooryards." Therefore, she continued, "may we not say that city housekeeping has failed partly because women, the traditional housekeepers, have not been consulted as to its multiform activities?"[12] Maternalism also provided strong motivation for Wald's activism. Wald saw some aspects of reform as child conservation, comparing her work to other environmental reforms during the Progressive Era. In helping to justify the creation of the Federal Children's Bureau, Wald pointed out "the grim fact that whereas the Federal Government concerned itself with the conservation of material wealth, mines and forests, hogs and lobsters, and had long since established bureaus to supply information concerning them, citizens who desired instruction and guidance for the conservation and protection of the children of the nation had no responsible governmental body to which to appeal."[13]

Facing the disenfranchisement of African American men and the legal institutionalization of Jim Crow laws across the South and racism in the North, African American women also incorporated very different reform rhetoric and goals into their agenda. As early NACW leader Mary Church Terrell stated, "Not only are colored women with ambition handicapped on account of their sex but are baffled about on account of their race. They are continually forced to fight the opposition born of a cruel prejudice, with they cannot subdue."[14] This led African American women activists into areas significantly different from many white women, including protests against racial stereotypes, segregation of railroad cars, and lynching.

The NACW strongly promoted its agenda of remaking stereotypes through activism. In one of their first actions in 1895, the organization passed a resolution condemning a letter from John Jacks, president of the Missouri Press Association: "the man has not only slandered women of negro extraction but the mothers of American morality, on a question that not only involves the good repute of the present generation, but generations to come."[15] In addition, Mary Church Terrell, in 1901, wrote furiously in reaction to "The American Negro," penned by Hannibal Thomas: "In order to prove the utter worthlessness and total depravity of colored girls, . . . [the author states that] under the best educational influences they are not susceptible to improvement."[16] Terrell then reiterated the group's commitment to remolding negative stereotypical images through their activism.

Despite its radical agenda, the NACW generally maintained a rather conservative rhetoric, stressing maternalism to justify women's activism and adopting Booker T. Washington's more cautious approach to race relations. The organization had good cause to espouse Washington's philosophy over the more strident demands of W. E. B. DuBois. Washington's wife, Margaret Murray Washington, was a founder and early president of the NACW, and the creator of the group's newsletter, the *National Association Notes*. Both Washingtons stressed the need for African Americans to obtain an "industrial"

education and to learn and practice lessons of moral uplift, thrift, and cleanliness as a solution to race relations. Through maintaining an acceptable job,
bathing regularly, saving money, and being patient, the Washingtons felt that
African Americans would demonstrate their fitness to whites for better treatment and political rights. Many in the organization interpreted DuBois's
work, especially during Washington's heyday, as divisive and negative. In 1899,
one woman described DuBois's work as showing "the deplorable condition of
the unclean and nauseatingly immoral Negro." She suggested instead, "let us
confer among ourselves and replace bad conditions with good."[17]

By 1910, NACW members began to incorporate specific environmental
reforms into their activism.[18] Concurrently, the NACW's literature developed
a theory of the home, consistent throughout the Progressive Era, as the source
of morality, peace, and stability for African Americans in highly uncertain
times.[19] In 1897, the first year of the *National Association Notes* newsletter, the
organization discussed the role of the home in African American life. An article stated: "the homes of a people determine, to a great extent, the character
and destiny of that people," and "progress of the colored people can be assured
as only as their homes are improved."[20] Later writers continued this theme,
developing the theory of the home into not only a place for character development, but a place of safety and comfort from the outside world. Alice White,
who had been "conducting one of the largest and most successful mothers'
meetings" in Montgomery, Alabama, described the ideal home as "the shelter
not only from all injury, but from all terror, doubt and division. As it is not
this, it is not home. So far as the anxieties of the outer life penetrate into it, and
the inconsistently minded, unknown, unloved or hostile society of the outer
world is allowed by either husband or wife to cross the threshold, it ceases to
be home."[21] As late as 1916, this image of the home as a place of supreme happiness and peace persisted. One woman described home this way: "Where associations cluster sweet with beautiful memories, where the ills and sorrows of
life are borne by mutual effort, and its pleasures equally divided. Where the
whole year round is a scene of cheerful and unwearied effort to swell the tide
of domestic happiness. Where sweetness breathes as naturally as a wild flower,
There, there is home."[22]

The mother, of course, figured as the primary agent in this theory of the
home. She was seen as "the rock upon which the home is built" or the "queen"
of the home.[23] The NACW also took considerable pains to equate the queen of
the home with expert status and knowledge. Members of the NACW force-
fully stated their opinions of a mother's pivotal and expert role in the fight
against society's problems, including environmental problems. To NACW
members, the urban environment existed as the source and cause of evil: They

decried the prevalence of crime, filth, and debauchery within overcrowded areas. Women expressed the most concern over the effects on children. One woman noted succinctly, "'the city streets are the devil's kindergartens.' The pupils are apt, going from bad to worse, till detected in some crime."[24] Others saw cities as sources of temptation to evil. Members of the Investigative and Police Committee of a Chicago club split up certain portions of the city for study. The enterprising women especially attempted "to prevent the walking up and down [by young boys and girls on] the streets at night, a prey to the worst temptations and influences."[25] As a result of this dangerous environment, one woman noted, city children "roam the streets at will, associate with bad companions, acquire no systematic knowledge save that of vice, no self-control save that which helps them to take advantage of others."[26] H. G. Miller, member of an NACW club in New York, described the conditions within cities for newly arriving African American migrants. Employment agents, she stated, "not only fail to make good on their promise [of employment] but rob their victims of their money, and then leave them to the cold charity of the city, or, worse still, induce helpless females to enter wicked dens of vice as a mean [sic] of livelihood."[27]

If NACW members saw the city as evil, they saw nature as wholesome and healing: the antidote to the city's corruption. This view of nature incorporated both the Jeffersonian concept of that term as well as elements of a transcendentalist nature. Thomas Jefferson reflected, perhaps better than anyone else, the standards and accomplishments of the Enlightenment. He strove to explain and uncover through science and logic what had been thought of previously as shrouded in mystery. His views of nature reflected this trend. The best use of nature, according to Jefferson, was for man's benefit. In a letter written in 1814 to Thomas Cooper, he wrote: "Botany I rank with the most valuable sciences, whether we consider its subjects as furnishing the principal subsistence of life to man and beast, delicious varieties for our tables, refreshments from our orchards, the adornments of our flower borders, shade and perfume of our groves, materials for our buildings, or medicaments for our bodies."[28] Certainly, Jefferson saw some aspects of nature as beautiful and wondrous. He described Natural Bridge, located near his home, as "the most sublime of Nature's works . . . springing as it were up to heaven, the rapture of the spectator is really indescribable!" Yet nature without the presence of man's hand, Jefferson noted, could produce pain and confusion as well as pleasure: "looking down from this height about a minute, gave me a violent head ach[e] . . . the view from the top [can] be painful and intolerable."[29] Generally, for Jefferson, the best nature produced commodities for human consumption or enjoyment, rather than undeveloped or untamed land.

NACW women generally defined nature by what the city was not—rural areas with green, open spaces and fresh air. Certainly, nature did not mean undeveloped, unpopulated wilderness. The NACW never advocated that its members take long, solitary retreats to the depths of Yosemite or the Sahara, provisioned only with their wits, for example. Humans figured largely into their version of nature. The women's retreats to rest spots and camps for children included cultivated gardens, playgrounds, and buildings. For example, the "House of Refuge" near Philadelphia, Pennsylvania, gave "poor, ignorant children a home where they will be sheltered from temptation [of the city]." This positive, healthy environment included "410 acres, with fifteen comfortable cottages . . . an administration building, a chapel . . . a gymnasium" along with the farm.[30]

Although the NACW's views of nature seemed to reflect a Jeffersonian ideal of a rural, agricultural space, the women also attributed to nature qualities similar to those described by transcendentalists like Ralph Waldo Emerson and Henry David Thoreau. In contrast to Jefferson's views of the wild as something to be dominated, used, controlled, and subdued, the nineteenth-century transcendentalist movement portrayed nature as beautiful and worthwhile in its own right. Transcendentalists also saw nature as a source of escape and renewal, which would bring men closer to their own souls. Emerson, for example, stated, "if a man would be alone, let him look at the stars. . . . The stars awaken a certain reverence, because though always present, they are inaccessible; but all natural objects make a kindred impression, when the mind is open to their influence."[31] Transcendentalists also viewed nature as beneficial to man's health. "In the woods, is perpetual youth," Emerson explained:

> Within these plantations of God, a decorum and sanctity reign, a perennial festival is dressed, and the guest sees not how he should tire of them in a thousand years. In the woods, we return to reason and faith. There I feel that nothing can befall me in life,—no disgrace, no calamity, (leaving me my eyes,) which nature cannot repair . . . all mean egotism vanishes . . . I am part or particle of God. . . . In the wilderness, I find something more dear and connate than in streets or villages. In the tranquil landscape, and especially in the distant line of the horizon, man beholds somewhat as beautiful as his own nature.[32]

Similarly, Thoreau expressed views of nature as spiritual, healthful, and renewing. He stated: "Our village life would stagnate if it were not for the unexplored forests and meadows which surround it. We need the tonic of wilderness. . . . We can never have enough of Nature. We must be refreshed by the sight of inexhaustible vigor, vast and Titanic features, the sea-coast with its wrecks, the wilderness with its living and decaying trees, the thunder cloud, and the rain which lasts three weeks and produces freshets."[33]

NACW members mimicked, unconsciously or not, the transcendentalist view of nature. Different actions reflected their views of nature as beneficial to health and spirit. For example, the Lend-a-Hand Circle of King's Daughters and Sons of Boston, an NACW club, donated over eighty dollars to charitable purposes in 1898. Some of the beneficiaries reflect these women's views about how nature, outside of the cities, provided a place of healing for the sick: "$5.00 to the Gordon Rest, a place in the suburbs where convalescents may go to regain health; $5.00 to the Floating Hospital, established that poor mothers with their sick babies might be benefitted by the sea breeze."[34] Other clubs organized methods of bringing nature to the sick, rather than bringing the sick to nature. One ailing member of the Lucy Thurman Union "longed to help those in like conditions bear their burdens; so she conceived the idea of sending little bouquets of flowers to the sick in hospitals and orphan homes to brighten and cheer them." This idea quickly gained acceptance among members, who even appointed a "Flower Mission Superintendent," responsible for organizing visits with flowers to hospitals, orphanages, and poor houses.[35]

NACW members also believed that vacations or retreats to the country were beneficial to the spirits and bodies of city residents, especially children. The Colored Empty Stocking and Fresh Air Circles in Baltimore, Maryland, led by Ida Cummings, played a leading role in the African American portion of the segregated Fresh Air Movement.[36] As one of its major operations, the Baltimore club purchased a ten and a half acre farm in Delight, Maryland, for $1,750. The club took the poor children of Baltimore for one-week periods to live "amid the best environment that tact, love and skill can procure; they come from the hot, stuffy alleys, dirty homes, where food, sunshine and pure air are scarce." Through this change in environment and contact with nature, Cummings asserted, "a wonderful change is noted after they have been there a day or two. Three wholesome meals, baths and pure air build up [their] run down bodies, and gives these little ones a chance to get strong, and to make a fresh start for another years battle." Cummings invited other club women to visit the farm, where, she promised, "you will find happy hearts and happy faces; happy children in grassy places." By 1912, almost 1,100 young men and women had the opportunity to visit the farm.[37]

White, middle-class club women demonstrated similar views about nature and the city. Jane Addams felt that the establishment of parks remained a vitally important effort for the city's youth. Along with many other female reformers, Addams felt that the city streets, theaters, and bars held moral dangers for young men and women. A solution to these threats, she noted, could be found in open, natural spaces: "Well considered public games easily carried out in a park or athletic field, might both fill the mind with the imaginative material constantly supplied by the theater, and also afford the activity which the cramped muscles of the town dweller so sorely needed." In addition to establishing playgrounds within the cities, Hull House also worked to provide both children and adults with "vacations" from their urban lives. Among their many other projects, Addams expressed pride in her involvement in having "vacant lots made into gardens, hiking parties organized for country excursions, bathing parties established on the lake front."[38] Other women also thought that children should be able to enjoy nature, rather than work for wages. Instead of laboring in industry, one woman stated that children should "enjoy the freedom of the bird and the butterfly . . . and all that the sweet breast of Nature offers so freely."[39]

Lillian Wald also reflected attitudes about nature as a place of rest and regeneration. Perhaps one of Wald's proudest accomplishments involved allowing poor, urban children more recreation time and "wholesome" time with nature. Her childhood, in the wide open spaces of Ohio, consisted of "storytelling, of housekeeping with all the things in miniature that grown-ups use," and of playing in the barn with her siblings. She lamented that urban children, instead, were constantly interrupted in their games by the activity of the streets, slept on fire escapes during the hot summer nights and played near garbage containers.[40]

African American club women never advocated wholesale flight from the evil that plagued the city, but frequently worked for improvements of environmental conditions. As had white women, African American women had begun to understand the role of germs, dirt, and insects in spreading and carrying disease and to participate in the public health movement. Thus, African American women worked not only to help children spend time in the countryside, but also to improve sanitary conditions within the home and through better city services. Moreover, African American women's activities included protecting animals from cruelty and planting trees or gardens.

If, as both groups agreed, the city corrupted, and if the mother should play a role in solving society's problems, the logical progression of these ideas propelled these African American women into urban environmental reform. Indeed, NACW women articulated a specific rationale for "municipal housekeeping," or the geographic enlargement of women's responsibility in the home:

It is necessary then that housekeeping be extended to encompass the city. The health and welfare of the public need such vigilance as only one of domestic tending and training can give. . . . The careful inspection of [a mother's] sewerage is merely keeping the city cellar clean. The care of the city's food and water supply, her sanitation; the caring for her children is simply extending the family housekeeping into community housekeeping. The education of the city's children are reaching out from her own. The work of beautifying parks, vacant lots, and river banks, keeping clean the streets and alleys, is supplying the art and sanitation which she studies at home, to the city's educational influence. No nature is so base that it is not elevated and refined by beautiful surroundings.[41]

In addition to articulating specific reasons for entering a broader field of environmental activism, NACW articles also provide evidence of African American women's interest and involvement in a wide array of municipal reforms outside the home. Many of these reforms, in fact, paralleled the activities of white women in urban areas.

Urban environmental activities gained currency with the NACW after 1910, but ideas for "cleanup days" had been around for some time among middle-class African American women.[42] In 1896, Mattie Sykes of Atlanta stated that, since women could purify and elevate society, they should become involved in reforms such as temperance and schools. She also stated that as part of this role, each woman "must begin at her own door and establish a Village Improvement Society to keep her town or city looking beautiful."[43] Scattered numbers of local clubs had already begun beautification projects by 1899. The National Association Notes held up many of these clubs as examples to men who thought "women's clubs amount to nothing. [This type of man] must well concentrate his eagle vision to grasp the fact, the significant fact, that they are working for the public good this year more than ever." The public good, in this case, involved developing gardens and parks, weeding, and removing stray posters. "In Brooklyn, they are introducing successfully the system of Pingree gardens in the poor districts," one article began. "In Philadelphia, they are transforming a pier on the Delaware River into a beautiful waterside park, where they have arranged for a series of popular concerts; in Lincoln, Nebraska, they have a 'weeds committee' which makes war on roadside weeds, and like the Chicago Club, are making a campaign against odious bill-posters."[44] City beautification would not gain much attention at the national level until the next decade, however, perhaps because of the NACW's simultaneous efforts to reform the stereotype of African American women.

In 1912, the NACW sponsored a "Swat That Fly" campaign. African American women, through reports of doctors, had become convinced of the danger many insects proved in spreading disease. At the national level, Dr. Mary F. Waring, chairman of the NACW Health and Hygiene Department, contributed numerous articles on the dangers of flies, mosquitoes, and fleas in spreading disease and increasing the death rate among African Americans. The year after the first "Swat That Fly" campaign, Waring reported much success, but lamented that the program had not started earlier in the year. In July 1913, she advocated that women start with the cleanup of individual homes. Waring listed various methods to reduce the number of flies: "Cleaning the back yard, the porch, washing dirt out of the corners and crevices, screening the doors and windows." In addition, she recommended further action, specifically with regard to garbage. She urged women to "provide covers for the garbage can; all waste, decayed food should be destroyed. When you know that the female fly lays about 150 eggs at a time, even though her life is short, see what a multiplicity of flies will be produced if conditions are favorable. Therefore, clean up; clean your basement, your yard, your gutter, and your garbage can." Manure, she continued, should be quickly sprinkled with "chloride of lime" to kill off some of the eggs. To impress her audience with her seriousness and their responsibilities, Waring justified her campaign for cleanup days with maternalistic reasons. "Flies cause so many of the intestinal diseases that carry off so many young children during the summer. If we *clean up* more there will be less white coffins to buy. The work of prevention of disease is the work of everyone. The care of children is properly the work of club women."[45]

In her annual address of 1914, Margaret Washington, then president of the NACW, listed several environmental areas for continued work, including establishing playgrounds, holding cleanup days and participating in "civic house cleaning."[46] In the spring of 1915, the Tuskegee Woman's Club, led by Mrs. G. S. Ferguson, along with the National Negro Business League, initiated a cleanup week in March. The women's club sent out numerous letters to African American institutions, including area churches and schools, offering a prize for the best work. Taking advantage of some of the existing structures of these organizations, the women urged "the ministers to preach a health sermon, impressing upon the people the necessity of co-operation in the campaign." The club requested that schoolteachers have their students use one day for indoor cleanup and another for outdoor work. Although not specific about all the types of work to be done, the club suggested "whitewashing fences [and] outbuildings."[47]

As the local efforts to improve the environment and neighborhood life became more widespread, they attracted attention at the national level. One NACW member, Christine Smith, noted that where African American women organized clubs, the community benefited. Much of the argument centered around aesthetic reasons for the cleanup work, but African American women also recognized significant health effects. Smith praised club women for the "beautifying of the once neglected back yards of our homes, the destruction of uninhabitable tenements, landscape gardening, in relation to public grounds, improved highways, both city and country, pure water, public play grounds, public baths." She also advocated increased levels of city beautification type activities, particularly in the poorer areas. "In each one of our cities and towns a civic improvement league should exist. You can almost intuitively tell the location where the poorer classes of our people are, and the work of such a league could be directed toward beautifying these localities." She even described a specific course of action for the club women interested in such issues, including involving the local neighborhood. "Hold meetings with the inhabitants," she suggested, "make personal visitation and demonstrate the influence of paint, soap, water and flowers. No dwelling, however so humble, but could be made a beauty spot if the change could be made necessary in the eyes of the householder."[48]

By the 1917 cleanup week, Waring seemed optimistic about the effects of the African American women's efforts, stating, "the war on flies has become effectual." Despite this progress, she again urged women's clubs to "go into the backways and the tenement houses, into the alleys and basements, into the places unfrequented by garbage wagons and street cleaners and help teach and preach 'cleanliness.'" Group activity, she reminded, should be supplemented by good individual habits and cooperation. She exhorted members to "clean your backyards, and hoist your screened windows at night . . . [and organize boys clubs to] pick up all the waste paper, fold it and sell it; you will spade up waste places and plant seed." By setting this example, Waring believed, entire neighborhoods would follow suit.[49]

Cleanup days became the most common form of environmental activism among African American women during the Progressive Era. In each of these projects, NACW members used reforms to improve conditions and present a better image of African American lives. However, the NACW's rationale also drew women into other activities. With duties to protect and nurture, some African American women worked to protect animals from harm. In 1899, the Tuskegee Band of Mercy reported that they had investigated and taken action on a "number of cases of cruelty to stock (the school property) as well as individual cases." In addition, they used a portion of their fundraising to purchase medicine for Tuskegee's animals.[50] Another group in Washington DC organized a "Band of March" as part of their Mother's Club to educate children on kind and humane treatment of animals.[51]

City beautification projects by several clubs also extended to the planting and preservation of trees. Although rarely mentioned in the minutes or notes, the NACW had a forestry department for much of the decade between 1910 and 1920, led at one point by Mrs. George Warner. She was a Californian, and forestry work seemed most active in her home state. In 1911, California listed two superintendents of forestry work, one from Los Angeles and one from Oakland. No other state listed any women participating in this capacity. At least part of the Forestry Department's duties included the purchase and planting of trees in various areas. The California State Federation of the NACW reported in December 1911 that it had "purchased two dozen shade trees for beautifying the Booker T. Washington Park, in the Allensworth Colony. We are also going to place some of these trees in front of the Old Folks' Home in Oakland."[52] This evidence reveals that these African American women actively participated in the conservation and preservation of trees in at least a minor way, an activity previously attributed only to elite white women. However, despite the examples of animal protection and conservation, activities involving issues other than city services remained more the exception than the rule for most African American women.

Cleanup of the city remained a high priority for middle-class white women as well. Jane Addams took a special interest in garbage pickup in her Chicago neighborhood. Citing disease and high death rates as a result of standing refuse, Addams organized the women of her area to collect information on violations. Because of her relentless interest, the city appointed her to the position of garbage inspector. Other white middle-class women participated in smoke reform efforts to clean up the city. Concerned about the health of their children and cleanliness of their homes, women in major urban areas worked successfully to change prevalent attitudes about smoke. Once thought to be a positive sign of industrial growth, women's clubs raised awareness of smoke as detrimental to health and safety.

The scope of environmental activities in which African American and white women engaged varied by ethnicity in certain ways. Upper- and middle-class white women, armed with more leisure time and resources, battled national-level environmental problems. They campaigned for the preservation of forests across the country, and for the preservation of the Hetch Hetchy Valley, for example.[53] Local environmental problems consumed middle class African American women. Not that African American women neglected national issues, however. Racism and Jim Crow remained a staple of concern to the NACW. In environmental issues, however, local problems for African American women paved the way for the improvement of their group as a whole.

Both middle-class African American and white women exhibited strikingly similar—that is, biased and patronizing—attitudes toward their poorer sisters. Club women attempted to force middle-class values onto the lower classes, often demonstrating a complete disregard for the others' situations and cultures. Middle-class NACW members frequently portrayed the poor in amazingly negative ways: they were "dependent" and "credulous," living lives of "debauchery" and "shame." Their homes and neighborhoods were seen as places of crime, laziness, illness, and death. Poor, urban African Americans were unfit parents: they allowed their children to roam the streets, purchase alcohol, smoke, and commit crimes. They had no respect for privacy: one woman criticized poor residents for living in crowded, one-room homes. Middle-class women frequently criticized the poor's aesthetic sensibilities, reflected in their music and dress. They also lacked the appropriate aesthetic sensibilities of the middle class. NACW member Christine Smith told club women that they would "almost intuitively tell the location where our poorer classes are" in the cities, and that these areas should be a focus of beautification efforts. In this context, her aforementioned statement about bringing the "influence of paint, soap, water and flowers" to the "inhabitants" of such neighborhoods takes on a different tone.[54] The poor were so debased that some middle-class women wanted to avoid them entirely. One of the reasons one club member worked against Jim Crow, she said, was to avoid sitting with the lower class "refuse" in one train car.[55] In many ways, for the middle-class women of the NACW, the poor were analogous to the city in the way that the elite were analogous to nature: the latter's characteristics, values, and benefits were simply better than those of the former.

White women exhibited similar biases against lower-class women. Addams, for example, remembered with horror the conditions around Halstead Street, where the new immigrants, she believed, "are densely ignorant of civic duties." Because the residents refused to take initiatives, Addams noted: "The streets are inexpressibly dirty, the number of schools inadequate, sanitary legislation unenforced, the street lighting bad, the paving miserable and altogether lacking in the alleys and smaller streets, and the stables foul beyond description. Hundreds of houses are unconnected with the street sewer . . . many houses have no water supply save the faucet in the back yard." Addams blamed the poor residents for the problems surrounding them. Had they been more cognizant of their "duties," poor neighborhoods would have fewer problems. She also criticized immigrants for their use and disposal of waste. The usual waste in urban areas, she stated, "was much increased by the decayed fruit and vegetables discarded by the Italian and Greek fruit peddlers, and by the residuum left over from the piles of filthy rags which were fished out of city dumps and brought to the homes of rag pickers for further sorting and washing."[56] Again, Addams takes an insensitive approach, blaming immigrant practices based on necessity and poverty for the increased level of waste.

In broad strokes, middle-class African American and white club women shared much in common in their environmental activism, from rhetoric and rationale to class biases. The way African American and white women used gender stereotypes, however, sharply differentiated these two groups, demonstrating that race played an important part in how women of the Progressive Era interpreted and attacked environmental problems. White women used and worked within their stereotype—that of idealized housewife and mother—to gain larger access to the public sphere. African American women, on the other hand, had to reform and remold the stereotype of lazy, overtly sexual degenerates to gain access to the prestige accorded far more readily to white women.

What does this tell us about women's activism in the Progressive Era? First, the use of a maternalist, or family-centered, rhetoric stretched across ethnic boundaries as a universal characteristic of environmental activism. In a time when society limited women's accomplishments in the public realm, women chose a nonthreatening argument to enlarge their sphere. Since men believed women to be experts in the home and with children, they could hardly object to women attempting to care for children in the best way possible. Women's environmental activism also tells us something of the adaptability and empowerment of women. Rather than submitting to stereotypes, both African American and white women chose to manipulate, reform, and redefine those stereotypes to suit their desires. Yet despite the fact that middle-class African American and white women resisted or stretched their stereotypes, they remained wedded to class-based hierarchies. Unable to see past their middle-class views and cultures, both groups saw the poor as victims and lesser beings—as uneducated, uncivilized, uncultured, dirty masses only needing the benefit of middle-class ways to join the prosperous. Environmental activism revealed both paths for possible ethnic unity and huge gaps in intra-ethnic understanding.

🌿8

Nature and Blackness in
Suburban Passage

CHRISTOPHER SELLERS

In the study of his house of forty years in Wyandanch, New York, Eugene Burnett, a longtime veteran of Long Island's civil rights movement, leaned back in his chair and summed up what he thought of environmentalists. "I've had some fundamental disagreements with them," he recalled. "Just to focus on that . . . that's a white issue . . ."[1]

Burnett's sense of a divide between the causes of the environment and civil rights has a long history. Ever since Earth Day, many civil rights leaders have looked askance at self-identified "environmentalists" as promoting an agenda at odds with their own. The environmental justice movement, rooted as it was in black as well as working-class communities in Warren County, North Carolina, and elsewhere, gave organized voice to this sense of conflict, bringing greater attention to African Americans both from environmental agencies and from environmentally minded scholars, including environmental historians. From those such as Andrew Hurley, Mart Stewart, Dianne Glave, and Ellen Stroud, we are learning much more about the historical shaping of African American environments, both by external forces and increasingly, by African Americans themselves. The oral histories of Eugene Burnett and his wife Bernice, which I culled through interviews in 1999 and again in 2004, help to extend this diversifying of environmental history to a less studied group, the black, suburban middle class, and its sometimes fraught relationship with the "environmental impulse."

That Eugene Burnett perceived environmentalism as "white" seems paradoxical, for his own story matches up perfectly with Samuel Hays's account of the genesis of environmentalism. Hays has argued that after World War II, new economic opportunities and affluence enabled a quest among the American middle class for "environmental quality."[2] The Burnetts' move to the suburbs in 1950, after years of living in New York City, exemplifies how this affluence spread to some blacks as well as whites: they were able to buy a single-family detached home of their own in a Long Island suburban development called Ronek Park. When Eugene became involved in local politics, however, it was through a chapter of the National Association for the Advancement of Colored People (NAACP), over issues ignored by an emergent environmentalism.

The Burnetts' political experiences also illuminate civil rights and African American history. The movement with which they engaged was not just a product of the American Southeast, as emphasized in most narratives of the civil rights struggle; it happened in the North, and in a suburb rather than a city. Activism such as theirs has received so little attention in part because of how black suburbanites have disappeared in generalizations about post–World War II "white flight." Not all migrants into northern cities become trapped in urban ghettos, but only recently have historians begun to study black experiences along the urban edge. Recent work such as that by Andrew Wiese points to the pre–World War II existence of black communities on America's urban fringes; the Burnetts' Ronek Park experience suggests what postwar black suburban migrants owed to these earlier arrivals.[3] Yet in several respects, the Burnetts' migration toward the country looks less like those of their black predecessors than those of their white contemporaries, the young, less well-off but hopeful white couples who moved into what became known as the prototypical mass suburb of the postwar period, Levittown, New York.

The Burnetts' move from Harlem to Long Island was only the final leg of a longer, cross-generational journey that began in a foreign countryside, the American Virgin Islands, and that brought them through the city and back out again. They settled on a landscape whose hybrid nature—its mixture of the urban with the rural under the name of suburbia or exurbia—opened up new options for them. But in part because of their evolving identity as African Americans, they found themselves torn between embracing and shunning the "country" and its ways.

Stories such as the Burnetts' shed light on how African American experiences with land, place, and nature could lead to worldviews in stark contrast to those of their white suburban neighbors.[4] Not only did African Americans face obstacles to the enjoyment of environmental amenities that white Levittowners could take for granted, they also devised different ways of remembering their experience of suburban migration. Most pointedly, African Americans gravitated toward a concern that their white contemporaries did not have—the pigmentation of their own skin. Over the course of their youth and early adulthood, the Burnetts came to highlight race, rather than nature or environment, as the main conceptual pivot around which their politics and many of their life stories turned. Heeding this prioritization and its history can prove tricky for the environmental historian. It compels a widening of focus from those nonhuman and material surroundings to issues of human skin color that belong, it would seem from most environmental history, to some other historical specialty.[5] Yet to write an environmental biography of the Burnetts without addressing these issues would strike them as a "whitening" reduction of their story and it would miss how profoundly interwoven their evolving perceptions of race and environment actually were. In order to better encompass the Burnetts' own sense of what was at stake in their environmental biographies, this essay explores not just the settings through which they passed but also the ways in which their passage crystallized their consciousness of what it meant to be black.

That race is socially and culturally constructed has become a truism in academic circles; even biologists, still the frequent targets of critiques of race, have long since moved from scientific racism and eugenics to stress the environmental basis and genetic triviality of skin color.[6] Expanding the purview of environmental history to include popular concepts of race helps illuminate just why it could become even more visible and central to the worldview of those such as the Burnetts, even as academics of all stripes were increasingly treating race as only skin-deep. In a time and place where biologists' as well as social scientists' views of race hardly seemed to matter, the Burnetts came to insist on the importance of their skin color because of the way whites reacted to it. Much of what kept blackness alive for them, what made it into such an organizing principle of their politics and their memories, was just how superficial and unnatural these responses seemed. Convinced that it did not signal any biological or other inferiority, they nevertheless found their own migration profoundly shaped by white readings of their skin color that barred them from neighborhoods, schools, and upper-level jobs. Gradations in skin pigment acquired new significance because of the lines drawn by real estate developers, local governments, and employers. In a landscape where the urban and the rural were so ambiguously mixed, continuing distinctions between city and country bolstered racialist thinking. Just as its ties to any deeper genetic differences were being rejected in scholarly circles, the distinction between black and white gained further footholds in the imaginations of blacks and whites because of how it was being hard-wired into the land itself.

Country to City

Only decades before the Burnetts' parents had moved there, Harlem itself had lain on New York City's fringe, attracting Irish and German immigrants who worked in the city but could not afford the rents of midtown. Improvised shacks arose where property titles remained tenuous or unenforced, and truck gardens and farm animals abounded, so much so that the area acquired the name of "Goatville." A less agricultural style of suburban settlement arrived with the streetcars of the 1880s and 1890s. The multistory brownstones erected on top of Harlem's Goatville remained a far cry from the single-family detached homes of mid-twentieth-century suburbia. The inhabitants remained white until a collapse in real estate markets after 1905 opened the door to the uptown transplantation of blacks newly arrived in New York City from the American Southeast as part of the Great Migration. By the time the Burnetts' parents arrived in the city sometime in the early 1920s, white panic and blockbusting as well as the successful exclusion of blacks from other areas had made Harlem the largest colony of African Americans in the United States.[7]

Most new black arrivals hailed from southeastern states, but some, like Eugene and Bernice's forerunners, also arrived from Caribbean locales. Like many from the American South, Eugene and Bernice's Virgin Island progenitors had been poor. Bernice's grandfather had owned a home in an area where urban services remained as sparse as in nineteenth-century Harlem. Bernice's family relied on rainwater collected in a cistern for cooking, bathing, and washing clothes. Outhouses served as bathrooms. Like residents of Harlem's Goatville, "everyone" had chickens and the birds "walked around free" in the streets. Some also kept goats, though less so close to the towns. The income-generating work available for men was mostly manual labor in the local industries of sugarcane extraction and fishing, or in the case of Bernice's grandfather, masonry. The limited opportunities for women to work outside the home contributed to what some observers saw as a traditional sense of gender roles. When Bernice's mother moved to New York, got a job, and returned to work after giving birth, she felt compelled to send her new daughter back to St. Thomas to be reared by her own nonworking mother

Bernice, growing up in her grandfather's house, lived mostly among those "who looked like me." She had little exposure to the island's whites, confined to a quarter of the city know as Frenchtown, or to mixed bloods or mulattoes, numerous on the island since Danish colonial days, who also enjoyed separate and more privileged niches. "You never found a dark-skinned black owning a business on St. Thomas," she recalled, "all the stores were light-complected." In the face of such divides, darker-skinned families nourished a legacy of resentment and resistance. Eugene's grandmother told stories about a slave rebellion against the Danish King, likely in 1848, in which three women leaders fended off the Danish until the British, French, and Americans merged their fleets to restore the colonial order. By the early 1920s, the Americans had purchase the island and lowered the barriers to stateside travel. Opportunities for work remained limited in an island economy still centered largely around sugarcane. Eugene and Bernice's parents then undertook their own acts of resistance: they decided to immigrate. Like so many of their fellow islanders, all four young adults, acting separately, cast their lot in distant New York City.

Upon arrival, they encountered barriers regarding where blacks could live, and so were funneled uptown into Harlem. In this increasingly crowded corner of Manhattan, where most had darker skin colors, the Virgin Island origins of both Eugene's and Bernice's mothers and fathers distinguished them from the native-born majority. Their past carried over in patterns of speech and food, in the homeland and heritage they regarded as their own, as well as in their social ties. Both couples met and soon married in Harlem, a strong indication of the intense social bonds that arose among newly arrived American Virgin Islanders who discovered one another in the midst of Harlem's black community.

That Harlem grew so large and that it harbored such foreign-born immigrants differentiated New York's black community from those in many other cities, such as Chicago and Cincinnati, that provided destinations for what Joe Trotter has described as a black urban proletariat. By 1930, Harlem had 285,000 dark-skinned inhabitants, some 35,000 of them born outside the United States. The largest group came from the British West Indies; the next largest from Latin America (preceding the later immigration from Cuba), and a smaller group came from the American West Indies. The first and third groups had the advantage of knowing English, though Eugene's parents alternated between Dutch and English in their Harlem apartment. As early arrivals eased the immigration of extended family members, Virgin Islanders in Harlem recreated close ties with one another resembling those back home. Eugene's parents, for example, made it possible for Eugene's grandmother to come to New York in 1928 or 1929 and live in the family's apartment. Although his family was not active in island-oriented Harlem groups like the Virgin Islands Civic Association, Eugene remembers seeing "a lot" of others from St. Thomas and St. Croix during his early years.

Despite these social carryovers, the material environment in Harlem nevertheless differed starkly from immigrants' island experiences. The streets were paved, the dwellings multistory, and city water and sewer systems, largely in place by the 1930s and 1940s, meant that many arrivals from the Virgin Islands enjoyed running water and flush toilets for the first time. The black housing market nevertheless had its own peculiar distortions. Demands for shelter among the new arrivals encouraged high rents in the relatively few places open to blacks, and their lower incomes meant that, on average, 30 percent of their pay went into landlords' pockets. The result was also overcrowding, in buildings that, while not as old as many downtown, were gradually deteriorating. In one 1932 study, 52.1 percent of Harlem households had from five to ten members, 2 percent of them more than ten, and lodgers averaged more than one per household.[8] Neither of the Burnetts' families had a separate room for the bathtub, which, in each case, sat beside the kitchen sink. Aside from Central Park to the south, there were few or no trees or yards, only buildings and paved streets.

Around the neighborhood, the Burnetts recall no farm animals and, in fact, few animals of any kind. Yet the animals of St. Thomas and St. Croix retained a place in the lives of the Burnetts' families in Manhattan through the media of story, metaphor, and song. Eugene, who spent much time with his grandmother, listened as she reminisced about the men of her day as "the baddest fish in the sea" and sang about a mongoose that "run up in this big fat kitchen" and "grab up one of our big fat chickens." Their evenings in aging brownstone apartments harkened back to "a life where there were chickens and the men from there went into the sea and brought back the fish."

As a child, Eugene read tracts written by Ashley Totten urging his fellow Virgin Island immigrants to not forget their homeland, especially the travails of the people they left behind. Once their elders had arrived, however, neither Eugene nor Bernice can remember anyone talking about going back. Aside from the limited socioeconomic opportunities that had driven them stateside, Bernice's mother worried "that a lot of these islands are volcanoes."

At this time, some observers of Harlem noted "a sharp struggle for place and elbow room between the educated West Indians and native-born Negroes."[9] The minimal tension recalled by Eugene suggests that he, like most ordinary West Indians, was "more inclined to think of African Americans as Negroes like themselves than as native-born Americans." He did remember the "ridiculous" accusation of some that West Indians "didn't know they were black." Bernice, once she made the move back to Harlem at age nine in 1939, also felt immense pressure to abandon her West Indian accent and habits for more Americanized ways. Eugene himself later regretted that his East Harlem upbringing had not acquainted him better with customs native-born black friends seemed to take for granted, from the Negro National Anthem to collard greens. His schooling also never gave him much sense of the long, deep legacy of slavery and racial discrimination in the United States. He did gain some acquaintance with the work of A. Phillip Randolph, who spearheaded the labor union known as the Brotherhood of Sleeping Car Porters, and whose chief lieutenant was the West Indian activist Totten. Though Eugene remembered feeling "assimilated," only after leaving Harlem would his own sense of "blackness" become more fully welded to that of native African American traditions.

Also solidifying his sense of blackness as a child and youth were his encounters with various white ethnic groups. Eugene remembered: "We were always fighting with [the] Jewish and Irish and the Italians [who] lived over on the east side," especially in the Italian American neighborhoods east of Third Avenue, where he went to school. Yet he also recalls formative relationships that crossed racial lines, in particular, with a Jewish syrup maker for whom he worked, Benjamin Jerzavitz, who trusted him with tremendous responsibilities for a ten-year-old, passed along entrepreneurial acumen, and defended Burnett against insulting customers. Many of Eugene's fondest as well as his bitterest recollections of his city upbringing emphasize not so much the thoroughgoing blackness of his own neighborhood as the ethnic and racial mixing it afforded.

Bans against black tenants in most other parts of the city nevertheless ensured that by 1942, 95 percent of Harlem's 285,000 residents were "considered Negro," according to the City-Wide Citizens' Committee on Harlem. The many moves Eugene's family made between apartments, especially after his father suddenly died, also pointed to the housing difficulties faced by blacks at this time, half of whom had incomes less than $837 per year. Eugene's mother had to go on welfare for a while, as the family shuffled between apartments. The city government's efforts to alleviate housing problems sometimes made things worse, as when, in the early 1940s, the Burnetts' apartment house was condemned to make way for one of New York City's early "urban renewal projects," and they had to move once again.[10] No doubt a sense of contrast between his parents' and grandparents' island upbringing and his own urban one shaped Eugene's sense of himself as a city dweller. His identification with the city, more enduring than that of Bernice, did not preclude qualms, for instance, about its crime. A burglary of his most valuable clothes in 1946 left him "disgusted," and spurred his decision to enter the military at age sixteen. Enlisting, he left behind school and home as well as his then-girlfriend Bernice, who went on to complete her course at a New York City commercial high school and, after working in a garment district factory, found it "pretty easy to get a job" in Manhattan's office district in "merchandising and sales."

Eugene's army experience opened his eyes to American racism, by his recollection, yet mainly in places he saw as distant from his own home. Thrown in with young men from all around the nation, his own sense of origins hinged on how he saw blacks from different places handling what he soon realized was "a segregated army." As a "boy of the streets" at Camp Stone in California, he wouldn't allow what the "old soldiers" had tolerated, and "got into a thing" with the white "commander" of his black regiment, a private from the Southeast. Burnett's time in the service disabused him of much naivete about white racism, with one glaring exception: "the racism in the service I always pictured as a southern phenomenon." He headed back home under a conviction that would undergird his willingness to venture out from the city once more in search of a home: that fundamentally fairer attitudes toward race reigned in the greater New York area.

Spreading City

Once Eugene Burnett returned to New York in 1949, he married Bernice, and they soon joined a massive demographic movement toward home ownership. As home ownership spiked from 43.6 percent to 62.9 percent of householders over the postwar decades, the rising tide of home building along the urban edges of major American cities like New York was truly phenomenal. Between 1940 and 1970, a growth rate of 332 percent for housing in Nassau, Long Island, far exceeded those in New York City boroughs like Queens, where the growth was only 179 percent. A Nassau County firm named Levitt and Sons led the way with a development of seventeen thousand homes launched in 1947, aptly called Levittown. By the start of the 1950s, home building had surged out from Levittown eastward across the Nassau County border into Suffolk, to meet up with new developments out from Amityville that included Ronek Park, where the Burnetts would eventually settle. Contrary to contemporary depictions of suburbia and exurbia as white, based on straightforward statistical aggregates, postwar urban-edge migration included a striking rise in black arrivals. Between 1940 and 1960, national rates of black homeownership doubled from 20 percent to 40 percent, with most gains occurring in urban centers.[11] Proportionally speaking, black gains during those years in Nassau County nearly equaled those of whites, and their 379 percent increase in Suffolk County actually outstripped the 339 percent rise in white residents. The biggest geographic difference in migratory patterns was that while whites generally settled all over, in neighborhoods defined by home value and income, the Burnetts and other new black migrants increasingly clustered in just a few locales. These included inland town centers, most notably Hempstead toward New York and the newer Brentwood in central Suffolk, as well as the unincorporated areas to the north and east of Amityville, such as North Amityville,

Copaigue, and Wyandanch. In racial terms, Long Island's urban-edge transformation proved more multicolored than most of the literature on suburbia
recognizes, even if intensifying segregation helped hide its blacker dimensions
from many whites.

As a greater range and variety of Long Island land came under the bull-
dozer, what surrounded and underlay subdivisions guided builders and
realtors in the ways they linked their construction, packaging, and marketing
of properties. With so many different kinds of homes and lands for sale, with
so many new potential customers, builders and realtors seized upon features
of local land and water as part of a complex sorting calculus to determine
what kind of home buyers belonged where. Picturesque nature figured far
more prominently in advertisements for upper-end properties than in those
for the lower-end properties most often available to black buyers. In a sample
of 113 ads for Nassau or Suffolk houses in the April 6, 1952, issue of the *New
York Times,* some 67 mentioned characteristics beyond the house itself and the
size of its lot, most often "landscaping," "waterfront" or other proximity to
water, and "tree-studded" or "wooded" lots. Far more reflective of the housing
possibilities open to the Burnetts were the "Long Island" real estate listings in
the April 5 issue of the *New Amsterdam Times,* a newspaper of Harlem's black
community. Of 69 ads, none alluded to woods or trees on their property, and
only 2 made mention of nearby water, one offering "beach bathing" and
another "overlooking bay," likely not on the waterfront. "Landscaping," was
mentioned in 5 ads, but descriptions included only the size of the plot or a
"big backyard." Most depicted the land accompanying houses as raw and
shorn, reduced to the purest and most abstract of commodities. The *New York
Times* ads assumed that their customers were car owners looking for the
single-family detached houses, while ads targeting black buyers were sprinkled
with references to whether they were for "fully detached" or "two-family"
structures and whether they were "near transit." In these respects, ads for the
African American market differed little from those for the middle and lower
ends of the white suburban housing market, as exemplified in a sampling
from the April 5 real estate section of *Newsday.* Such differences said far more
about the economic and transportation limits to the black home-buying
market, and the ways realtors generally imagined the African American
"consumer," than about the meaning of advertised properties either for home
buyers or for builders.

The land where Ronek Park arose was representative of places post–World
War II developers contemplated building for African American buyers. Importantly, it arose around an area where an enclave of non-whites had long
clustered, in this case including Native American as well as African American

families. Along the northern edge of the small, south shore town of Amityville, across the railroad tracks from the town center, the neighborhood had
remained beyond the city limits drawn by those who incorporated Amityville
as a village in 1894. An appeal from one of North Amityville's leaders allowed
"coloreds" of both races into the village school district, yet otherwise, the geographic separateness of the black community came to be expressed in the
moniker for the east-west thoroughfare Dixon Avenue—the "Mason-Dixon
line." During the 1920s and 1930s, much of this flat, low-lying area to the
north of the town had retained the characteristic pitch pine and scrub oak of
Long Island's Oak Brush Plains. African Americans like the Leftenant family
moved into this Albany Avenue area because it was "peaceful" and "green."
Even if jobs were hard to come by and urban services remained minimal, it
seemed to offer the chance "of just being free." The Leftenants were like many
of the pre–World War II suburbanites described in Andrew Wiese's article,
"The Other Suburbanites," who built their own houses, often out of the scrub
pine around them; relied on well water and outhouses; kept their own chickens and livestock; and grew their own vegetables. Many of these residents reportedly were brought in from the South to work for the local farmers. They
lived alongside, and sometimes intermarried with, local Native Americans.
They also took up domestic and other service work for white Amityvilleans,
and during the 1940s also began to find jobs in local aircraft factories.[12]

After World War II, the Romanos, two Italian American brothers from
Islip who had worked together with their father as contractors, bought farm-
land just north of Amityville for subdivision and home-building.[13] Moder-
ately favorable for agriculture, the land they bought had none of the waterfront views favored by wealthy home seekers. Zoned by the township of
Babylon as a second-tier or "B" residential area, which allowed for multiple- as
well as single-family dwellings, North Amityville's scattered homes and small
farms were loosely surrounded by industrial zones in corridors along the
railroad and a new Sunrise Highway. The area extended up to airfields and
surrounding undeveloped land on its northerly edge. Whether or not the
Romanos were aware, the flat inland glacial moraine that underlay North
Amityville, quite unlike north shore land, remained vulnerable to high water
tables. Natural features as well as its preexisting zoning and uses helped make
the land more affordable for the Romano brothers.

Just like Levitt and Sons, and in stark contrast to the reigning practices in
pricier developments, the Romanos built a subdivision of tract homes on lots
that were 50'x90'x100'. The builders projected one thousand homes but later
scaled back to around four hundred; still, Ronek Park was one of the larger
residential building projects on Long Island, even if dwarfed by the Levitts'

massive operation. Ronek Park most dramatically departed from Levittown and so many other mid- and lower-end housing developments of that time and place in its deliberate openness to customers of "all races." So unusual was "nonracial" housing on Long Island that the builders held a luncheon announcing its opening at the posh Belmont Plaza Hotel, which drew higher-ups from the Greater New York Urban League and the NAACP as well as the racial relations adviser of the Federal Housing Administration. The latter publicly praised the development as "one of the first 'concrete answers' to the problem of providing housing for all groups in the New York area."[14] The phraseology and fanfare surrounding this nonracial policy for sales reflected just how deeply ingrained was the practice of characterizing neighborhoods by race.

The Romanos may well have been making a virtue of necessity. Only the largest-scale builders like the Levitts had the luxury of distinguishing their handiwork more completely from the areas in which they built. Glances at the occupants of the surrounding neighborhoods to Ronek Park would likely have undermined any sales campaign to whites alone. Long after the Supreme Court's 1948 ban on explicitly racial restrictive covenants, builders and real estate agents often simply refused to sell to blacks, on Long Island and elsewhere. William Levitt's public acknowledgment of a whites-only sales policy at Levittown throughout the early 1950s was a case in point. The Romanos likely shaped their own policies of advertising and sales largely to take advantage of the Levitts' refusal. Rising rents in African Americans' long-established enclaves on the north shore also undermined the viability of these communities during the postwar years, as more southerly places like Ronek Park and neighboring Wyandanch increasingly emerged as havens both for those residents and for African American suburban migrants like the Burnetts.

As with Levittown, the huge response to Ronek Park reflected the pent-up demand for lower-cost postwar housing. More than eight thousand potential buyers converged upon the Ronek Park model home on the first weekend it opened, in late January of 1950, and by the following Monday some 140 units had been sold. Demand for suburban homes by blacks looked to be every bit as hefty as that among whites who could move into Levittown. The Romanos promised many of the same features as their larger-scale and more famous predecessor: inside, an "electric kitchen with washing machine and refrigerator" and outside, "grounds—*at least* 6,000 square feet—with landscaped lawns, flagstone walks, concrete sidewalks."[15] Yet unlike the Levitts, but more like other builders who sold in the six thousand to seven thousand dollar price range, the Romanos planned no public parks or playgrounds. The larger environmental impact of their work lay not in what they failed to do but what they had already done to the informal commons North Amityville residents had long enjoyed. As trees were cut, soil removed, and the roads, pipes, and foundations laid to erect a subdivision as large as Ronek Park, its 147 acres were stripped bare both of the potato fields and of the remaining patches of oak scrub brush that had drawn earlier North Amityvilleans. While those who had grown up in this area during the 1920s and 1930s regretted this erasure, Ronek Park's new black suburbanites themselves harbored little sense of what had been lost in its building. Their country predecessors would nevertheless figure importantly in how the Burnetts and their neighbors crafted their own sense of what it meant to be black in a suburban, as opposed to an urban, place.

The Blackness of the Burnetts' Search for a New Home

The pathway by which the Burnetts arrived in this transformed place after World War II forced further cognizance of the melanin in their skin. In 1950, Eugene and Bernice Burnett were twenty-one and twenty, respectively, just married, and seeking to buy their first house. In all these respects, they looked much like the stereotypical images of suburbanites that began appearing in the mass media over the early 1950s, exemplified, according to many journalists, by the mass suburbs of Levittown. Yet their experiences reflected their differing origins and the more limited suburban options they faced.

As with so many of those moving into Levittown, what stirred the Burnetts' resolve to move was the prospect of starting a family. While job prospects in suburban aircraft factories proved a drawing factor for some white Levittowners, for the Burnetts, it was the prospect of a home rather than a job—the sphere of reproduction rather than production—that steered them eastward. In 1949, Eugene "came back as a serious young man thinkin' about family and life and all those sort of things." He moved into a small apartment in the Bronx with his brother and a sister-in-law, looking to get married to his longstanding girlfriend, and start having children. They didn't consider moving back into Harlem, which they saw as having moved "out of its Renaissance," and which Eugene's mother had already left for the Bronx. Aside from the continuing problems with its housing market, the crime and "gangs" that had spurred Eugene's enlistment made regular headlines in Harlem's newspapers, as did a rising threat from "dope." Eugene did not want to go back "because at the time . . . heroin had . . . posed its ugly head . . . and I saw a lot of my childhood friends getting caught up in that." This kind of intrusion threatened not so much neighborhood aesthetics and property values—less a consideration among renters—as the life chances of their own familial future generation. "We said . . . we want to raise our children somewhere else other than in Harlem," Eugene recalled. "So I started looking."

Helping to spur the Burnetts' thoughts of home ownership was the income they both earned. Bernice, in particular, had found success as one of the first African Americans to be employed at Consolidated Edison's headquarters in Manhattan. Eugene, meanwhile, though kept out of white-collar jobs by his lack of a high-school diploma and, likely, his skin color, worked at two jobs upon his return, at the post office and as a chauffeur, to save money for their house purchase. Proud of the education and prestigious, well-paying position of his wife, he also expressed discomfort with her working: "I was one of those kinds of husbands: I'll get another job, do the work . . . I didn't like that job." Searching for property out from New York City meant finding a place where Bernice, once they began to have children, could "retire" to full-time motherhood. Suburban home ownership seemed less a reflection of their jobs than an independent means to enhancing their status; as with many Levittowners who had lived in New York City apartments, moving out to Long Island meant, for the Burnetts, "moving up."

Burnett gathered information about the Long Island housing market not through any real estate broker but through the newspaper. In early 1950, he remembers scouring the real estate ads of the New York *Daily Mirror* and coming across notices for Levittown. Intrigued, still naively not suspecting that he might be turned away, he called up the only person he knew out on Long Island, an old army buddy who lived in Corona, Queens, then in transition into a black enclave. Corona was some fifteen miles to the east of Levittown, but his friend there was the closest Burnett had to a local informant. This friend also had a car, a rarity at this time in Burnett's circle. Eugene, Bernice, and he drove together out to the Levittown model homes. When they arrived, they realized they were the only black people in sight. "I noticed that everyone was staring at us," Eugene remembered. The real estate salesman promptly turned them away, saying "It's not me . . . but the owners, the builders of this development have not as yet decided to sell this to . . . Negroes."

The Burnetts came away fuming with indignation at this treatment. Clearly the kind of prejudice Eugene experienced in the army was not confined to the South; "I don't know why I didn't start World War III." At the same time, in retrospect, the Levittown model homes further crystallized his vision of who he was and what he wanted. Arrival into manhood seems to compel not just a change of place, but home ownership. "I was a ghetto boy who always lived in apartments and to see a plot of land and the outside of a house and this is mine and I can buy this . . . that's what I mean by beautiful. That's a whole new experience. I knew no one that owned their own home and so forth. That was a big step in the life of a young black man." Bernice recalls being "on the same page" as Eugene about the importance of ownership. Her recollections of that fateful visit to the Levittown model home nevertheless bore a feminine accent. She was more impressed more by the "modern devices" inside: "we were washing clothes by hand, and now you got a washing machine?!" She remarked not so much on the land as the "airiness" of the place, which contrasted starkly with the "closed in" apartment interiors and city spaces of the Bronx. With all the open, unbuilt space, she said, "you could really dream."

Property ownership has been much maligned in environmental history scholarship as an alienating commodification of land. For the Burnetts in this moment just after World War II, however, it boded new and meaningful possibilities of reconnection with land and air. For Eugene, not just the house but the "plot of land" he saw at Levittown held great significance. It did so not because of its soil or flora but because of how it contrasted with the floors and stairs on which he and his family and friends had become accustomed to stepping outside their apartments. Seeing this house from the outside, imagining himself as its owner, he read into the prospect of purchase a transformation in his heretofore place-bound, masculine identity as a "ghetto boy." What he found "beautiful" in the prospect of buying a Levittown home was precisely the mobility, as well as the extended sense of selfhood and maturity that property ownership promised. Bernice's emphasis on the house's interior and its modern devices reflected her own gendered view. But her greater stress on its "airiness" reflected something else besides: a popular counterpart to the many official declarations of "overcrowding" in urban places like Harlem, especially as new and less crowded living possibilities emerged elsewhere. Bernice also echoed a still earlier place in her past, those outskirts of Charlotte Amalie on St. Thomas, where she had lived until age nine.

Ownership of such a home thus prefigured a new connection with land (for Eugene) and air (for Bernice) and a move into more natural version of domesticity (for both). Compared to an apartment, it provided a more stable gendering of domestic spaces, with a kitchen and laundry room for women and a yard for men. More bodily privacy was also built in: rather than in the kitchen, bathing could now be done in private bathroom. As with many Levittowners, as well as other African Americans searching for an urban-edge home during this time, the home with a yard also provided a safe setting "for kids to run around in." Beyond the yard itself, some who had grown up in the rural South also sought a setting with the "open spaces" they were "used to."

Along with his army times, Burnett's frustrated experience of seeking a house on New York's urban outskirts further confirmed a self-image defined more by skin color than ethnic origin, not so much West Indian as black. This sense of his own blackness was a far cry from the biologically rooted racism of the eugenicists; instead, and perhaps especially at this forward-looking stage in his life, it was radically environmental—an appreciation of how, even in the urban Northeast, the physically superficial characteristic of skin tone could determine one's socioeconomic as well as geographic fate. In comparison with the whites who were welcomed into Levittown, fewer African Americans had moved to the suburbs because real estate agents turned them away and because of the many other levels at which discrimination operated in the urban Northeast. Limited information about available houses reached the places where blacks lived, even as discrimination in many job markets restricted the amount they could earn. Mortgages posed a further barrier. Banks and insurance companies, following the long-standing "wisdom" of federal loan officers and realtors, were reluctant to lend to African Americans, and when they did so, usually demanded a considerably bigger down payment than they asked of white customers. The Romano brothers had to go to Chicago to find a lender who would lend most of the initial down payment as well as the remaining principal to their prospective customers, then a standard option for cash-strapped white buyers. When James Merrick, also a future Ronek Park resident, tried to buy into the Nassau Shores development in nearby Seaford, he was told that the bank collaborating with this developer would never give him a mortgage. When he suggested he could get his own mortgage, they told him, "This bank is handling all our mortgages."[16]

Despite bad experiences, the Burnetts as well as Merrick and many others persisted in their search for a house. Not long afterwards, they found out about Ronek Park, where prices were slightly less than those in Levittown (starting at $6,990 versus $7,500). The model home stood out less in the Burnetts' memories than its Levittown counterparts, perhaps because there were fewer brand-name fixtures or appliances and the landscaping and community services were less elaborate. There were no signs of fruit trees or emphasis on the "garden community" that Levitt and Sons advertised; plantings were confined to a front lawn, a few shrubs and no more than three pine saplings per home. There were no fire hydrants or streetlights. The streets were oil and dirt rather than asphalt. "Playgrounds and community center" and a "shopping center" were only "contemplated" rather than built. Still, these differences only brought the Romano brothers' offering more in line with the Levitts' competitors for the white working- to middle-class market.[17]

Both Ronek Parkers and Levittowners were made up primarily of young families who had been living in apartments or with relatives. In the wake of recent upheavals associated with wartime, both sets of new homeowners sought what they imagined as more stable and natural living quarters for themselves and their children. For most Levittowners, however, property ownership did not seem quite as exotic as it did for Eugene Burnett, who sought the first single-family detached home owned by anyone he knew—parents, grandparents, siblings, or friends. Arguably the biggest difference in the respective suburban migrations of black Ronek Parkers like the Burnetts and white Levittowners lay in the extent to which they connected their experiences with their own skin color. For the whites who moved into Levitt homes, race itself hardly ever figured into their memories about achieving middle-class home ownership. But for those such as the Burnetts, the consequences of skin color loomed large. Even as their earning ability brought high hopes of middle-class status, they came to realize that a color line etched across Long Island's suburban landscape determined what opportunities were available to them and what were not.

The Lens of Race in North Amityville

To Edward Green, a retired New York City policeman and current realtor whose rant before the Babylon town board made local headlines in 1953, the unincorporated areas to the north of Amityville were a "shanty town" that needed cleaning up. Though he had been "selling Suffolk County for years" and was "proud of it," "now we're going into the housing conditions of the share-croppers." Green did not have to mention blacks or "Negroes"; it was enough to tie the "conditions" he could see "from the train window" with rural destitution, signified by the southern system of tenant farming. "Those who want to live like pigs, let them live like pigs, but we don't want them in the town." While Green began by implicating all of North Amityville, later in his testimony, he admitted that he had actually observed a more confined area to the north of Ronek Park, which was visible from trains on the Long Island Railroad's Central Branch.[18]

Green's remarks suggested the dilemmas faced by those like the Burnetts who were just moving into places like Suffolk County. Even though they came from the city, white neighbors found it easy to associate them with rural poverty, not only because of the nearby housing of long-time black residents, but also by metaphor, through the local connotations of their skin color. Even as the Burnetts sought opportunities to own "a plot of land" available to them in the Long Island countryside, their migration rendered them vulnerable to stereotypical linkages made by whites between skin color, slovenliness, and a southeastern sharecropper background. At the same time, the Burnetts and their fellow Ronek Park residents, more so than Levittowners, rubbed elbows with a preexisting community in North Amityville that they considered to be more rural. This evolving relationship between newcomers and older residents helped Ronek Parkers define and forge their own ways of living on the land. Even life in modern Ronek Park could be driven as much by the perils of country living as by its pleasures. That the blessings of the local countryside proved so decidedly mixed helped consolidate race, rather than nature, as the prevailing lens through which the Burnetts remembered North Amityville.

From the beginning, Ronek Parkers, living a couple of miles from the pricey waterfront, encountered water in all the wrong places. A gap between the chimney and the roof in many of the houses allowed rainwater to drip into their living rooms. The builders had not graded the streets to handle enough of the runoff from storms, and with the high water tables, water pooled in many the crawl spaces underneath the houses. To make matters worse, the Romano brothers had failed to check the absorbance of the underlying soil in their first round of homes; missing beds of clay prevented cesspools from draining. Seeping up after rains, the wet, stinking pools in peoples' yards drove out at least one family permanently. On top of these problems, by 1952, the builders had not followed through with promises to pave the roads and put in streetlights and fire hydrants, even though the often faultily wired development lay some twenty minutes from the nearest volunteer fire department in Amityville.[19] The resulting senses of grievance among these home buyers sparked much early civic activism in Ronek Park. As stories circulated about how much of the subdivision was built on a swamp or "underground stream," individuals wrote to the county health department, appeared before the town board, and even sued the builders over the unmet promises and unanticipated problems. As in Levittown and many other white neighborhoods, the Burnetts and their neighbors pulled together a Ronek Park Civic Association, which gave a collective voice to their protest.

Even as they appealed to government officials on the local, county, and national levels, Ronek Parkers took to tending their own homes and lands. However little care the builders devoted to topsoil and horticulture, those living in these homes took to planting. Burnett recalls Ronek Park lawns as "some of the most beautiful lawns I've ever seen anywhere." For some, it took a while, even as they watched neighbors "rushing" into lawn care. James Merrick remembers that he had neither the money nor the time to fix up his lawn over the first couple of years, yet fix it up he eventually did, by bringing in topsoil, along with grass seed, peat moss, and other fertilizer. Merrick was unusual in that he turned to the county agricultural extension agent for advice in the unfamiliar practices of lawn making; as in Levittown, most turned to their neighbors or relied on experience. Eugene picked up much of his knowledge of cultivation from Jimmy Leftenant, who had grown up in North Amityville and who was a coworker during his brief stint at the Republic aircraft plant. Burnett remembers using "phosphorus" to make his grass "very, very thick," even as a neighbor "used to put nitrogen on his lawn." As with Levittowner recollections, "there was a kind of competition goin' with that."

Beyond their lawns, Ronek Parkers planted around their homes more of what Levitt and Sons had provided its customers: shrubs and foundation plants, as well as fruit trees. At least by some recollections, like Burnett's, "all of them" grew their own vegetables. Unlike the African American gardening Dianne Glave has studied in the rural South of the early twentieth century, mid-twentieth century gardening on Long Island had become a predominantly male endeavor. The Burnetts and their neighbors bought many plants from nurseries, including City of Glass, a large nursery "supermarket" also frequented by Levittowners. For Eugene, the search for horticultural material helped to further contacts with the longer-standing residents of the North Amityville area. "We used to get a lot of plants from the old timers that lived in the neighborhood." Northward from Ronek Park, North Amityvilleans new and old could be even more agriculturally inclined. Eugene Reed, a black dentist who had recently moved from Glen Cove on Long Island's north shore and would later become an NAACP leader and Eugene Burnett's best friend, made gardening his "main hobby" during the 1950s. He kept chickens, turkeys, and ducks in his backyard, a practice he had learned from his father when growing up in Glen Cove's black enclave. "I just liked it. . . . We got fresh eggs." Interspersed between the residential neighborhoods of North Amityville, some small farm plots remained, tilled by at least one black plowman for hire, even as much of the land flooded with new houses.

The clearest version of rural appreciation surfacing in Eugene's recollections, and Reed's, had a consumerist tilt: his relish over foods that came from local land. In season, he and others would go knocking on the doors of local farm families to buy the harvest, sold directly from the house rather than a farm stand. "I couldn't wait for the corn. Their corn was just out of this world." Reed too "loved corn," and not only bought it from local farms, he grew his own. Women also had roles in the leisure-time efforts to cull local crops, especially once these reached the kitchen. Even after moving from Ronek Park into a more expensive house with a larger yard, Jane Kopchinsky took to canning preserves from their blackberry and other plants. Using the local land in another way, Eugene's friend, "country boy" Jimmy Leftenant, took him out into the shallow bay water off Amityville and showed him how to dig for clams, how you "felt it with your foot and then pulled it out."

For Burnett as for his friends Reed and Kopchinsky, an essential characteristic of gardening and other yard work was that these were, "more than anything else . . . hobbies." Unlike the farm work they imagined had first brought
those such as the Leftenants to settle there, they worked their land neither for
pay nor as a necessary supplement to the dinner table. Instead, they spoke of
rewards such as the visual appeal of their green lawns, or how good their
homegrown corn tasted. Even as it harkened back to a rural heritage that for
some men such as Burnett was more distant than for others, this leisure-time
land work was now a matter of choice, appreciated in terms of "enjoyment,"
that contrasted with what they did in their own work lives. Occupationally,
they saw themselves and their Ronek Park neighbors as "professionals and so
forth," whose jobs as local authorities—doctor, dentist, and policeman—reinforced their "progressive" and "aggressive" sense of what needed to be done in
North Amityville.

Further augmenting this sense of status over against their predecessors as
well as neighbors was how their incomes became sufficient to allow their wives
to give up paid work. Once Bernice became pregnant with her first child, she
gave up her job with Consolidated Edison in Manhattan, and as Eugene was
able to secure a steady job with the police department, she did not return to
work until nearly two decades later. While other women in Ronek Park and
the rest of North Amityville took on full- or part-time jobs while raising their
children, Bernice and Dr. Reed's wife also struck up a friendship, in part because they were some of the few women in the community who became full-
time housewives.[20]

Like so many others whom environmental historians such as Samuel Hays
have seen as forging middle-class demands for "environmental quality," the
Burnetts and their friends traveled deeper into the countryside. During sum-
mers, the Reeds rented a house on Long Island's East End, near where his sis-
ter and brother-in-law and some mutual friends had built homes. "It was
down on the water. It had the beach right there. It wasn't very crowded. It was
very country at that time." The Burnetts also traveled, "to Canada and up New
York State . . . the White Face Mountains [White Mountains, a national forest
in New Hampshire] and the North Pole [a Christmas-oriented theme park]
and this one and that one." What sticks out in Eugene's recollections is not the
countryside or wilderness experience itself but the "racism upstate . . . [it was]
very difficult to find a place to stay. . . . [W]e had been to about five motels . . .
and . . . they all tell you, 'no we're full,' . . . we had just about had it and I walked
in and [invoking his own authority as a policeman, told the woman at the desk
in one of them] . . . 'Call the state troopers and if you have a vacancy here, I'm
going to lock you up for violating New York State antidiscrimination laws.'"

They got to stay. But when the children went out to swim in the motel pool, full of people, all the whites then promptly left. "So one of my nieces said, 'fine, now we have the whole pool to ourselves.'" The Burnetts' enthusiasm for sojourning into the countryside was tempered by such experiences.

They nevertheless remember Ronek Park as the "best" neighborhood situation they ever had. Among the communal efforts undertaken by the new arrivals to North Amityville after they had settled in were initiatives to develop the public spaces such as playgrounds and a community center that Levitt and Sons had provided their white counterparts to the west. Toward these ends, the Romanos only donated an old, unreconstructed farmhouse and its lot. The Ronek Park Civic Association took over the deed, and through members' donations of lumber, paint, and furniture for the house; desks and books for a library; a fence and shrubbery for the playground; along with their "sweat equity" of volunteered time, labor, and skills, transformed it into a public gathering place.[21] Awareness of the discrimination they had all faced undoubtedly help drive the self-reliant character of Ronek Park's community-building efforts. New arrivals also joined networks of preexisting civic life in the larger North Amityville area, a vibrant array not only of churches but of other social groups, from gardeners to veterans to "chit-chatters" and sportsmen, who expanded another, older community center, named for Benjamin Banneker, and set up a community chest and volunteer fire department.[22] Most of these groups and initiatives had counterparts in rapidly growing white suburbs with similar home values such as Levittown. But there was one group in North Amityville that had no Levittown equivalent, one whose existence and strength marked this place as African American: a local chapter of the NAACP.

The Amityville NAACP chapter, chartered in 1946, seemed to Eugene Burnett and his friend Eugene Reed, when they first began attending in 1951 or 1952, to be controlled by the community of North Amityville "old-timers." Led by a man named Major Braxton, who was not native to the area, the chapter seemed to these newcomers largely a social club devoted to dances and baby contests, while raising money for the legal defense fund. The arrival of a group of younger residents associated with Ronek Park, including Burnett, Reed, and Harold Kopchinsky, whose offices lay next to the new subdivision, brought rapid change to the group. Broadening its geographic reach, they changed the chapter's name from the "Amityville" to the "Central Long Island" chapter, and began to engage in more active confrontation with local discrimination. To support and help publicize their efforts, local leaders also brought in nationally known figures to speak, including Eleanor Roosevelt, Thurgood Marshall, and Roy Wilkins, and undertook energetic membership campaigns. By 1956 they had registered some 1,339 members from all over western Suffolk County, about half of whom lived in the Amityville area, where Eugene Burnett had directed the campaign.[23]

Along with his involvement with neighbors, working with the NAACP helped to consolidate Eugene Burnett's sense of how much he and Bernice shared with blacks from other national traditions. Reflecting the cross-national arc of the African diaspora, NAACP leaders' families came from "all over"; those tracing their black ancestry to the American South, like the Reed family and some strands of the Kopchinsky family, did not dominate. Most of the men close in age to Burnett were, like him, veterans. What had made them neighbors in North Amityville, as they came to see it, boiled down to the shade of their skin. As many white descendants of southern and eastern European immigrants who moved into Levittown felt that they were thereby becoming more American, people like the Burnetts, whose transnational migrations of family now brought them into Ronek Park, became familiarized with the African American experience. The exchanges went both ways; Eugene shared his own West Indian traditions with interested people of more native backgrounds such as Eugene Reed. Living in Ronek Park also brought Burnett a deepening familiarity with what he had missed in his New York City upbringing: things such as collard greens as well as the long and varied American tradition of racial discrimination. Perhaps because of this exchange, as well as some (not all) of their origins, Ronek Parkers within North Amityville, like the Burnetts, acquired a reputation as a diverse crowd "from the city."

The new NAACP chapter began its political efforts by combating local discrimination in housing. One of Reed's first actions as group leader was to organize members to guard a house being built by an African American family on a property in Copaigue, which had been burned down "three or four times." Once New York State passed a law forbidding racial discrimination in housing in 1955, the group attempted to publicize the new law and monitor local violations. Respecting local members' leadership on this issue, the New York State NAACP promoted Ronek Parker Laska Strachan to become its housing chair.

Schools also provide a focal point for the local NAACP's activities. So thoroughly had Ronek Park and other developments reconstructed the neighborhood landscape in the northern part of the Amityville school district, however, that here, the "neighborhood school" principle provided the license for school officials' new version of a color line. In 1954, the Amityville school board proposed to build two new elementary schools to handle the overflow of new students in the northern parts of the district. However, the attendance plan they proposed, which limited one of the new school's catchment areas almost entirely to Ronek Park and surrounding neighborhoods, seemed destined to make the new "Northeast" school in North Amityville almost entirely black.[24] Coming in the same year as the *Brown v. Board of Education* decision by the Supreme Court, this avowedly "colorblind" plan brought quick attacks from NAACP leaders, but was then approved by the local majority white electorate, as well as the state education board. By the early 1960s, the resulting all-black school elevated school desegregation into the most explosive and energizing of all the chapter's chosen issues.

In the meantime, the Central Long Island chapter had also opened up a third front, the restricted job opportunities for blacks. Burnett's own workplace experiences pointed in this direction. He recalled little or no prejudice during the years he worked for Long Island manufacturers including the huge Republic Aircraft, but when he became a Suffolk County police officer, that was another matter. His white bosses made it plain that he had been hired mainly to service the "beat" of expanding black neighborhoods in North Amityville. Repeatedly passed over for advancement, he was also given undercover work on Long Island's east end that made plain the inclinations of higher ups to lump all "blacks" together, aspirants to middle-class status such as himself alongside the least well-off. He posed as a black migrant worker seeking cheap alcohol as part of a sting operation against liquor-runners. However far removed the agricultural plight of his own forerunners may have seemed, the assignment brought him face to face with the similar circumstances then prevailing in Long Island's burgeoning potato fields, not so far east of Ronek Park. For police higher-ups, a shared skin tone made Burnett perfect for stepping into the shoes of these toilers on Long Island's remaining countryside, most of whom traveled up from Georgia or Florida only for the harvest season. But for Burnett himself, it was hard to miss the parallels between their plight and his own family's enslaved past.

Crafting an agenda distinct from that of their southern counterparts, against a segregation that was de facto rather then de jure, New York NAACP members remained wary about race relations not just in the Southeast, which was perceived as rural, but in their own countryside nearby. Their suspicions steered them toward a terrain utterly neglected by a local branch of the Nature Conservancy that arose in this same period to "preserve" land: Long Island's working farms. Early in the 1950s, the NAACP became a chief promoter of better treatment of migratory farm workers, in the New York State legislature and on a local level. In the years prior to the arrival of subdivisions and more industrial jobs, some of the "old-timers" in North Amityville had indeed labored on the local farms during harvest time, but by 1960, only a handful at best still did so. They had little to do with the Ronek Park core of the NAACP. What got the NAACP involved in the issue of migrant farm work was not self-

interest so much as memory—reports of hiring practices and working conditions conjured up a painful rural heritage shared by their own families. What
was happening out on Long Island farms seemed to verge on slavery, or what
the labor secretary of the group, Hill, called "peonage."[25] Ronek Park residents
assisted in a statewide study of conditions in migrant camps of the 1950s, and
pitched in to push through state legislation to better migrant workers' condition. Some NAACP members, like Eugene Burnett, took it upon themselves to
provide donations of food to migrant families who stayed over on Long Island
during the holiday season. They were shocked by what they saw. "They were
living in a barn and we just couldn't understand how you could live like that."

In the mental map that united and drove those in the NAACP, the local
countryside harbored the most egregious instances of prejudice, but suburban
areas like Amityville were next in line. Whereas white Levittowners saw their
movement out from the city in mostly positive terms, the Burnetts' suburban
passage, even as it brought more rural and neighborly pleasures, also cultivated suspicions about this middle landscape. Around Amityville itself, the
Central Island Chapter of the NAACP took arms not just against housing and
school policy but also against the local job discrimination—at agricultural
processing firms like Sealtest, at health clubs, and in the local public schools.
If Eugene Burnett later came to acknowledge naivete about the depth and per-
vasiveness of the discrimination in his Harlem youth, this awareness itself was
largely a product of his countryward move, and the experiences of racial solidarity as well as prejudice that it brought. Not just the agricultural past of
southeastern cotton but its reminders, both in Burnett's West Indian past and
his postwar Long Island present, restrained his enthusiasm for the rural or the
pastoral.

Departure and Return

The minimal influence that the NAACP's Central Long Island branch
proved capable of exerting on local government policy during the 1950s, most
notably on the issue of school desegregation, undoubtedly influenced which
battles its leaders picked to fight. While the NAACP's Central Branch did seek
further government interventions against "slums" and "peonage," it devoted
most of its energies toward abolishing racial barriers in the private sector, in
markets for homes and jobs. Beyond the branch's collective initiatives, for the
Burnetts and Reeds, private and individual acts of consumption, such as "buying up" into a larger house and neighborhood, seemed of a piece with their
political programs, a way of taking on those racial boundaries that structured
the suburban status quo. In 1960, the Burnetts sold their Ronek Park house
and bought another that was a few miles further east, deeper in the Long

Island countryside. They saw this move not just as political but, like many of their white counterparts, as part of a natural progression, joined as they were by, according to Reed, "most of the people . . . that had a leadership position— the progressive people moved out of there as soon as they got on their feet and could afford to." Starting with the difficulties so many of their neighbors had had with Ronek Park houses, but especially once steadily rising incomes brought more options, those such as the Burnetts came to see the two-bedroom houses as "not well built," with "very little land around them." Aiding these impressions was how their three children had been growing, with the oldest just arriving at school age. Skeptical about how the Amityville school district would treat his children, some eight years after buying into Ronek Park, Eugene Burnett once again went shopping for a new home, scoping out different neighborhoods on his police car rounds.

He and Bernice settled upon a larger house in a white, working-class neighborhood some five miles to the northeast. Not only were there more rooms and floor space, it came with a half-acre of land. There were as yet only two other houses along the street, which ended in a patch of woods—not a public park, but a more informal and rural commons. These "environmental" amenities far surpassed those of Ronek Park, yet what sold Eugene Burnett on it were the better prospects it offered for his children's education. The school district in which it lay, he found out, sent more of its graduates to college than any other district in New York State. Buying this new home, they once again met with those same obstacles they had first faced at Levittown, and had continued to battle through the NAACP. Their first effort to buy into the area had been stymied by the local neighborhood association, which raised one thousand dollars as a binder to prevent the purchase. Eugene's coworkers at the police department chided him about "why in the world" he would want to move there. The only reason the Burnetts were finally able to purchase a house there was that the seller was embroiled in a quarrel with her neighbors. To avoid active hostility from those next door, the Burnetts moved in during the dead of night. The people in New York City who Eugene recalled as reaching across racial lines to befriend and protect him in his childhood seemed a distant memory indeed.

After a while, the Burnetts got on tolerably well with their new white neighbors, but the socializing was not nearly as friendly or congenial as in Ronek Park. The Burnetts, the Reeds, and the Kopchinskys continued to see one another socially, in part through their continuing involvement with the Central Long Island NAACP. The harassment and other race-related "hassles," meanwhile, soured Eugene on his job with the Suffolk County Police. In 1963, he quit, and with his two brothers in New York City, pooled enough starting capital to open a restaurant. Starting with a property in New Rochelle, Long Island, then adding others in Brooklyn and elsewhere, the Burnett brothers served their customers a cuisine characteristic not so much of Virgin Islanders but of African Americans born in the Southeast, "soul food." A stranger to collard greens during his Harlem youth, Eugene Burnett returned cityward nearly a decade and a half later to making his living off of selling them.

Once again trekking across the New York City line, into Brooklyn, if not Manhattan, Eugene now sojourned to and from a business oriented to African Americans, in which he shared both title and profits. Though he no longer thought of himself as a "ghetto boy," his identification with city life had been affirmed, rather than eroded, by his suburban passage. As Bernice notes even today, Eugene "becomes a different person when he crosses that city line." Bernice herself, having grown up outside the city, was also reflecting on a continuing sense of difference between Eugene and herself. Holding her own reservations about the countryside, she herself found the "city line" less transformative or inspiring. Mobility, along with the hybrid character of the land on which they lived, allowed a "city" person and a "suburban" person to coexist under one roof, with their geographic identities undergirding their sense of gender differences. Where the Burnetts had come to define themselves as more alike was in the significance of their skin color.

Mixing Places, Constructing "Races"

The Burnetts' sense of location by the 1960s reflected not just the places through which they had passed but a resulting transformation in how they thought about "blackness." Eugene's and Bernice's urban and suburban sojourn had shorn away many ties to the Virgin Islands that they had initially taken for granted, as well as a childhood naivete about the colorblindness of fellow New Yorkers. It had brought a new appreciation of the many constraints imposed on themselves and others in this country who shared their skin color. They learned more about what it meant to be African *American*, about how much American blacks shared, whether their families had come from the Virgin Islands or the Northeast or the Southeast, whether they lived in city, country, or suburbs. This knowledge arguably fed, rather than diminished, their efforts to pass along to their children a sense of their own Virgin Island roots: in 1969, they made their first trip back since Bernice had left at age nine. From what they had learned, though, Eugene and Bernice Burnett found it difficult to entertain the longing and nostalgia of many of their suburban contemporaries for a vanishing countryside, on Long Island or elsewhere.

Both saw their movement eastward as a progressive triumph of socioeconomic mobility, of "moving up." They also appreciated the land, space, and "country" nature that it brought within their reach. But their pleasures from these "environmental amenities" remained tempered and private, largely detached from their political engagements. As the more activist member of this couple, Eugene had committed to securing economic and social opportunities for Long Island's blacks, and found few reasons for switching gears toward problems of land use, parks and open space, or air and water pollution, that on Long Island and elsewhere in the mid-1960s were collectively becoming known as "environmental" issues.

The fate of North Amityville, meanwhile, suggests the limits of this political agenda. So long as private developers did not exclude blacks from their houses or job sites, their plans for individual properties in the area proceeded without contest. Fondly recollected by those who moved out, Ronek Park itself crossed ever more into an ungainly urbanness. New homes and developments continued to spring up, especially in the more sparsely built northerly reaches, as trailer parks spread in from the west. The shopping areas that the Romanos and others tried to establish closed down, and the industry that had loosely encircled the area when the Burnetts had lived there edged closer to its residential neighborhoods. Rezoning by the town of Babylon and the village of Amityville enabled this encroachment. By 1970, North Amityville's degradation had drawn the attention of local planners, not as a "return to the conditions of the share-croppers" but as a suburban version of Harlem: a "blighted" area, thanks to "scattered . . . housing in dilapidated and deteriorating condition" and "scattered commercial and industrial uses" in "residential areas," as well as "an insufficient amount of recreational acreage and facilities." The worst of the city, in these planners' view, had crept into the suburbs. Additional "blighted areas" had cropped up in Wyandanch, just south of where the Burnetts had subsequently moved.[26] Even on their own street, an informal commons of woods and vacant lots had been almost entirely replaced with houses, and other hazards loomed.

In his 1999 interview with me, after insisting that environment was a "white issue," Eugene Burnett shifted gears: ". . . but it is a common issue . . . particularly [for] us . . . we are ones that are inundated in our communities with all these negative things . . . the landfill, the high voltage system, right here." Picking up on a critique pioneered by the environmental justice movement, he was also reflecting back about the successive places from which he and Bernice had made their escape: from Harlem after World War II, and, a decade later, from the Ronek Park area that would soon take on the same "blighted" stigma, in theirs as well as the planners' eyes. Though the Burnetts had changed their place of residence, though they had physically removed themselves from the most besieged of places, Eugene nevertheless could speak of all these "communities" as "ours," in the present tense. Even though he and Bernice had been fortunate enough to insulate themselves and their family from the worst of these incursions, they had not avoided others, and he still felt tied to those in the neighborhoods that were hardest hit.

As historians delve deeper into the environmental dimensions of the African American experience, it is vital to study changes in and uses of the land around a place such as North Amityville, including those private and public dynamics that have driven environmental injustices. But it is an equally vital task to consider the makings of that "blackness" that rendered Eugene Burnett and so many others receptive to the "environmental justice" critique. Here, the memories culled through oral history may serve the historian as allies; for people such as the Burnetts, shifts in racial identity remain one of those "regions of the past that only memory knows."[27] Taking memories such as the Burnetts' more seriously can open up new environmental avenues into the popular versions of those racial distinctions that have proven so important and influential in American history as a whole. Their stories suggest that, at least in post–World War II America, popular notions of race themselves may well have less to do with genes or biologists than historians have yet imagined. Instead, blackness—along with the racial unconsciousness of so many of the Burnetts' white contemporaries—may have much more of an environmental history.

9

Environmental Justice, Ecoracism, and Environmental History

MARTIN V. MELOSI

Influenced by European Romanticism, Americans have thought and written about their relationship to the physical world at least since the beginning of the nineteenth century. The earliest works of environmental history, concerning the United States at least, were written primarily in the 1930s and 1940s and focused on the West. But American environmental history as a distinct field of study that possessed a wide range of nuance and topic did not take shape until the late 1960s with the emergence of the modern environmental movement.

Although it drew enthusiastic support from college students and others caught up in the political and social turmoil of the 1960s, the modern environmental movement was rooted more deeply in the American experience. Attracting major support from the middle and upper-middle classes, and bolstered by the maturing of ecological science, it functioned politically as a coalition of groups with a variety of interests, including natural-environment issues such as outdoor recreation, wildlands, and open space, and in concerns over public health and environmental pollution.

Older preservationist organizations, such as the Sierra Club and the National Audubon Society, experienced a revival in the early 1970s. Newer groups reflected a range of political and social objectives, from the corporate-backed Resources for the Future to the more militant Friends of the Earth and, later, Greenpeace. Their political views, consequently, were not necessarily compatible, nor were their reform tactics similar. Some accepted governmental intervention as a rational way to allocate resources or to preserve wild-lands; others were suspicious of any large institution as the sole protector of the environment. Some worked within the existing political and social structures; others blamed capitalism for promoting uncontrolled economic growth, materialism, and the squandering of resources.

Since the emergence of environmental history was so strongly influenced by political and social goals of environmental activism in the 1960s and 1970s, some in the academic community were quick to dismiss it as a "fad" or to brand it simply as "advocate history." To be sure, many budding environmental historians did not shy away from advocacy, and much of the scholarship rings with conviction. But by compelling its practitioners to study the past through a combination of science, environmentalism, and history, and by asking grand questions of its data, the new works of environmental history had the potential to address important issues long neglected by other fields.

In tone, substance, and topic, much of the scholarship of the late 1960s and 1970s reflected the spirit—if not the breadth—of the new environmental movement, focusing on the cultural and intellectual roots of environmental thinking or sometimes on the political implications of the older conservation movement. Only rarely in this period did historians venture into the realm of ecological sciences as expressed in Rachel Carson's monumental *Silent Spring* (1962).

The young discipline of environmental history, therefore, took much of its inspiration—if not its execution—from the modern environmental movement. In doing so, historians often shared a common set of values, including a biocentric (or more precisely an "'ecocentric'") worldview, a belief in the intrinsic value of nature, a faith in ecological balance, and skepticism about—if not contempt for—uncontrolled economic growth.

Into the 1980s and beyond, the field of environmental history began to find many new voices that examined a wide variety of themes—from the environment of the human body and questions of gender to perceptions of nature and the wilderness, from the modification of the land by agriculture to the transformation by urbanization and industrialization. The focus on the United States increasingly expanded to encompass the whole world, especially through the intellectual stimulation of the members of the American Society for Environmental History, the European Society for Environmental History, and several other scholarly and professional organizations.

Of the questions that challenge the contemporary world as well as the human past, race is an issue that is confronting the environmental movement and is destined to help reshape it. Until quite recently, race is a topic that has been largely missing from the literature of environmental history. Consideration of racial issues was implicit in a variety of studies, but at least through the 1980s explicit only in the extensive work on Native Americans. In the literature on the United States historical treatment of African Americans, Hispanics, and Asians with respect to the environment has been limited. Although, with the publication of this volume, Sylvia Hood Washington's *Packing Them In,* and an array of recent articles and paper presentations at academic meetings, the discussion of race is germinating within the field of environmental history.

Aside from the intrinsic importance of race as an issue for further scholarly inquiry, the public debate over questions of environmental justice, ecoracism, and environmental equity are changing the focus of the environmental discourse in the United States and in other parts of the world. Just as the environmental movement of the 1960s and 1970s helped to shape the burgeoning field of environmental history, the more recent public dialogue over equity and environmental justice ultimately will have a similar impact.

The appearance of the environmental justice movement in the late 1970s and early 1980s offers a medium through which to examine the question of how race has been introduced into the debate over environmental goals and policies in recent years. The movement also suggests potential shifts—or even basic changes—in perspective which challenge traditional notions of environmentalism. Amidst the diversity of contemporary interests and goals, those individuals in the environmental justice movement seem to be most strident in questioning older environmental thinking of the 1960s and 1970s.

The environmental justice movement found its strength at the grassroots level, especially among low-income people of color who faced serious environmental threats from hazardous wastes and other toxic material. Women have been key leaders in the antitoxics effort, including Virginia civil rights activist Cora Tucker; Lois Marie Gibbs, leader of the protest at Love Canal; and Sue Greer, organizer of People Against Hazardous Waste Landfill Sites (PAHLS). According to sociologist Andrew Szasz, "The issue of toxic, hazardous industrial wastes has been arguably the most dynamic environmental issue of the past two decades." By 1980, he said, "the American public feared toxic waste as much as it feared nuclear power after Three Mile Island."[1]

The reaction of local groups to toxics (such as lead poisoning or exposure to pesticides) and to hazardous wastes (through landfills and other disposal sites) may have begun locally, but evolved into something much more expansive. As Lois Gibbs stated, "our movement started as Not In My Backyard (NIMBY) but quickly turned into Not In Anyone's Backyard (NIABY) which includes Mexico and other less developed countries."[2]

A radical environmental populism—ecopopulism—emerged within the larger tradition of American radicalism rather than as an outgrowth of the modern environmental movement. One estimate suggests that almost 4,700 local groups appeared by 1988 to oppose toxics. Before the publicity over Love Canal, which began in 1978, contact between the groups was scant, but in the 1980s a more vibrant and better-networked social movement appeared to be arising. Some scholars, including movement leader and sociologist Robert D. Bullard, argue that the struggle for environmental justice for people of color predates the 1970s, but these efforts generally were contested under the rubric of "social" as opposed to "environmental" problems.[3]

For those defining the goals of the movement, grassroots resistance to environmental threats is simply the reaction to more fundamental injustices brought on by long-term economic and social impacts. According to Cynthia Hamilton, associate professor of Pan African Studies at California State University, Los Angeles, the consequences of industrialization "have forced an increasing number of African Americans to become environmentalists. This is particularly the case for those who live in central cities where they are overburdened with the residue, debris, and decay of industrial production."[4]

For African Americans and other people of color in the movement, struggles against "environmental injustice" are, as Bullard noted, ". . . not unlike the civil rights battles waged to dismantle the legacy of Jim Crow in Selma, Montgomery, Birmingham, and some of the 'Up South' communities in New York, Boston, Philadelphia, Chicago, and Los Angeles."[5]

Within this context, activists in the movement claimed a full range of rights for any social group, including fair public treatment, legal protection, and compensation. Bunyan Bryant and Paul Mohai of the School of Natural Resources at the University of Michigan took the argument a step further, contending that the civil rights movement that faltered in the late 1970s and 1980s was seeing its resurgence in the area of environmental justice.[6]

The environmental justice movement has its historic roots in civil rights activism, and its members and leaders have openly disclaimed connection to the traditional, or mainstream, American environmental movement. A focus on more immediate human-oriented—or anthropocentrist—goals, as opposed to more generalized ecocentrist values, is characteristic of the movement. For example, there is substantial mistrust over attention that environmental groups have given to global population issues (with their racial implications), and frustration over the little attention given to apparently mundane public health issues. As Robert Gottlieb has argued, some alternative environmental groups "have begun to shift the definition of environmentalism away from the exclusive focus on consumption to the sphere of work and production."[7]

In October 1991, a multiracial group of more than six hundred people met in Washington DC for the first National People of Color Environmental Leadership Summit. In a document called "Principles of Environmental Justice," conference participants asserted the desire "to begin to build a national and international movement of all peoples of color to fight the destruction and taking of our lands and communities . . ." and for the reestablishment of "our spiritual interdependence on the sacredness of our Mother Earth." Another goal was: "to secure our political, economic and cultural liberation that has been denied for over 500 years of colonization and oppression, resulting in the poisoning of our communities and land and the genocide of our peoples."[8]

The "Principles of Environmental Justice" document, interestingly, overlaps with many of the values found in the literature of other environmental groups. However, leaders in the environmental justice movement have been prone to characterize mainstream environmentalism—especially as represented by the so-called "Group of Ten"[9]—as white, often male, middle- and upper-class, primarily concerned with wilderness preservation and conservation, and insensitive to—or at least ill-equipped to deal with—the interests of minorities. The movement's priority issues were predominately urban-based: siting of toxic facilities in minority neighborhoods and public health problems such as lead poisoning. A concern over the use of pesticides in the produce industry is a link to farm workers and migrants, who represent the rural equivalent of the urban underclass. Bryant and Mohai concluded: ". . . [Environmentalists] are viewed with suspicion by people of color, particularly as national environmental organizations try to fashion an urban agenda in the 1990s. To champion old growth forests or the protection of the snail darter or the habitat of spotted owls without championing clean safe urban environments or improved habitats of the homeless, does not bode well for future relations between environmentalists and people of color, and with the poor."[10]

Token representation of people of color in mainstream environmental organizations is an additional reminder of the gap between the movements. Clearly, there is much to justify such criticism. Frederick D. Krupp, executive director of the Environmental Defense Fund noted, "The truth is that environmental groups have done a miserable job of reaching out to minorities."[11] Nevertheless, politics makes strange bedfellows, and within the environmental justice movement there has been division of opinion over whether to join forces with mainstream environmental groups and cooperate with them in areas of common interest, or simply to follow a separate path.

The rift among those committed to environmental reform can be traced in part to the failure of mainstream groups to reach out, fired by the suspicion of those in the environmental justice movement that "people-centered" environmental issues have low priority among the Group of Ten. However, an additional reason for the rift is the once widely held—but largely unsubstantiated—belief that people of color and low-income groups marginalize environmental issues, especially if economic survival is at stake.

To counteract the assumption that people of color lack an interest in the environment, supporters of the movement have addressed that issue frontally. Dana A. Alston, director of the Environment, Community Development and Race Project of the Panos Institute in Washington DC, situated environmentalism in a larger social context: "Communities of color have often taken a more holistic approach than the mainstream environmental movement, integrating 'environmental' concerns into a broader agenda that emphasizes social, racial and economic justice."[12] In an effort to dispel the notion of environmental advocacy as "a white thing," several studies have pointed to the strong environmental voting record of the Congressional Black Caucus and the commitment of minorities to key clean-air and clean-water legislation.[13]

In analyzing the evolution of the environmental movement, Dorceta E. Taylor wrote that existing environmental groups have largely failed to attract minorities due to the particular appeals and incentives they have promoted. For instance, the argument that minorities struggle to meet basic needs and thus place environmental issues low on a list of priorities assumes that the priorities are permanently fixed: "The argument does not allow for the possibility that environmental issues could become high-priority issues for minorities by redefining environmental issues in terms of basic needs, or that individuals might seek to meet high-order needs before all of their basic needs are met. Because many of the environmental problems facing minorities are immediate and life-threatening, it is predicted that they will become involved in environmental organizations and groups, if and when these groups deal with issues of survival and basic needs."[14]

Taylor analyzed several studies conducted in the 1970s and 1980s concerning the different levels of black/white involvement in environmental issues and concluded that the environmental "concern gap" between blacks and whites can be understood by exploring the disparity between "concern" and "action." First, previous studies may mask levels of black concern because of measurement errors. Second, blacks have a history of higher rates of affiliation with voluntary social, political, or religious associations than whites.[15]

A persuasive argument about the relationship between people of color and environmental concern is the notion that environment is culturally constructed, and participation must be understood from that perspective. Barbara Deutsch Lynch's study of Latino environmental discourses sheds light on contrasting views of the environment between U.S. Latino peoples and Anglo-

American environmentalists. The study takes into account the role of "the garden and the sea" as traditional sources of livelihood for Spanish-speaking peoples—as well as instruments of bondage to dominant economic systems such as plantation life—and contrasts these perceptions with such images as the frontier, wild rivers, and forests in the Anglo-American community. "The ideal or utopian natural landscapes of Latino writers," Lynch observed, "are peopled and productive." She concluded: "looking at the impact of environmental ills or mitigation programs on U.S. Latinos solely in terms of end points determined by Anglo environmental agendas (siting of toxic waste facilities, for example) only perpetuated the silence of Latino voices on the environment and postponed fundamental changes in the U.S. environmental discourse."[16]

In light of the context in which environmentalism among people of color has been cast, the environmental justice movement's focus on ecoracism is not surprising. Some in the movement connect class and race, but many others view racism as the prime culprit.[17]

Some observers look back to the 1970s for the start of the environmental justice movement, when black residents of the Northwood Manor subdivision in Houston filed the first class-action lawsuit challenging the siting of a waste facility in their neighborhood as a violation of civil rights, resulting in *Bean v. Southwestern Waste Management Corp.* (1979). But the event that succeeded in "racializing the antitoxics agenda" was the Warren County, North Carolina, protest in 1982.

Reverend Benjamin F. Chavis Jr., former head of the NAACP, is credited with coining the term "environmental racism" while executive director of the United Church of Christ's Commission for Racial Justice (CRJ).[18] One-time reverend Chavis became interested in the connection between race and pollution in 1982 when residents of predominantly African American Warren County, North Carolina asked the CRJ for help in resisting the siting of a polychlorinated biphenyl (PCB) dump in their community. The protest proved unsuccessful, resulting in the arrest of more than five hundred people, including Chavis, Dr. Joseph Lowery of the Southern Christian Leadership Conference, and Congressman Walter Fauntroy of Washington DC.

The Warren County incident and others—some affecting middle-class blacks as well as the poor—convinced Chavis and his colleagues that a national study correlating race and toxic waste dumping was in order. After five years of work, the CRJ produced *Toxic Wastes and Race in the United States: A National Report on the Racial and Social-Economic Characteristics of Communities with Hazardous Waste Sites.* The report was the first comprehensive national study of the demographic patterns associated with the location of hazardous waste sites. The findings stressed that the racial composition of a community was the single variable best able to predict the siting of commercial hazardous waste facilities. Minorities, especially African Americans and Hispanics, were overrepresented in communities with these facilities. Furthermore, the report concluded, it was "virtually impossible" that these facilities were distributed by chance and thus race must have played a central role in location. Supporters of the report's conclusions argued that other, less comprehensive studies conducted as far back as the 1970s generally corroborated the findings.

The CRJ report—especially its strong inference of deliberate targeting of communities because of race—gave powerful ammunition to those interested in broadening a concern over ill-defined "environmental equity" into the movement for environmental justice. Later statements by Chavis demonstrated more depth in the call for environmental justice: "Millions of African Americans, Latinos, Asians, Pacific Islanders, and Native Americans are trapped in polluted environments because of their race and color. Inhabitants of these communities are exposed to greater health and environmental risks than is the general population. Clearly, all Americans do not have the same opportunities to breathe clean air, drink clean water, enjoy clean parks and playgrounds, or work in a clean, safe environment. People of color bear the brunt of the nation's pollution problem."[19]

The question of deliberately targeting communities of racial and ethnic minorities is viewed by some leaders of the movement as indispensable in keeping the focus on the relationship between race and pollution. Also critical are efforts to reject the notion that siting decisions are most often based on distinction by class not race. The perceived culprit in deliberate targeting is not simply private companies, but also government. "In many instances," Bullard asserted, "government *is* the problem." He argued that a "dominant environmental protection paradigm" has been in operation which, among other things, institutionalizes unequal enforcement of laws and regulations, favors polluting industries over "victims," and delays cleanups.[20]

Efforts by the federal government to address some of the concerns over environmental racism and inequity have been viewed with skepticism by those within the movement. A June 1992 report issued by the Environmental Protection Agency (EPA)—*Environmental Equity: Reducing Risk for All Communities*—supported some of the claims of the exposure of racial minorities to high levels of pollution, but it linked race and class together in most cases. In November 1992, an Office of Environmental Justice (originally called the Office of Environmental Equity) was established within the Environmental Protection Agency. Its purpose was to ensure that communities including large numbers of low-income families and people of color received protection under environmental laws.[21] EPA administrator Carol Browner designated environmental justice as one of the agency's top priorities in 1993. In September of that year, the National Environmental Justice Advisory Council (NEJAC) was created as a forum through which activists and communities could bring their concerns to EPA.

Nevertheless, a study conducted by the *National Law Journal* in 1992 questioned the EPA's environmental equity record up to that time, pointing out that in the administering of the Superfund program, disparities existed in dealing with hazardous waste sites in minority communities as compared with white neighborhoods. William Reilly, EPA director under presidents Ronald Reagan and George Bush, was strongly criticized for not attending the People of Color Environmental Summit. And although President Clinton signed the Executive Order on Federal Actions to Address Environmental Justice in Minority Populations and Low-Income Populations, many have been disappointed because an Environmental Justice Act has yet to pass Congress.

Environmental justice claims, however, vary widely because they derive from an increasingly diverse body of supporters, a loosely knit national coalition of grassroots organizations, and a variety of leaders from several walks of life. There is little doubt, nonetheless, that the movement has broadened the issue of equity as it relates to environmentalism. The movement has persuaded—or possibly forced—environmental groups, government, and the private sector to consider race and class as central features of environmental concern for Americans as well as for people of color in developing countries. It has helped to elevate the toxics and hazardous waste issue to a central position among a vast assortment of environmental problems. It has shifted attention to urban blight, public health, and urban living conditions to a greater degree than earlier efforts by predominantly white environmental reformers. And it has questioned the demands for economic growth at the expense of human welfare. Whether or not the environmental justice movement grows larger, it has altered the debate over the future goals and objectives of American environmental policy.

The movement, however, is not without its limitations, particularly its stance on the issue of race versus class; its underestimation of its friends and sometimes mischaracterization of its foes; and its own exclusivity. After all, the environmental justice movement, although born at the grassroots, is first and foremost a political movement with an agenda questioning many traditional practices and values, and attempting to define new ones in order to change the law and the regulatory apparatus of the nation.

The core view that race is at the heart of environmental injustice is born of an intellectual and emotional attachment to the civil rights heritage of the past several decades. Few—including the EPA—would deny that poor people of color are often disproportionately impacted by some forms of pollution. But the qualifiers are significant. Outside the movement, there has been serious questioning: Is the issue really environmental racism or just poverty? Even within the movement there are those who cannot cleanly separate race and class in all cases. Given the political goals of the movement, the unbending assertion of the centrality of race may prove unworkable if broadening the constituency is to be achieved.[22]

Because of its controversial nature, and not despite it, the emergence and persistence of the environmental justice movement suggests several points of inquiry worthy of deeper historical analysis: (1) environmental equity, especially as it relates to race, class, and gender; (2) environment as a cultural construct; (3) the clash between anthropocentrism and ecocentrism; (4) the importance of urban environmental problems, especially as they impact human life; and (5) the nature of the environmental movement itself, including its short-term and long-term goals. Of these five areas, more exploration of the first three may offer the freshest insights, since historians have devoted substantial attention to the last two in recent years.

The environmental justice movement, because of its stances on race, class, and the environment and its skepticism about the goals and objectives of mainstream environmentalism, has played a historic role in reintroducing equity into the public and academic debate over environmental policy. Equity, however, has been transformed into environmental justice, with a particular focus on the traditional American underside caught beneath the wheels of an avaricious economy. From the historian's vantage point, this is but one aspect of a larger issue, which has already been addressed broadly by philosophers and social scientists—especially sociologists and economists—concerned mainly with distributional effects. Sociologist Allan Schnaiberg, for example, argued that the redistributive element (such as a windfall profit fund to provide cost offsets to the poor) has been largely absent from most of the history of environmental movements through the 1970s, "despite rhetorics that have been vaguely populist," and that environmental movements "are simply not welfare-oriented to the degree that a stable sustained coalition-building effort will be possible.[23] Such a conclusion leaves us to speculate if and how concerns over environmental equity can be uncovered in the historical record, especially if they were not a priority in various environmental movements over time as Schnaiberg argued.

In *Forcing the Spring*, Robert Gottlieb pointed to a few historical episodes of "environmental discrimination" with respect to workplace hazards, espe-

cially the Gauley Bridge episode which led to the death of hundreds of miners—white and black—working for Union Carbide in West Virginia during
the Great Depression.[24] Industrial accidents, workplace hazards, and community pollution problems offer potentially good data for examining questions
of equity with respect to exposure to health risks.

Clayton Koppes suggested another approach to addressing the equity issue
in his article, "Efficiency, Equity, Esthetics: Shifting Themes in American Conservation." Koppes maintained that three ideas dominated the American conservation movement in the Progressive Era: efficiency (management of natural resources); equity (distribution of the development of resources rather
than control by the few); and esthetics (the preservation of nature free from
development). Of the three, efficiency held the greatest sway. Supporters of
the "gospel of efficiency"—proponents of applied science and environmental
management—did not want to undermine development per se, but questioned short-term private gain at the expense of long-term public benefit. Although this view was not wildly popular among all capitalists, it certainly was
less threatening than strict preservationism. Koppes argued further that for
many conservationists of the Progressive Era, "efficiency was not enough; they
were also concerned for greater equity." In this context, "equity" implies that
natural resources remain in public control so that their benefits could be distributed fairly. "The equity school," Koppes stated, "saw wise use of the environment as a tool to foster grass-roots democracy." By the 1960s, the efficiency
school remained dominant, the esthetics school at least had successfully protected the national park system, but the equity branch wallowed. Without
grassroots organizations to press for change—and with resistance to redistributive efforts at every turn—equity moved little beyond the conceptual
stage.[25] Equity, in Koppes's study, has clear definitional limits—more in line
with the concerns over distributional issues than class or race questions. It is,
nonetheless, a useful starting point for asking some key questions about the
intent and direction of national policy expressed in terms of the impartial distribution of resources.

Andrew Hurley's influential *Environmental Inequalities: Class, Race, and
Industrial Pollution in Gary, Indiana, 1945–1980* is a model monographic
study that goes to the heart of environmental justice and environmental racism. Applying the twin perspectives of environmental and social history, he
argued that industrial capitalists and wealthy property holders had "a decisive
advantage in molding the contours of environmental change. Those groups
who failed to set the terms—African Americans and poor whites—found
themselves at a severe disadvantage, consistently bearing the brunt of indus-

trial pollution in virtually all of its forms: dirty air, foul water, and toxic solid wastes."[26]

The cultural construct of environmentalism opens up another world of possibilities, and has been receiving substantial attention from environmental historians, especially at recent meetings of the American Society for Environmental History. Leading the way have been several works on Native Americans and women. Also of particular significance has been Alfred Crosby's biohistory, *Ecological Imperialism: The Biological Expansion of Europe, 900–1900*, which identified European models of environmental practice and how they clashed with indigenous approaches. Despite these fruitful efforts, there is room for more and for a wider range of studies, especially those dealing with the environmental values and goals of a wide variety of racial and ethnic communities. Since environmental historians have never feared borrowing methodological approaches from other disciplines, the notion of culturally constructed environmentalism begs for a greater range of methods, including studies on the use of language.

The question of anthropocentrism versus ecocentrism is not new, but can be brought to bear more directly on issues concerning race and class. Also important are questions about the practical objectives of environmental reform. Human-centered issues offer an immediacy and accessibility to environmentalism that global warming, ozone depletion, overpopulation, and so forth do not possess. Because the environmental justice movement is political at its core, the concreteness and immediacy of its environmental agenda is understandable. But there are some significant longer-range issues underlying the embrace of this brand of anthropocentrism. In *Who Pays the Price? The Sociocultural Context of Environmental Crisis,* applied anthropologist Barbara Rose Johnston argued that environmental quality and social justice issues are "inextricably linked." She explained: "Efforts to protect a 'healthy environment' may, in some cases, result in human rights abuse, and depending upon subsequent social response, may ultimately fail to meet original environmental integrity objectives. And conversely, responding to human rights needs while ignoring the environmental context infers temporary intervention rather than substantive solution; it may thus serve to initiate or perpetuate a cycle of human rights abuses." To lessen victimization from environmental threats, Johnston and other authors in the book promoted the need for more citizen empowerment.[27] While the emphasis in the book is clearly policy-related, the subject of the human-rights dimension of environmentalism begs for more of the historian's scrutiny.

Of all the faults we may possess as scholars and teachers, for all the personal biases and secret passions we may indulge while pursuing our research projects, no shortcoming is more deadly than complacence. If the emergence of the environmental justice movement has shown us anything, it clearly has demonstrated that the foundations of environmentalism laid many years ago are not unshakable; the connection between environmental rights and civil rights have to be taken seriously. We have an obligation to ferret out what is happening to the theory and practice of environmentalism over time. We have the training and the interest to make a contribution to the incredibly complex interface of humans with their world. We have a duty to expand the historical horizons of our field whenever possible. The question of race is central to environmental history.

10

Identity Politics and Multiracial Coalitions in the Environmental Justice Movement

EILEEN M. MCGURTY

The environmental movement, like other social movements, has succeeded, in part, by representing and reinforcing a collective identity of members and potential members. People join because the movement "expresses something essential to their sense of self."[1] Yet the environmental movement long excluded the poor and people of color and neglected to address the potential for disproportionate impacts of environmental risks either directly from pollution or indirectly through unintended consequences of regulations.[2] Beginning in the early 1980s, environmental justice activists confronted the underlying elitism in the environmental movement and demanded that environmentalists address the characteristics, values, and experiences of people who had been victims of unjust environmental risk.

The month-long protest in 1982 against a chemical waste landfill siting in Warren County, North Carolina, a poor and predominately black county, was pivotal in initiating the challenge to environmentalists. The activists in Warren County articulated the heretofore unspoken problem of environmental racism and argued that solutions to this problem must include multiracial coalitions and expanded participation by people of color. Environmental racism purported that people of color were more likely to be exposed to environmental risks than whites. The solution of multiracial coalitions promised to help build a bridge between environmental issues and social issues. According to Dorceta Taylor, a vocal critic of elitism in the environmental movement, environmental justice should: ". . . mobilize community-wide coalitions built

across race, ethnic and class lines and between interest groups and factions
... [because] fairness and justice are issues all can agree on as ones which are
important in building a desirable society."[3]

Racial identity quickly became the primary organizing framework for the
political activism of the environmental justice movement, enabling people of
color to validate their experiences of environmental racism and to become
vocal members of an expanded environmental movement. Environmental
justice activists did not want to reinforce the static ideas of race that had enabled the construction of racism and its many manifestations. However, the
identification of environmental racism and the suggestion of multiracial coalitions created significant tension within the environmental justice movement,
resulting in expanded political participation in environmental decision making and a simultaneous contraction of democratic practice.

Warren County, the so-called birthplace of environmental justice, illustrates the tension in the movement and its impact of contradictory outcomes
in both Warren County and environmental policy making in general. The activism in Warren County occurred in two phases. First, the initial resistance to
the landfill (1979–1983) established the environmental justice activism frame
and became a critical event in the formation of the environmental justice
movement.[4] In the second phase, which is the subject of this chapter, activism
focused on remediating the environmental problems that emerged from the
landfill ten years after its construction (1993–2003). Throughout these two
stages of activism, the environmental racism framework empowered blacks to
be vocal advocates for environmental protection and transparency in environmental decision making. The potential for a disproportionate environmental
burden to be borne by one segment of the society attracted renewed interest
at the national policy level after the events in Warren County. In a 1983 report,
the General Accounting Office (GAO) found that commercial hazardous
waste facilities in southern states were more likely to be located in communities with a predominately African American population. The GAO report is
often credited with initiating the scientific investigation into inequitable distribution of environmental burdens, especially the oft-cited 1987 report by
the United Church of Christ's Commission for Racial Justice (CRJ), *Toxic
Wastes and Race.*

When the potential for an environmental and public health disaster from
the thirteen feet of water in the landfill was discovered in 1993, citizens built
on their success from earlier years. The multiracial coalition that was responsible for the initial organizing moved these activists onto the national
environmental justice stage and enabled them, ten years later, to gain major
substantive and procedural demands from the state regarding remediation at

the landfill. They created a citizen participation structure that surpassed a traditional advisory role and gave the residents significant input and near-veto power on all decisions made regarding the landfill. The citizens had access to outside, independent expertise, and were eventually successful at pushing the state to pursue treatment of the landfill contents to detoxify it. Moreover, the treatment process ensured that no contaminated materials would leave the site; there was no need to use the commercially available landfills or incinerators that were hosted by other poor communities or communities of color.

Eventually, however, the racial construction of the issues silenced dissent and fueled racial animosity among dedicated activists. These tensions led to several difficulties, including a near-breakdown of unity among activists, that almost squelched the goal of securing an environmentally sound and safe resolution of the risks from the landfill. In order to explore these difficulties and their implications, this chapter will first set out to present the events chronologically, and then return to some of the proceedings to focus on the specific issue of racial tension among the activists.

Coalition Building and the Expansion of Democracy

When water was first discovered at the Warren County landfill in 1993, the state proposed a two hundred thousand dollar plan to address the problem by installing a new pump, filtering the sediments contaminated by polychlorinated biphenyls (PCBs), spraying the filtered water over the top of the landfill, and shipping the residues to a facility permitted to manage PCB waste, either a landfill in Alabama or an incinerator in Arkansas.[5] Residents objected to this plan, and, more vehemently, to the fact that a decision was being made without input from the entire community of black and white residents. Thus, the second wave of activism began with a letter from Ken Ferruccio, a white resident living near the landfill and an influential leader in the landfill opposition. He wrote to Jonathan Howes, then secretary of the Department of Environment, Health, and Natural Resources (DEHNR), demanding a process to allow for citizen review and approval of any action taken by the state. He began by emphasizing the historical significance of Warren County and identifying the problem as tied to environmental racism: "We of Warren County . . . ignited the spark, that lit the fuse, that blew the powder keg in 1982 . . . The light and heat from those explosions fueled forever concepts that for too long had been kept apart: environmental justice, environmental civil rights."[6]

The state was not required by law to create a citizen participation process but agreed to do so, in part, because of the potential for recreating the events of 1982, when the ongoing battle over the siting of the landfill had produced demonstrations by civil rights leaders. Environmental racism claims gave residents of the county power to make demands for meaningful input into any decisions that affected the landfill. The secretary responded by promising to "create a first-of-its-kind joint advisory committee comprised of local citizens and State officials to develop a process by which the water can be removed."[7]

The initial group had a broad membership but was dominated by local residents. The most active and vocal community members were Ken and Deborah Ferruccio and Dollie Burwell, who had worked closely together in 1982 when the large protests were held, and had continued active involvement in the environmental justice movement. Ken and Deborah Ferruccio had moved to Warren County in 1976 looking for a rural setting in which to live and raise a family. The 1982 action in Warren had put them into contact with the antitoxic movement, especially the influential North Carolina Waste Awareness and Reduction Network (NC WARN) and the significant number of scientists who had become involved in the antitoxic movement. Since then, the Ferruccios had been involved in a variety of waste-siting conflicts throughout the state. Dollie Burwell had been elected as registrar of deeds for the county in 1982, in part because of her activism with the landfill. She sustained a connection with the CRJ during the time of its influential environmental justice study and was also an integral part of organizing the first National People of Color Environmental Leadership Summit in 1991, where the "Principles of Environmental Justice" document was formulated. Her prominence as a black woman leader in the all-important Warren County project gave her access to the environmental justice structures newly emerging in the national policy arena and became an active participant in the National Environmental Justice Advisory Council (NEJAC) after its formation by the EPA in 1994.

The joint advisory committee in Warren County was immediately renamed the Citizens/State Joint Warren County PCB Landfill Working Group, referred to as the Working Group. This change, while seemingly a semantic detail, reflected the citizens' demands to be equal partners in the decision-making process. With the aid of outside expertise, independent of the state, citizens forced a shift in the goal of the Working Group from overseeing the dewatering of the landfill to finding and implementing a detoxification process for the materials in the landfill. Moreover, the Working Group was able to ensure that no contaminated materials were removed from the landfill for shipment to another community. Concessions by the state to seek detoxification did not come easily. The initial purpose of the committee, as envisioned by Secretary Howes, was not to find a detoxification process, but for "citizens and the state together to develop, monitor and review the process by which the water will be removed from the landfill." Howes concurred that any movement of materials off-site would be unfortunate, but claimed, "no technically feasible means to handle onsite the sediment . . . has been identified."[8] In agreeing to the creation of the Working Group, the DEHNR acknowledged that "environmental justice/environmental equity is a major issue" but was also adamant that detoxification should proceed as "appropriate and feasible," not "at any cost."[9]

Jim Hunt was the governor of North Carolina during the original protests in 1982. He left office after eight years in 1984 (because North Carolina law prohibits more than two consecutive terms), then returned for two more terms in 1992 and again in 1996. In 1983, immediately after the landfill was capped, the governor appointed a group to examine the possibility of treating the soil in the landfill, but the composition, format, and structure of that group did not foster meaningful citizen participation. The report of the governor's group was issued in early 1984 and recommended proper upkeep, appropriation of enough funds for safe maintenance in the future, and the dissolution of the ad-hoc group with "continue[d] surveillance of developments in PCB detoxification, with representation from the appropriate state agencies as well as liaison with EPA, Warren County and the research community." No follow-up action was taken, but ten years later, in 1993, with the opportunity from the water emergency at the landfill, residents used the power of the environmental justice movement to create a much more inclusive and meaningful involvement process. The residents began their efforts in 1993 by focusing on the promise Governor Hunt had made in a 1982 letter to the citizens of Warren County: "The state will push as hard as it can for detoxification of the landfill when and if the appropriate and feasible technology is developed."[10] They never relented in their demand for detoxification, and the procedural concessions made by the state eventually led to this outcome.

The first substantive victory for citizens related to the water debacle in the landfill was the approval of an independent science advisor paid for by the state but answerable to the residents. While Secretary Howes had, in principle, agreed to "outside review," finding the funding for a qualified consultant was another matter. Eventually, in March 1994, after tenacious insistence by citizen members of the group, DEHNR funded one year of work for the landfill project with one hundred thousand dollars. This allocation was to cover capital improvements to initiate removal of water (still the official position of the state) and payment to the science advisor. The initial funding started a process that enabled residents to force the state to shift away from the dewatering plan and to accept the residents' detoxification plan.

In March 1994, Ken and Deborah Ferruccio contacted their antitoxics comrade Billie Elmore, director of NC WARN, who suggested Pauline Ewald for the position of science advisor. Residents were very confident in Ewald: she had strong science and community advocacy qualifications, a reputation for standing up to regulatory agencies, and experience with dioxin issues. The group attempted to draft a mutually agreeable sampling plan but could not agree on the inclusion of split samples to be evaluated at an independent lab and reviewed by Ewald. The state's resistance only fueled the perceptions that it had something to hide and did not, in reality, accept the idea of an equal partnership with residents. At the June 1994 meeting, residents confirmed their intensions to conduct an action of civil disobedience if split samples were not taken, and only then did the state acquiesce.

After the initial sampling, the state found no PCBs, dioxins, or furans in the leachate, but did report eleven to thirteen parts per quadrillion (ppq) of dioxin in the monitoring wells. They concluded that the positive results in the monitoring wells were due to either contamination from outside the landfill or lab error from contaminated equipment; they wanted to test again.[11] Ewald issued a damning report of dioxins and furans in surface soils outside the landfill and in sediments of the nearby stream. The Division of Solid Waste Management was furious, particularly because the conclusions in Ewald's report seemed biased and unrelated to the data. Her report focused on a general description of toxicity of dioxins without specific reference to the risks at the site and recommended a specific technology, Base Catalyzed Decomposition (BCD), to detoxify the landfill. The state contended that Ewald's conclusions could not be drawn from the data reported but were, in fact, predetermined.[12]

Citizen members of the Working Group agreed that choosing a particular technology might be premature but continued to insist that detoxification was the primary goal. The findings of the science advisor, in whom they had placed enormous trust, were enough for citizens to conclude that a serious risk from contamination did exist. The state never accepted the Ewald report nor believed that detoxification of the landfill was necessary for public health reasons. They did, however, partially agree to the principle of detoxification when they argued against selection of a particular technology in favor of full review of available technologies as a continuation of the initial effort of the governor's appointed group in 1984. Although the technical report began the state's shift away from the dewatering plan, the Working Group also called on the aid of powerful politicians. Eva Clayton, the congressional representative for Warren County, was a black woman who had won her first election after the 1982 protests, partially because of increased black voter registration and turnout. She wrote a scathing letter to the secretary of the DEHNR reinforcing that the landfill situation could become a national-level civil rights cause once again.[13]

In 1995, Ewald's contract was not renewed because the state refused to work with her. Citizens were convinced that Ewald had reported the truth and that the state did not want the truth to be known. Employing the argument that it would maintain credibility with the community, the citizens were able to keep the independent science advisor's position. Inclusion of an expert advisor continued to help drive the citizens' agenda, and the Working Group hired two science advisors, each with a different expertise, to address the multiple issues from the landfill. Joel Hirschhorn had a doctorate in materials engineering in addition to extensive experience with remediation, technology assessment, and risk assessment. Patrick Barnes was a geologist whose experience would be helpful in understanding the site characteristics and the current situation at the landfill. State officials were still strongly supporting dewatering and installation of an upgraded pump in the current leachate collection system, so, for the state, the geologist was potentially more appropriate. However, many citizens were impressed with Hirschhorn's expertise in and support of detoxification as well as his extensive qualifications in the area of "environmental technologies."

The state's resistance to detoxification continued: they argued that this expensive approach was not necessary because the landfill presented no real risks to the community. The regulators were schooled in the logic of risk analysis, and they wondered if detoxification might cause significant risks that would outweigh the very negligible risks posed by the landfill. Residents were particularly frustrated with this line of reasoning since they interpreted Governor Hunt's promise to detoxify as independent of the conditions at the landfill. Residents always felt the landfill posed serious health risks to their community, despite the formal risk analysis employed by the state. Of equal importance to the assessment of the landfill problem was the further decline in their already troubled economy that the standard risk-assessment techniques did not take into account. There are one hundred counties in North Carolina, and in 1980, Warren was ranked ninety-seventh in wealth—only three counties had a lower economic standard. By 1990, it had reached the bottom—it was the poorest county in the state. The inequities were highlighted by the economic boom in "the triangle" area (Raleigh, Durham, Chapel Hill), just sixty miles away. Massenburg Kearney, who lived adjacent to the landfill and was a member of the Working Group, expressed his concern: "Our neighbors died of cancer. We all use filtered water, but it didn't help them . . . I used to raise cows here, but I can't anymore because the contamination from the landfill . . . I just want my family to be able to stay on this land. The landfill is here because the community is poor. If we had more money, we could have fought the dump. Things just got worse after the dump was put in."

Any action that the state took, or did not take, that slowed detoxification was seen as obstructionist, and when Hirschhorn recommended further study of the landfill to determine its condition, citizens in the Working Group were completely frustrated. They had put their faith in one advisor, but now another one was telling them that the first one had not done an adequate job. Who were they to believe? Could it be that Hirschhorn was not their advocate but had sided with the state? Hirschhorn's challenge to the Ewald report, however, was tempered by his critique of the state's response to the report. On one hand, the state was not forceful enough in criticizing the report's deficiencies; on the other hand, the state ignored the possibility that dioxins were found offsite and neglected to attempt to find a reason for their presence.

Residents were eager to move forward with detoxification and wanted the BCD process, but Hirschhorn successfully convinced them that a full examination of the landfill's status was needed to determine the current risks posed by the landfill and to compare these risks to those involved with the different remediation processes. The formal risk-assessment techniques of environmental decision making also shaped his approach: "Every remedial action poses some risks. But if the landfill itself poses a high(er) risk, there will be a sound reason to detoxify."[14] Coming from the science advisors, this approach was now easier to accept.

Hirschhorn's assessment of the leachate collection system concluded that the water in the landfill was most likely from the heavy rains that occurred during the construction of the landfill. The state, he argued, was negligent in the construction of the landfill because they allowed the water to build up, and the EPA was also negligent for not monitoring the construction more closely. His most damning conclusion was that the design and operation of the leachate collection system was seriously flawed. The original plan for the landfill called for a perforated pipe system, but the "as-built" drawing showed that no such system was installed. Although the state claimed that they had received permission from the EPA for the change in design, neither the state nor the EPA ever located the documentation. The system that was installed, according to the Hirschhorn report, had never operated properly. The fluctuating water in the monitoring wells, he also argued, indicated that the landfill was leaking through the bottom liner. Since the original plan called for a more extensive leachate collection system and there was indication of contamination moving out of the landfill, Hirschhorn argued that the landfill never was a "state-of-the-art" facility as was promised by the state and EPA. Government agencies were culpable, therefore, in misrepresenting their actions, of making promises that they did not keep, and of putting the community at risk.

The highly critical report enabled citizens to move one step closer to their stated goal of detoxification. In April 1996, the Working Group approved a proposal for the two science advisors to conduct a full site investigation as a first step toward detoxification. Given Barnes's background in geology and experience in site assessments, his firm took the lead in conducting the investigation. The scientific investigation was grounded in the understanding that the selection of the Warren County site was not based on good scientific data. First, the report stated that, "the State selected the site, either in part or in large measure, because of an African-American community that could not effectively fight the site selection process." Secondly, "the location was complicated by a difficult to assess hydro-geological setting that was, in fact, never fully or accurately characterized prior to the decision to locate the landfill there."[15]

The investigation found data to indicate several problems with the landfill. The report affirmed Hirschhorn's earlier investigation, damning the leachate collection system and stated that, "the State had not complied with certain important legal requirements." Evidence from groundwater testing supported the claim that leachate from the landfill had moved into the subsurface immediately adjacent to the landfill. Evidence from the air-monitoring system suggested that PCBs were probably moving through breaches in the top liner. Analysis of the chemical composition of the landfill contents reported ". . . a significant amount of 2,3,7,8-TCDD was found, namely 24 ppq, which is unusual for dioxin/furan impurities for PCBs." This analysis resonated strongly with citizens who had long felt unsure of exactly what was put into the landfill. Most of the soil had been taken off the roadsides contaminated with PCB liquid from the illegal dumping in 1979, but some of it was obtained from Fort Bragg, near Fayetteville, North Carolina. Activists had argued that the material from Fort Bragg was different from the original PCB-contaminated soil. The report stated, "No specific data has been found in the files on exact chemical compositions of the Fort Bragg material," and concluded, "the possibility (exists) that there might be a source of the dioxins other than PCBs."[16]

The most problematic finding with respect to the water in the landfill, however, related to Barnes's analysis of water levels in the landfill and the monitoring wells in relation to seasonal rainfall variations. The evidence suggested a "very strong correlation between the natural hydrologic cycle and the water in the landfill," indicating that the materials in the landfill were not isolated from the environment as the engineering design had intended, but that rainwater was entering and moving through the landfill.[17] State officials were "taken aback" by this finding and for the first time thought perhaps there was evidence to suggest a breach in landfill integrity.

In the end, the information and assessments from both Hirschhorn and Barnes enabled the citizens to continue to push for their ultimate goal of detoxification. In particular, they provided extensive data leading to the "overall conclusion . . . that the landfill has lost integrity and containment efficiency" and that "detoxification of the landfill . . . (is) the only reliable long-term solution to address the threats posed by a low quality landfill containing large amounts of PCBs and dioxins."[18]

The pressure on the state to begin a detoxification project intensified as a result of these investigations. The citizens used the power they had gained through the environmental justice framework to redefine participation and garner significant levels of persuasive evidence to support their cause. The information from the science advisors enabled the Working Group to argue that the landfill posed a major risk to the community. At one very dramatic press conference in Raleigh, both science advisors presented a dire situation for which the state was culpable. By the time the site assessment at the landfill was completed in 1997, Governor Hunt was at the end of his political career, and his 1982 promise to Warren County citizens for detoxification was looming as a possible blemish to his historical record. The political costs were too high; he directed DEHNR to move ahead and make the problem go away. DEHNR's agreement was not so much an acknowledgment of a risk but what was characterized by Mike Kelly as "the right thing to do." The Working Group had chosen BCD as the appropriate technology, and Hirschhorn estimated a $24 million price tag for design, demonstration tests, treatment, and restoration.[19] Funding was the major sticking point, but it was a time of surplus state budgets, and the Working Group had a very strong ally, Frank Ballance, in the general assembly. Hunt included $15 million in his 1999 budget, pledging to fulfill the promise he had made. The state hoped to find the additional $9 million elsewhere.[20] The assembly approved $7 million, but $1.4 million of it was diverted to help with the cleanup from Hurricane Floyd in September 1999. An additional $1 million was taken from the state's white goods program, designed to divert appliances from landfills, and the general assembly approved $4.5 million more in 2001. It looked like a $24 million project would have to be whittled down to a $12 million project. Treatment of the soil began in August 2002 and was scheduled to be completed by spring 2003. The BCD process was designed to treat the soil to two hundred parts per million (ppm) for PCBs and dioxins/furans, a level ten times below regulatory requirements. The residents also achieved their goal of eliminating the need to send contamination to another community: all the treatment was done on-site, safeguarding other communities from contamination problems.

Dissolution of the Coalition and Contraction of Participation

While victorious in obtaining their stated goal of landfill detoxification, the Working Group was less successful in contributing to the goal of a movement built on fluid identities. The potential solution of multiracial coalitions was limited by the problematic definition of environmental racism, which created a rigid understanding of the identity of legitimate victims of environmental injustices. The Warren County citizens faced a daunting and complex problem: how to have a multiracial coalition while nurturing people of color in leadership positions in environmental decision making.

The idea of black leadership was vital to the environmental justice movement for three reasons. First, people of color had been systematically excluded from environmentalism. Second, since the experience of racism could not be translated, no one could validly speak for people of color. Lastly, if whites were leaders in the movement, people of color feared their own leadership would be usurped, as had happened in so many other situations in the past. The conflict between multiracial coalition building and the racial identity of leaders emerged in two contexts in the Working Group. The governance structure of the Working Group and the role of the science advisor both contributed to the dissolution of solidarity among the black and white citizen activists.

In March 1994, the initial structure of the Working Group allowed for a very broad participation by community members, including a total of sixteen members, eight of them residents of Warren County and one the chair of the County Commissioners. It was cochaired by Dollie Burwell and Ken Ferruccio. They were reasonable choices since both had worked together during the 1982 protests and had been involved in the UCC's Commission on Racial Justice report. Both were articulate, tenacious, and dedicated to the project of detoxification. When Henry Lancaster, a high-ranking black official in the Hunt administration, was added as a third cochair, he was supposed to help bridge some of the problems in communication encountered between the state and the citizens. Yet several members were wary of adding a state employee to an official position. Conflicts among the three cochairs intensified, and Ferruccio accused Burwell and Lancaster of pushing him out. The animosity heightened to a point where Ferruccio decided to leave the position of cochair at the end of 1996 but remained an active member.

The Working Group was initially scheduled to end its work in December 1996, but as the end came near and they had not finished the project, the group needed to reconstitute itself and gain the approval of the governor. The remaining cochairs, Burwell and Lancaster, proposed that the original eight

presented himself to the Working Group as a strong candidate because of his extensive work in site assessment, but also because he had: ". . . an understanding of the distribution of environmental contamination, especially as it relates to minority communities. As a black environmental consulting firm, BFA is dedicated to assisting Grassroots organization[s] as they seek answers to the environmental problems facing minority communities."[26]

Here was a perfect opportunity for the Working Group to contribute to the goal of increasing the number of people of color in technical and decision-making positions in environmental agencies and organizations. While tokenism was not desired, a highly qualified, black geologist was too good to pass up. However, not everyone was pleased with this approach to choosing a science advisor, particularly Ken Ferruccio who said: ". . . environmental justice in Warren County requires that we hire the most qualified person for science advisor, that we exclude racial and political considerations, and that we judge applicants only on documented merits."[27]

Of course, in the world of the black members of the Working Group, the idea of "excluding race" was impossible; race existed because racial discrimination persisted. Yet, how could they address the seemingly contradictory impulses in the environmental justice movement: nurture black environmental leadership while also developing a multiracial coalition?

The Working Group avoided a direct discussion of this tension. After they voted, nine to six, in favor of Hirschhorn, Henry Lancaster, a black deputy secretary for DEHNR, met alone with Bill Meyer, director of solid waste management and the lead state member on the Working Group, to craft a structure for a joint science advisor position.[28] The state was inclined to work with Barnes because he was more approachable, but they did not want to alienate the Working Group who had voted for Hirschhorn. Since Lancaster worked for the state, despite his legitimate voice in the environmental justice movement by virtue of his black identity, most citizens did not trust him. If Lancaster wanted to eliminate Hirschhorn, as many citizens perceived, then Hirschhorn must be the biggest threat and should be kept at all costs.[29] The state was able to garner support with the help of Burwell, who had favored Barnes, in part, because she was dedicated to encouraging African American leadership in environmental decision making. The proposal was not well received by Hirschhorn or Ferruccio, but in the interest of moving forward, the Working Group decided to hire both of the consulting firms, hoping to benefit from their complementary qualifications while also ensuring the involvement of an African American scientist.

The tensions over the science advisors were also related to different work

citizen members be reduced to four. However, at the December meeting, the Working Group not only defeated the decrease in citizen members but also prevailed in increasing the number to nine. They decided to place an advertisement in the local paper to find new people to work on the project and instructed Lancaster to submit the proposal to the secretary for approval. The group waited for the secretary's decision for six months, during which time they did not meet, despite several requests of members. When the cochairs informed the group that they had met with Secretary Howes on May 29, and the secretary was awaiting a proposal for a new structure of the Working Group, citizen members were perplexed and outraged. Why hadn't the cochairs represented the wishes of the group to the secretary? Could it be that the "first-of-its-kind" advisory committee, created to foster a new form of citizen participation in government decision making, was silencing potential members? When a meeting still had not been called by July, Ferruccio wrote a scathing memo to the cochairs, claiming that they had been co-opted by the state because they wanted to maintain their positions of power. Ferruccio, a white man from Ohio, claimed to be speaking on behalf of the marginalized residents of Warren County, victimized by: "policies [that] are discriminatory and are based on a willingness to enslave and sacrifice people, especially people of color, by keeping them in ignorance of the facts, often through the help of people of color."[21]

The Working Group was eventually reconstituted with eight members so that the broader membership could continue reviewing technology for detoxification of the landfill. Dollie Burwell continued as cochair and Mike Kelly, special assistant to Secretary Howes, took Lancaster's position as the other chair. Funding was secured from the general assembly. As the detoxification process moved forward, the state argued that the Working Group was no longer necessary and a more traditional Citizen Advisory Board (CAB) would suffice. Not everyone embraced the name change, and the Ferruccios, who had been a centerpiece of the entire effort, "work[ing] long and hard to get to this point,"[22] completely rejected it. For Ferruccio, "the state and federal government would continue to control the decision-making process through their state co-chair and through their NEJAC affiliated local co-chair. . . . The Citizen Advisory Board in Warren County is simply a function of the federally institutionalized environmental justice community, centralized . . . through NEJAC."[23]

These direct attacks on Burwell and Lancaster claimed "reverse environmental racism," and the challenge to leadership by a black woman and black man was deeply troubling to members of the group. Despite the real and difficult personality conflicts with the Ferruccios, the new format did demon-

styles. Hirschhorn had been unrelenting in his attacks on the state and was unwilling to work collaboratively. For example, he oversaw the state's air monitoring tests. While at the site, he observed but said nothing. The following day, he denounced the state's tests as incomplete and inaccurate. State officials were upset that he had spent the entire day at the site and did nothing proactively to improve the monitoring process, made no suggestions, gave no comments. Instead of taking the opportunity to make a change, the state saw Hirschhorn's actions as only trying to find additional reasons to bolster the argument that the state didn't know what they were doing.[30] Barnes was less confrontational even though the site assessment report that he oversaw offered severe criticism of the state and the EPA. Now that the group was moving toward detoxification, Barnes was more willing to work with the state. He did not always agree, often offering significant challenges to the state's position, but could more easily work out compromises.[31]

Black residents in the Working Group allied with Barnes, and the white residents with Hirschhorn, resulting in an additional racial division within the group. Hirschhorn felt that he was discriminated against because he was white and often claimed his qualifications were superior to Barnes's. Deborah Ferruccio concurred: "He is the national expert in detoxification technologies. He has a doctorate and many publications in peer-reviewed journals about these topics." The sense of superiority was particularly troubling to black members of the group, especially Burwell and Lancaster, who wrote to Hirschhorn castigating him for his "unfair and baseless" allegations. They continued to stress that each had different skills and experience to bring to the project—Hirschhorn's technical expertise in detoxification processes, and Barnes's geological expertise for site assessment. Dollie Burwell and Henry Lancaster wrote to Hirschhorn: "It is our opinion that neither of you are superior to the other and such comments have strong racist undertones. This is particularly distressing given the PCB landfill detoxification is such an important environmental justice project."[32]

Adding to this animosity, Hirschhorn rejected the economic development dimension of the project that was central to the Working Group's environmental justice mission. The plan for implementation included an Environmental Job Training program to "strengthen the ability of Warren County workers to compete for jobs associated with the PCB Landfill Detoxification and Redevelopment Project"[33] with funding from the EPA and HUD. Also, Barnes spent much of his time in Warren County meeting with local business to help them compete for construction bids at the site. Hirschhorn rejected these activities: "In my view the [Working Group] should and must remain

strate that the CAB was now part of the establishment. This position in the established order was possible, in part, because environmental justice had gained enormous power on the national and state level, and this power was directly related to partisan politics. Ferruccio took an extreme position on this development: "It is therefore to the economic advantage of the NEJAC nexus to link environmental problems to environmental racism as a rationale for justifying minority control of alleged liberation mechanisms . . . (and) polluters are protected and environmental problems perpetuated in exchange for trickle-down economic and political benefits to minority leaders."[24]

He was adamant that Burwell's political connections limited her ability to represent citizens because she was using her position to further her political career or the political career of others. After she lost her registrar of deeds position to Elsie Weldon in the election of 1996, she went to work for Congresswoman Eva Clayton. The Ferruccios were not the only citizen members of the group that felt uncomfortable with the close ties Burwell had to the political establishment. In November 1996, Burwell and Barnes met with Eva Clayton and state senator Frank Ballance without the knowledge of the Working Group or the participation of the other science advisor. Jim Warren, representing the state anti-toxic coalition, NC WARN, alleged that any contact with the government should be sanctioned by the other citizen members, lest there be secretive deals made and "hidden agendas" pursued that diverted the Working Group away from its main goal of detoxifying the landfill. Although Jim Warren was convinced that Burwell never "lost her commitment to detoxification," the meetings did not fit with the operating procedure used by the group.[25] The political connections of members of the Working Group created competing and contradictory reactions, reflecting the tension in environmental justice about the appropriate relationship of a social movement to the established political order. The close relationship Burwell had with both Ballance and Clayton did enable the group to move appropriation bills through the general assembly; however, just a month after these questionable meetings with elected officials the cochairs proposed a diminished role for citizen members in the Working Group. This timing was not lost on other members.

As the conflicts over governance deepened, tension about the science advisors also contributed to the dissolution of a fluid identity that enabled a multiracial coalition. A new science advisor was needed after the Ewald debacle, and the review of candidates left two choices. Patrick Barnes was a geologist with Barnes Ferland and Associates, Inc. (BFA), an African American owned environmental consulting business, and Joel Hirschhorn was an engineer who had worked on technology review and risk assessment. Barnes

limited to dealing with the safety and detoxification of the landfill. If people want to pursue civil rights, environmental justice and economic development, then they should use means other than the [Working Group].[34]

These comments perplexed members of the Working Group because they understood environmental justice to emphasize the relationship between economic justice and environmental quality. For these activists, any community work related to the landfill had to be tied to economic development efforts. If these activists knew anything, it was that environmental problems and issues of civil rights and economic opportunities could not be separated.

✹

The environmental justice framework, both through its problem definition and proposal for solutions, broadened participation in the decision-making about the landfill and led to major substantive successes on behalf of environmental quality for residents in Warren County. The soil was detoxified without shipment of contamination off-site, and investment in job training for residents in Warren County was obtained. The dedicated efforts of many activists over ten years made these outcomes possible.

Despite the many successes that can be enumerated, there is still some skepticism. Massenburg Kearney, while delighted that work is progressing, is holding off judgment on the success of the project until everything is finished: "I'll believe it when I see it." The Ferruccios still argue that the detoxification process will not yield the desired results because the science advisor, Patrick Barnes, is in the state's pocket. Without the independent oversight that Hirschhorn would have offered, there is no way to know if the activities at the site are safe and if the procedure will render the site clean.

Many involved in the process expressed some surprise that the detoxification had actually started because there were so many opportunities during the decade for the entire process to unravel. The animosity about leadership and science advisors was virulent, but an intra-citizen rift also grew as black members of the group grappled with the development of a unitary racial identity. When members wanted to send out a press release, pointing out the landfill problems and the need for funding for detoxification, Burwell claimed that newspapers were not the best form of communicating with residents of Warren County because, "my people don't read," suggesting that the majority of African Americans in Warren County were illiterate. Another black member of the group, a reticent but thoughtful man who lives adjacent to the landfill, stormed out of the meeting, telling Burwell, "I don't know about your people, but my people know how to read."

While distrust of the state contributed significantly to the tension and difficulty in resolving the issues, conflicts among citizens over the role of identity in environmental justice proved equally as troubling. These tensions were personality driven, in part, but were also tied to the politics of environmental justice. As Jim Warren reflected on the process, "they [blacks on the Working Group] were under enormous pressure from the environmental justice community. All eyes were on them. There had to be black leadership on this project because of that pressure."

Perhaps a direct and upfront discussion about the role of affirmative action in the project would have helped ease the tension, but in the end the racial animosity, driven by both racism and pressure from the outside, enabled the state to avoid the sticky problem of the risks from the landfill. The state never acknowledged that there was a significant risk from the landfill, and the decision to detoxify was driven by a desire to keep a lid on racial politics. The logic of siting, the inherent problems with attempting to entomb waste in perpetuity, and the perpetuation of waste policies predicated on expected waste expansion, therefore, never had to be brought into question. Not only did identity-based politics limit the ability for radical challenge to waste policy, the state's insistence that "of course it became a racial thing," belittled the legacy of racism. As the second phase of activism in Warren County illustrates, environmental justice, while an enormously powerful organizing principle, can have the unintended consequence of reinforcing the very problem it is attempting to dismantle.

✹ 11

Religion and African American Environmental Activism

MARK STOLL

In October 1991, three hundred delegates gathered in Washington DC for the People of Color Environmental Leadership Summit. Among the first to address the audience gathered in the conference room of the Washington Court Hotel were the leaders of two of the most prominent national environmental organizations: Michael Fischer, executive director of the Sierra Club, and John Adams, executive director of the Natural Resources Defense Council. Both these white men took great pains to profess their sympathy for the environmental problems of minorities, confess their organizations' historical failure to address minority issues, and assert the need for environmental racial unity. Often, said Fischer, the Sierra Club had been "conspicuously missing from the battles for environmental justice," but now was "here to reach across the table and to build the bridge of partnership with all of you." For his part, Adams also offered a "partnership" with minorities in fighting toxic waste, and concluded, "You can't win this battle alone."

Dana Alston, leading organizer of the summit, responded in an impassioned speech. An activist in poverty and racial issues since she served as president of the Black Student Organization at Wheelock College in the 1960s, Alston was a staff member of Panos Institute hired to develop a program relating to domestic environmental justice issues. She later went on to become program officer for the environment at the Public Welfare Foundation, and, since her untimely death in 1999, has come to be widely recognized for her important work in the environmental justice movement as well as her broader social activism. Alston did not speak directly to these representatives of the overwhelmingly white mainstream environmental movement. Environmentalism to her made sense only when put in a different context. "For us," she said, "the issues of the environment do not stand alone by themselves. They are not narrowly defined. Our vision of the environment is woven into an overall framework of social, racial, and economic justice."[1]

From one perspective, Alston had essentially rebuffed the proffered olive branch. Indeed, the speakers even seemed to be speaking different languages, the language of nature issues and the language of social issues. In fact, African Americans long have overwhelmingly responded to mainstream environmentalism in a way very similar to Alston's. Take, for instance, Carl Anthony, who is about as well connected with mainstream environmentalism as anybody, black or white: he is former president of David Brower's Earth Island Institute, a founder and former director of Urban Habitat, keynote speaker at the 1999 meeting of the American Society for Environmental History, and current program officer of the Sustainable Metropolitan Communities Initiative of the Ford Foundation. Even Anthony betrays a skeptical and cynical tone when discussing environmental issues that whites get passionate about. In an interview with Theodore Roszak about "ecopsychology," Anthony clearly could barely keep his patience, linking ecopsychology with something to him about as useless, deep ecology:

> Deep Ecology is in touch with something, but the desire of a tiny fraction of middle- and upper-class Europeans to hear the voice of the Earth could be in part a strategy by people in these social classes to amplify their *own* inner voice at a time when they feel threatened, not only by the destruction of the planet, but also by the legitimate claims of multicultural human communities clamoring to be heard. . . . Why is it so easy for these people to think like mountains and not be able to think like people of color? . . .

For their part, such mainstream environmental organizations as the Sierra Club have found it frustratingly difficult to get people of color to think like mountains. Anthony did acquire a growing appreciation of the John Muir tradition in his association with Brower and like-minded people, but he remarked in a 1999 interview, "I think that there is a fundamental problem within the John Muir mythology, for all that it's contributed—and it's contributed a lot—and that is that somehow we can save nature by separating it from human activity." In 1997 Anthony resigned as president and left the

Earth Island Institute over his white colleagues' resistance to the integration of social justice and environmental issues in the national forests of northern New Mexico.[2]

Perhaps surprisingly, this issue is anything but new. Two decades earlier, on Earth Day 1970, there was talk that environmental issues crossed class and racial lines, certainly a soothing notion after the tumult of the 1960s.[3] Yet in 1972, when the Conservation Foundation sponsored a three-day seminar entitled "Environmental Quality and Social Justice," leaders from the Sierra Club and other environmental groups met with union, urban, and minority representatives, and their remarks uncannily foreshadowed those of the 1991 People of Color Environmental Leadership Summit. According to the opening speaker, Illinois state senator Richard Newhouse of Chicago, "The urban social movement has been concerned with housing, welfare, unemployment, and youth problems. Insofar as the people in those activities are concerned, there is absolutely no connection between what they see as an environmental movement and what their problems are all about.... The conservation movement is much the same as women's lib and all the rest of the elitist operations that have come into being since people got sick and tired of fighting for the rights of black people."[4] Much of the discussion at the seminar dealt with building the bridges and fostering the cooperation that Fischer and Adams would talk about in 1991. In the same year, 1972, at the first United Nations Conference on the Environment, held in Stockholm, intense discussion between Western and postcolonial nations produced a declaration that insisted as its leading principle, before discussion of resources or pollution: "Man has the fundamental right to freedom, equality and adequate conditions of life, in an environment of a quality that permits a life of dignity and well-being, and he bears a solemn responsibility to protect and improve the environment for present and future generations. In this respect, policies promoting or perpetuating apartheid, racial segregation, discrimination, colonial and other forms of oppression and foreign domination stand condemned and must be eliminated."[5] Despite early national and international recognition of the necessary connection between social justice and the environment, almost twenty years of American environmental activism had narrowed the gap between environmentalist and African American concerns very little, if at all.

The irony is, of course, that environmentalists in general tend to be among the most broad-minded, well-meaning, politically progressive white people. The lack of people of color in the environmental movement has been a point of embarrassment to them since the 1960s. Yet even when white environmentalists invited local black activists to join in campaigns for parks and conservation, blacks often declined to take part. For example, Cora Tucker, who won national recognition when she organized local resistance to toxic waste dumps in her heavily black southern Virginia county, was asked to join in demonstrations to save a local park:

> This white woman from an environmental group asked me to come down to save a park. She said that they had been trying to get black folks involved and that they won't come. I said, "Honey, it's not that they aren't concerned, but when their babies are dying in their arms they don't give a damn about a park." I said, "They want to save their babies. If you can help them save their babies, then in turn they can help you save your park." And she said, "But this is a real immediate problem." And I said, "Well, these people's kids dying is immediate."[6]

Despite efforts to broaden the movement, environmentalism continues to have such a low profile in the black community that it constitutes barely a blip on the radar screen of black concerns. In editions of *The African American Almanac,* for instance, or any other standard African American encyclopedias or reference books, environmental issues merit barely a mention, a paragraph at most, and often do not appear in any form in the index. That more than two decades have passed since one-time reverend Benjamin Chavis coined the term and popularized the concept of "environmental racism" must surely add to the frustration of mainstream environmental groups. On the other hand, it is not the case that blacks do not care about the environment. The Congressional Black Caucus, for example, has one of the best environmental voting records on Capitol Hill. Why then does this gap between environmentalists and blacks exist, and why has it continued for decades, virtually impervious to all attempts to bridge it?[7]

There are many possible approaches to answering this question, because the issue is bound up with black historical experience in a nation that has always denied African Americans full equality and opportunity; with longtime black concerns and attitudes; and with the characteristic black moral viewpoint. In all of these—experience, goals, moral perspective—African Americans contrast with white environmentalists.

All of these are also intimately tied up with the history of the African American church. It represents a lens through which shine clearly and sharply the actions, perceptions, and moral assumptions that have historically guided and shaped African American politics and social action. The main issues of black history and politics, from abolitionism to civil rights to environmental justice, cannot be separated from the power and influence of the institution of the black church and of the peculiar realities of black Protestantism. The church was virtually the only institution to survive slavery intact. It was the center of the black community throughout the long night of Jim Crow segregation. It continues to be the single most important black institution in America today. The church has supplied most historical black leaders, who tended to be either ordained or very religious, including, for example, Frederick Douglass, Sojourner Truth, Booker T. Washington, Martin Luther King Jr., Jesse Jackson, and Al Sharpton, among many others. Benjamin Chavis himself was then a minister in the United Church of Christ. As the center of black communities across the South, the church has often played an essential role in organizing resistance to toxic waste dumps and toxic pollution. In Halifax County, Virginia, community activist Cora Tucker, a very religious member of the Crystal Hills Baptist Church, organized the black community through local churches to fight a nuclear waste dump in 1986. Local activists in Texarkana, Texas, used the Mount Zion Baptist Church to inform and organize a black neighborhood to act out against the poisoned soil upon which it sat. Black churches have played a role in community after community in rallying and organizing against environmental dangers.[8]

The centrality of religion to African American environmental activism stands out in strong contrast to other comparable social groups. Despite the examples of Pat Robertson and Jerry Falwell, no other ethnic, social, or religious group has as strong a tradition of clerical political activism. A most instructive comparison can be made with poor southern whites, who have had a similar economic status, who have also attended Baptist, Methodist, Holiness, and Pentecostal churches, and who occasionally have made political common cause with blacks, as in the Populist Party of the nineteenth century. Yet poor whites do not have a similar strong tradition of ministerial leadership and have rarely, if at all, organized their communities against the siting of toxic dumps or polluting industry. Lower-class southern white churches have played little significant positive role in local environmental activism.

While in the twentieth century many competing institutions have developed, in black communities, especially in the South, the church remains the communal heart. As such, it expresses central black values, and has been the locus for tensions in community and religion between radicalism, political activity, and resistance on one hand, and accommodation, otherworldliness, and the charismatic on the other. As Frederick C. Harris has noted, the "relatively mainstream" black churches—which currently comprise the African Methodist Episcopal Church, the African Methodist Episcopal Zion Church, the Christian (formerly "Colored") Methodist Episcopal Church, the National Baptist Convention, USA, Inc., and the National Baptist Convention of America, Inc.—have played a contradictory role in black history. These churches "serve[d] as a source of civic culture by giving African Americans the oppor-

tunities to practice organizing and civic skills and to develop positive orienta-
tions toward the civic order." Yet they also made available the resources and
mind-set to oppose oppression in ways that aimed for inclusion in society and
politics and rejected political violence and separatist black nationalism. By
nurturing both civic culture and an oppositional mentality, black mainstream
churches empowered believers by encouraging their self-worth and promoted
and facilitated political and economic activism within the system.[9] `

Just as importantly, black churches have always been politically active—
"the most activist sector of American religion," according to political scientist
Robert Booth Fowler. In the words of Cora Tucker, "The real organized groups
in the United States are churches." The National Association for the Advancement of Colored People (NAACP), the National Urban League, and the Southern Christian Leadership Conference (SCLC) have all relied on churches for
support and participation. The NAACP often met in churches after Sunday
services. The civil rights movement in the South drew strength, nourishment,
and material support from an already existing network of churches. So much
were they centers of agitation and protest during the civil rights era that at
least ninety-three were bombed or burned between 1962 and 1965. According
to one analysis, "African-American politics has always had and continues to
have a decidedly religious slant, while African-American religion is deeply
political." In a *Detroit News*–Gannett News Service poll of blacks in the early
1990s, a majority thought black churches met their needs more effectively
than the NAACP, the National Urban League, the SCLC, or the Congress of
Racial Equality, and 63 percent felt that black churches should "spend more
time" on social and economic problems of the community. When politicians,
black or white, seek the black vote, they visit black churches and woo the black
clergy.[10]

Among the historically central themes of African American religion are
the key ideas of blacks as a people apart, chosen by God, and of the search for
social justice as the goal of moral action. The distinctiveness of the African
American church arose from the interplay of three historical factors: a generalized African cultural influence lacking boundaries between religion, politics,
and culture; a heritage of exploitation and injustice based on race; and the
enduring character of the church as an institution. Take, for instance, the central role of the minister in southern black communities. In Africa, each village
viewed its ruler as the supreme priest who ruled by favor of God. Africans required exemplary moral character of rulers because of a perceived correspon-
dence between his character and the community's well-being. African Americans transferred the spirit of African kingship to the clergy. W. E. B. DuBois
called the "Priest or Medicine-man" the most significant institution to survive

the voyage from Africa: "He early appeared on the plantation and found his function as the healer of the sick, the interpreter of the Unknown, the comforter of the sorrowing, the supernatural avenger of wrong, and the one who rudely but picturesquely expressed the longing, disappointment, and resentment of a stolen and oppressed people."[11] Because churches were blacks' primary institutions, ministers took on an essentially political role to become leaders of local communities, often due to their charismatic and oratorical skills, and acquired great social status and some material benefit. The duties of these leaders revolved around the maintenance of harmony with God, and with whites. As de facto community leaders, black ministers had no qualms about giving political sermons or, when possible, acting in the political arena themselves. Note that both major African American presidential candidates, Jesse Jackson and Al Sharpton, are ordained ministers.[12]

The political orientation of black churches similarly grows from African and American roots. Like many premodern religions, African religion assumed a unity of the sacred and profane. Music, dance, and stories found their place in work and play as well as religion, and continue to find a place in contemporary African American Christianity. In the early nineteenth century, slaves circumvented religious prohibitions against dancing by a half-dance known as the "ring shout," in which participants would half shuffle, half walk in a circle to the rhythm of religious song, often all night long. Despite white denunciations that such behavior was "heathenish," "savage," and "barbaric," black congregations moved, swayed, and clapped while singing in church. White understanding of the separation of behavior appropriate to the spheres of church and the world found no counterpart in black culture. African Americans have also never hesitated to see political meaning in biblical stories. When slaves heard these narratives, most particularly those from the Old Testament, they interpreted them politically. The God of Moses and the Hebrews was a liberator deity who freed oppressed peoples and opposed the oppressors.[13]

Among the churches, these themes have historically manifested themselves most notably in the "relatively mainstream" churches, which all trace their origins to the days of slavery or Reconstruction. Black Methodist and Baptist ministers have long been social and political activists, and although their theology and ecclesiology differ, their social thought is the same. Members of the African Methodist Episcopal Church, the oldest black denomination, were early abolitionists and have a strong tradition of racial consciousness. In addition, Methodists have always concerned themselves with social services, education, and social justice. (White Methodists, too, share an ethic of social concern, exemplified by their strong support in all parts of the country for the Social Gospel of the early twentieth century.) Examples of leading black Methodist activists are many: Sojourner Truth, Harriet Tubman, and Mary McCleod Bethune (graduate of Moody Bible Institute and would-be missionary to Africa) were devout Methodists; Frederick Douglass was a licensed preacher, the three major black revolts of the nineteenth century, the Prosser, Vesey, and Turner revolts, were all associated with black Methodists; Reverend Hiram Revels was the first black senator in Congress during Reconstruction, joined in politics by several other clergymen; Reverend Oliver Leon Brown sued the Topeka Board of Education to integrate the school system; and Methodist civil rights activist James Farmer had a divinity degree.

Traditional Baptist congregational independence—and the vast majority of rural southern black churches are Baptist—made Baptist pastors, especially of large congregations, less vulnerable to civil and economic suppression, and hence leaders in political activity and community advocacy. The Baptist church has supplied a preponderant number of civil rights leaders as well as the majority of membership in civil rights organizations. Booker T. Washington functioned as an unordained Baptist preacher. Martin Luther King Jr., King's father, and his maternal grandfather, all Baptist ministers, were also all social or political activists. Large urban Baptist churches might also provide social services, such as New York's Abyssinian Baptist under Reverend Adam Clayton Powell Sr. and his son, the latter of who was also active in politics and served in the House of Representatives. The leadership of the SCLC was heavily Baptist, and Baptist ministers led the campaign against segregation in the civil rights era. Soon after Reverend Al Sharpton was precociously ordained a Pentecostal minister at age ten, his mother began taking him to Bethany Baptist Church, a politically very active congregation in Bedford-Stuyvesant in New York City whose pastor, Reverend William A. Jones Jr., assumed a mentorship role for the boy and set him on the path of politics and protest.[14]

Among other black denominations and clergy, the record of social and political activism has been more mixed, or lacking altogether. On the one hand, although comparatively small in number, black ministers in Presbyterian and Congregational churches (now the United Church of Christ, or UCC) have fought for racial and social justice since before the Civil War. Indeed, the UCC sponsored the study that first documented environmental racism in the 1980s, and sponsored both the First and Second People of Color Environmental Leadership Summits. On the other hand, sects like the Nation of Islam (Black Muslims) have been too alienated and separatist to engage in mainstream politics, and Pentecostal and Holiness churches tend to be otherworldly, conservative, and apolitical. Of the Pentecostal churches, the

Church of God in Christ (COGIC) is today the largest and the most politically engaged. Nevertheless, no Black Muslim mosque or Pentecostal or Holiness church seems to have led a fight against environmental injustice. For example, when opposition developed to an incinerator in a mostly black neighborhood of Philadelphia, Black Muslims expressed initial interest and showed up for an early meeting, but never returned or participated in any political activities.[15]

Along with a strong tradition of church-based activism and clerical community leadership, African Americans have had a distinctive moral orientation. Black morality is a social morality. Africans had a reciprocal, covenantal relationship with their deities. God sustained and protected Africans in return for loyal obedience. As members of different African communities coexisted in New World plantations, where slavery and racism set blacks apart from white society, racial identity replaced previous affiliations. God now served the well-being of the race, and of any other people in covenant with him. Again, the Hebrew Bible, particularly the story of Exodus, inspired blacks to think of themselves as God's chosen people whom he would lead to the Promised Land—a well-established symbol from the sermons and spirituals of slaves to the speeches of Martin Luther King Jr. In consequence, the well-being of the community was of the highest value. Individualism in the sense of autonomy from the community had no moral sanction in African values, and African American individualism never upheld the individual apart from the community. Black church services have always had many elements that reinforced the community: the vocal congregational responses to the chanted sermon; the call-and-response style of singing; the identification of the audience with soloist or preacher; and the communal creation of songs and spirituals in nineteenth-century churches and singing at all times.[16]

For two centuries, white observers have noted the extraordinary communal unity of feeling and emotion in black congregations, and often found themselves caught up in the mood despite themselves. In church, during the sermon and especially while singing, the individual became one with the community. Clifton Furness left a vivid description of a prayer meeting he attended in 1926 in the old slave cabins of a remote South Carolina plantation, at which he witnessed communal unity come alive and sacred song emerge. The preacher began speaking slowly, but gradually both tempo and intensity increased until he declared, "Gawd's lightnin' gwine strike! Gawd's thunder swaller de ert!"

> Gradually moaning became audible in the shadowy corners where the women sat. Some . . . began swaying backward and forward. Several men moved their feet alternately, in strange syncopation. A rhythm was born,

almost without reference to the words that were being spoken by the preacher. It seemed to take shape almost visibly, and grow. I was gripped with the feeling of a mass-intelligence, a self-conscious entity, gradually informing the crowd and taking possession of every mind there, including my own.

Furness recounts that someone called out, "Git right—sodger! Git right—sodger! Git right—wit Gawd!"

Instantly the crowd took it up, moulding a melody out of half-formed familiar phrases based upon a spiritual tune.... A distinct melodic outline became more and more prominent, shaping itself around the central theme of the words, "Git right, sodger!"
... The general trend was carried on by a deep undercurrent, which ... bore the mass of improvised harmony and rhythms into the most effective climax of incremental repetition that I have ever heard. I felt as if some conscious plan or purpose were carrying us along, call it mob-mind, communal composition, or what you will.[17]

The black church also created a feeling of self-worth and empowerment that carried over into politics and society. This likely carries over from African practice, most especially in Baptist churches, whose extreme congregational polity along with white indifference toward black worship forms allowed African religious and ritual influences to survive more than in other churches. According to the influential analysis of Walter F. Pitts Jr., black Baptist rituals, chanted sermons, and songs not only transmitted African antecedents, they also imbued participants with divine assurance and the self-confidence born of doing the work of God. According to many who experienced it while speaking before a church audience, the chanted affirmations of "Well!" or "Hallelujah!" or "Isn't it the truth?" also gave a tremendous psychological boost to the speaker. This kind of communal self-affirmation gave the speaker a sense of elation, fluency, and power. This sense of power, of possibility, and of divine protection extended to believers as well. "God can make a way out of no way" is still a characteristic attitude of preachers and believers. It deflects any blame from themselves to outside forces and gives godly sanction to opposition to ungodly laws and mores. Many participants in the civil rights movement took with them divine assurance and confidence in divine justice as they went from the churches to the places of protest and action.

Other elements of black Protestantism served to heighten group identity and separation from whites. Blacks saw white religious services as cold and overly intellectual, and often asserted that shouting and emotion were essential to both salvation and proper worship. When forced during slavery to listen to white preachers, slaves amongst themselves would reject any parts of the ministers' message that rang untrue or conflicted with their own sense of God's justice. Blacks might rejoice at the prospect that the death of a particularly hated slave owner or white meant he or she would be going to eternal punishment. The coming apocalypse, when the innocent and suffering believer would be elevated over their oppressors, held strong appeal and gave comfort during the days of slavery and segregation.[18]

A common ancestry in Africa has also helped to unify blacks: Africa has come to represent the Promised Land for African Americans. This view results from an alienation of a landless race from the land, and therefore from the land myths that have animated European Americans from Jamestown and Plymouth Rock to the modern environmental movement. Herein lies another reason for the racial split in environmentalism. This land was *not* their land. This is not to say that the Promised Land has not at times had other metaphorical meanings for African Americans: during slavery it indicated the free states, in the late nineteenth century Kansas and Oklahoma, and then in the early twentieth century northern and western cities. Yet it is certainly true that nowhere in this country have African Americans felt a pride of full possession, of mythic origins tied to the soil, of confidence in a divine destiny manifest in the land itself, such as is symbolized for whites by Plymouth Rock, Yosemite Valley, or even Stone Mountain. While it is true that "wilderness" in general held meaning for blacks, particularly during slavery, as a place of freedom both for hunters and for runaways, a place of magic and spirits, a place for secret religious meetings, and a symbolic place in religion and sacred song, it never acquired a significance requiring its preservation or veneration. The great monuments of black sacred history are human, not natural, and the dominant metaphor has been Moses in the wilderness, not Adam in Paradise.[19]

The environmental justice movement, especially but not only in the South, yields numerous examples of all these aspects of black Protestant social morality and the central community roles of the minister and the church. At the environmental justice protest in Warren County, North Carolina, in 1982, hundreds gathered every day for six weeks at the Coley Springs Baptist Church and marched to the dump to protest or block the trucks. Reverends Joseph Lowery of SCLC and Walter Fauntroy of the Progressive National Baptist Convention, Inc. (PNBC) joined the protests, and were arrested along with Reverend Benjamin Chavis of the UCC and Reverend Leon White, director of the North Carolina–Virginia field office of the UCC Commission for Racial Justice. From his experience there Chavis sponsored the United Church of Christ study that in 1987 brought attention to "environmental racism" in the siting of dumps and polluting industries. In 1992, in a complicated and doomed fight against a waste-to-energy incinerator in the poor city of Chester, Pennsylvania, a black minister, Reverend Strand, cochaired the group Chester Residents Concerned for Quality of Life, which had been organized to oppose it, and Reverend Commodore Harris of the West End Ministerium also spoke in opposition. Aside from toxic dump and pollution issues, church activism has been so rare that the water conservation program of the First AME Church of Los Angeles to upgrade showerheads and toilets stands out.[20]

The National Council of Churches, in cooperation with the mainstream black denominations and COGIC, held a National Black Church Environmental and Economic Justice Summit in Washington DC in 1993. The summit sent six requests to Vice President Al Gore, including "the naming of a Black Church representative to the Sustainable Communities Task Force of the President's Council on Sustainable Development" and the "involvement of local Black church congregations in major environmental decisions undertaken by the administration." The summit issued a declaration that assumed the unity of social and ecological justice: "We, African-American Church leaders, historically committed to justice issues, affirm the unitary nature of life and commit ourselves to the ministry of converging justice and environmental issues that are critical matters of life and death for our Church and for our community." The summit created a Black Church Environmental and Economic Justice Network, and the three black Methodist denominations joined the Environmental and Economic Justice Working Group.[21]

The dominant southern white Protestant ethic contrasts on environmental issues in nearly every respect. The South has historically had a very strong tradition of individualism. In the realm of religion this has produced churches that have a sect-type relationship with society—that is, they are apart from society, not identified with it—even as Baptist and Methodist churches, in particular, have strongly shaped white social attitudes and morality. White Protestants' belief is that society will only improve with the individual conversion of all of its members, and that a universal, personal, puritanical ethic will then solve all social problems. Until the evangelical resurgence in the 1970s and 1980s, itself the product of social, cultural, and demographic change, white churches and ministers tended to stay aloof from politics. In addition, white evangelicals incline toward conservatism, while black evangelicals lean towards liberalism. As a consequence, southern white evangelical churches have tended to oppose or ignore environmentalism and most social reform programs. Circumstances have never made the church the primary institution of white communities. The denomination that historically did try to encompass all of society, the Episcopal Church, was abandoned to a small number of elite in the aftermath of the American Revolution and has little influence. In any case, the South has produced disproportionately few white environmentalist leaders, authors, or thinkers.[22]

Those northern churches with a Puritan or Lutheran pedigree—primarily the Congregational Church or UCC, Presbyterian Church, Unitarian Church, Disciples or Churches of Christ, American Baptist Church, and the Lutheran churches—produced various traditions that have strongly influenced the American environmental movement. Concisely put, the Puritan goal of a godly society shaped and guided by a partnership of minister and magistrate produced secular offspring in the form of the American social and political reform movements. Puritan Calvinist theology encouraged respect for wild nature as the direct creation of a good and wise Creator and the place where God draws nearest to us. Puritans therefore began a tradition of solitary meditation in natural settings. These ideas, nurtured by post-Calvinist churches and transmitted by post-Calvinist environmentalist heroes like Ralph Waldo Emerson, Henry David Thoreau, and John Muir, continue to powerfully influence modern white environmental attitudes. Conveniently emptied of its original human inhabitants and regarded as the pure antithesis to exploitative American capitalist corporations and corrupt, degraded cities, the Edenic American landscape with its original flora and fauna thus has constituted a moral resource to be owned by the people and preserved in parks and reserves for the benefit of society. The anticapitalist, antiurban analysis tends to direct environmentalist attention away from analyses focusing on racism or urban problems.[23] Many of the churches in the Puritan and Lutheran traditions continue to place great emphasis on the protection of creation, although for the past three or four decades, churches and theologians in such liberal Protestant denominations as the UCC and Presbyterians have been drifting towards the social justice left.[24]

It is no wonder, then, that the black and white environmentalists have had difficulty communicating. African American environmentalists are most concerned with issues that directly impact their people. They often resemble "situation-environmentalists" motivated by simple "NIMBYism" ("Not in my backyard" campaigns), indifferent to environmental issues except for those that show up in their own communities or literally in their own backyards. They tend less to blame amoral, faceless capitalism than to blame decisions they allege deliberately or systematically target their communities and other communities of color. African American environmentalism has paid little attention to such issues as endangered species, nature parks (as opposed to urban parks), and nature preservation, which do not directly affect the black community. The moral discourse of environmental ethics comes in different dialects, and mistranslations and misunderstandings will continue to be inevitable and divide the environmental movement.

Religion has served African Americans well in their environmental fights. It has supplied them with leaders, instilled confidence, and fired resolve. Their churches have become centers of organization and agitation, and their communal sense of social ethics and morality have given them a way of conceptualizing, identifying, and attacking toxic threats to their communities. However, the black church tradition as it emerged from the rural South is fragmenting and transforming. Most blacks do not live in small towns or rural southern areas any longer. The Great Migration of African Americans to urban areas shattered the communal identity and, with it, the near monopoly of the Baptist and Methodist churches. No one church could speak for the new huge black urban constituencies. Alienated and isolated by city life, blacks sought refuge in Pentecostal and, to a lesser degree, Black Muslim congregations. African American Catholicism, source of no conspicuous political activism, has also grown quickly. Essentially creations of urbanization, these groups together have surpassed the "mainstream" churches in numbers. Yet because of their pietistic or inward orientation, they have had little of the social and political influence of the older denominations. Unlike churches in the rural or small-town South, few churches in large urban areas have led or facilitated local fights for environmental justice. In any event, declining political activism has matched the declining numbers in mainstream denominations. The rise of Black Power and the death of Martin Luther King Jr. broke the confidence and purpose of church activists. Environmental justice has been but a faint echo of the glory days of the civil rights movement. A white environmental ethic founded on love of wild nature survived secularization of the Puritan tradition, and most likely so will the black environmental justice ethic grounded in a social morality. Carl Anthony himself epitomizes that evolution, in that as the agnostic son of a deeply religious, Bible-reading mother, he has ascribed his "very strong . . . sense of moral principles" to her influence.[25] No secular organization, however, is likely ever to replace the black rural church as the heart, soul, and voice of the black community, and the black environmental justice movement seems likely to suffer in the future as this traditional source of communal organization and mobilization steadily erodes.

12

Politicized Memories in the Struggle
for Miami's Virginia Key Beach

GREGORY BUSH

On numerous occasions from the late 1950s until the end of his life, Martin Luther King Jr. visited Miami. He stayed at Hampton House, the all-black resort in Brownsville, relaxed with friends, went fishing in Biscayne Bay and swam at the area's only "colored beach," Virginia Key, a one-thousand-acre island between Miami and Key Biscayne. From 1945 until the late 1950s, it was the only place that blacks could officially go in order to bathe in Biscayne Bay. King loved coming to Miami to relax. He is even reported to have made an early version of his "I Have a Dream" speech at Hampton House, which is presently being restored. The champion of civil rights found Miami an exciting and warm place to recharge his soul.

For many African Americans, Miami was America's urban tropical paradise, combining modern excitement, natural attractions, and an increasingly cosmopolitan flavor. Yet in the years after the integration of Miami's parks and King's own death, the park on Virginia Key became neglected and underused, and eventually closed. For more than twenty years it remained largely abandoned and forgotten, seemingly a fit prize for commercial development and revenue generation for a bankrupt city. Then in 1999, by reviving the memories of their younger days on Virginia Key, older African Americans became an important component in redefining the public purpose for the park.

Miami's experience as a tourist and recreation location provides a unique window into the confluence of racial politics, developmental pressures, and environmental consciousness, raising important questions about long-overlooked land-use questions and the meaning of public space in modern culture. A successful attempt by African Americans at the end of World War II to demand access to the water had been largely forgotten by the 1980s. Then, by the late 1990s, that history was reclaimed, linked to a threatened park, and, ultimately, transformed into a part of the multicultural struggle associating civil rights with public space. The leadership role played by African Americans, predominantly older professional women seeking to retain Virginia Key Beach, helped forge new forms of public input into the use and design of public space and highlighted the long-obscured government neglect of public land. It also illustrates how memory has been used to confront public apathy in urban America, and how land use is increasingly redefining notions of public purpose in our times. The challenge is not over.

Academics are citizens and not merely observers. Too many fellow academics have become far too removed and uninvolved to understand the places in which we live, especially in South Florida. I acted as president of the Urban Environment League of Greater Miami from late 1998 until 2002. As a historian, director of the University of Miami's Institute for Public History, and interviewer for a series of oral histories, I came to appreciate the need for more local research into the history of various local people as well as for more public advocacy for parks. The Urban Environment League and its dedicated supporters put research to use and grew unapologetic about using highly charged rhetoric to revive the public quality of parks. A commitment to building a constituency among African Americans to save this threatened park became imperative.

Miami-Dade County contains a large number of people who are curiously cynical or unreflective about the environment in which they live or the history of its development. The media is dominated by spectacle and celebrity and provides inadequate reporting on local politics or land use. No comprehensive political or planning history of the area has ever been written. Gradually the profound ramifications of a culture of cynicism and ignorance about local political and land-use history have become apparent. Complacence becomes costly. For older African Americans who remembered earlier days of segregation, community solidarity, and struggle, reidentifying with Virginia Key helped revive their memories of place within a political culture where black historical consciousness and power had been limited. Their actions have helped refocus the city's notions of the public purpose of parks.

By the mid-1990s, environmental activism across the nation increasingly linked the loss of urban public space to racial inequality and the need for broader inclusiveness in planning. In cities like New York, Detroit, Los Angeles, and Berkeley, issues of homelessness, environmental justice in the location of toxic dumps, eroded funding for urban park systems, and access to public space were addressed by such national organizations as the Trust for Public Land and the Project for Public Spaces, as well as local activist organizations, many of whom were using the powerful new organizational tool of the Internet. Voters overwhelmingly favored bond issues for parks and open space. Retaining community gardens became a celebrity-led issue in New York City, thanks to Bette Midler, while serious scholarly efforts such as those of Gerald Kayden challenged the utility of older public land deals in New York that allowed builders to lift height restrictions in exchange for the donation of public spaces.[1]

The public realm was becoming the focus of research by urban and environmental historians as well as suburban planners, some of whom were associated with the work of the New Urbanist movement. The Urban Environment League of Greater Miami (UEL) was founded in 1996—mostly by architects and planners—to stop waterfront park giveaway for a basketball arena. It was originally led by planner Jorge Espinel and strongly assisted by New Urbanist leader and University of Miami School of Architecture dean Elizabeth Plater-Zyberk, who sought to stimulate a new constituency focused on planning, good urban design, and broadened consideration of public space. The UEL did not win that battle for the downtown waterfront and an arena was built for the Miami Heat. However, by examining that failure, it became clear that the group's work would have to become both more practical and contextualized.[2]

The fate of Virginia Key was thus part of a larger set of local challenges. After the loss to the Heat and the founding of the Urban Environment League, there was a weak effort to build a planning constituency. Later controversies, including the battle to stop development of a high-rise on top of the Miami Circle, gained national attention and proved important in preserving what is arguably one of the oldest archeological sites in the southeast. The Miami Circle is a two-thousand-year-old, thirty-eight-feet across foundation of a Tequesta Indian structure buried under an old building at the mouth of the Miami River that surfaced a long-forgotten past. On this ground, sacred to Native Americans, a politically connected developer wanted to build a large apartment building. Street demonstrations and the support of the African American head of Dade Heritage Trust, prominent local artist Dinizulu Gene Tinnie, and an important, Internet-led coalition of multicultural advocates for public space galvanized the community's attention—just as the Virginia Key issue was coming to a head.

Ultimately, the struggle for Virginia Key preserved public land by reasserting cultural memory and advancing an alternative model for public development confronting the long-held patterns of official neglect and public cynicism. Public inclusion in the planning process became a successful mantra, sending signals to the wider community about the need to preserve and enhance parks, notably in relation to the cultural history of African Americans. Reclaiming land by reclaiming memory is a growing trend in this country as sprawl and increasingly contentious fights for public land are heightened. Through all these time-consuming fights, it became clear that one of the central issues involved the community's civil rights to public space—an issue that bridges color, class, and ethnic identity. No longer an elite issue, this struggle possesses significant symbolic importance in terms of ways to rebuild a more educated political community on the subject of land use, while striving for fair growth, tangible power, and social justice.[3]

Public Land in Florida

The conveyance of public land from the federal government to the state of Florida and from the state to local governments has a long, torturous, and important—yet largely overlooked—modern history. The federal Swampland Act of 1850 began the process by which final decisions about transferring land from the state to local communities are made by the Internal Improvement Fund Board, consisting of the governor and cabinet. The reality has been that the complex process at the lower levels of government has effectively paved the way to reassign much public land to commercial use. This has been done through the influence of locally prominent lawyers, developers, and elites, or government bureaucrats who have often defined waterfront parkland as merely an economic asset, overlooking enforcement of deed restrictions. Little creativity has been unleashed in terms of developing public space as public space, while the major news media have often ignored these issues. The largely nonexistent institutional memory and community vigilance in dealing with public lands has taken a huge toll on Florida's land as well as its residents' sense of civic involvement. Nowhere can this be more clearly seen than along Miami's waterfront.

Ironically, as its population growth was exploding during the Cold War era, Florida became one of the nation's leaders in growth management legislation. Starting with initiatives from Governor Reuben Askew that followed a severe drought in the early 1970s, new laws were enacted and later refined under the leadership of Governor Bob Graham. The Growth Management Act of 1985 mandated that a Comprehensive Development Master Plan (CDMP) was to be formulated by each city that included a listing of park acreage. Each plan, regularly updated, was sent to the Florida Department of Community Affairs, which acted as overseer, assisted by the South Florida Regional Planning Council. As our group gradually discovered, however, there was little staff to provide oversight to the plans sent by the cities, and few enforcement actions were ever taken against cities that did not follow their own plans—especially when it came to park land.

While possessing more than one hundred parks, including famed (and long segregated) Bayfront Park, city officials had grown negligent in the face of demands for greatly increased funding for the police and fire departments, and by the apparent lack of popular interest in parks. The city lapsed into embarrassingly dire political and financial straits by the late 1990s, including vote fraud charges in the mayoral race, the firing of the longtime and corrupt city manager, and the state mandate requiring a financial oversight board of city of Miami operations. Such conditions led to heightened interest by officials in leasing out what was so often seen as derelict waterfront parks for commercial ventures and increased tax revenues.

The fate of Miami's parks has been compounded by civic apathy, the relative weakness of advocacy groups, the diverse array of issues faced by those groups, and the fact that residents have had such a weak sense of local identity. Environmental advocacy in Miami, for example, has long been limited by an alternative focus on threats to Everglades National Park, most often associated with the great work of Marjorie Stoneman Douglas. Historic preservation of buildings has been led by the Dade Heritage Trust and the Miami Design Preservation League; the latter group was startlingly effective in helping to rebuild South Beach beginning in the 1980s. Yet both were largely focused on buildings, not open space. Historically, civil rights organizations such as the Congress of Racial Equality (CORE) and the National Association for the Advancement of Colored People (NAACP) as well as the Civil Rights Congress had focused on voting rights and desegregation of such public places as lunch counters and schools. There was one longtime fighter for public parks in Miami: Dan Paul, a brilliant lawyer who had long advocated funding of waterfront parks, waterfront setbacks (often waived by compliant commissioners), and a county charter amendment that prohibited commercial development of more than 1,500 square feet in county parks. Yet he eschewed organizing a continuous constituency for parks and worked largely alone in his quest to retain and enhance public waterfront parks.[4]

All in all, by the late 1990s, Miami was home to arguably the worst park system in the nation. The *Miami New Times* of January 27, 1999, featured a humorous front-page story entitled "Take Me Out to the Parking Lot," in which park advocate Bob Weinreb showed a reporter around different city parks, illustrating how the parkland counted toward overall acreage in the CDMP was often bogus. Submerged land, parking lots, a medical center, and other facilities were all dutifully included in the figures of open space for the

CDMP. Numerous parks were closed or derelict. Historic Virginia Key Beach was closed to the public.

By 1998, it was clear to park observers that budget constraints seriously affected staffing, security, maintenance, and programs. Parks were also impacted by the conscious neglect of many officials who looked at the poverty, depopulation, and ravished condition of the inner cities and convinced themselves that many parks were useless public space, largely superseded by beaches and sports fields, suburban malls and private yards. City parks director Alberto Ruder worked valiantly to keep the parks in serviceable condition, but the lack of staff, resources, or power available to him, in contrast with the force of demands for economic development, promoted the perspective to many officials that parks were to be leased to the highest bidder. Within this context, Miami's patterns of racial segregation, homelessness, widespread poverty, and the desperation for development eroded concerns for the quality of public spaces. Downtown Miami was widely seen as a ghost town, notably at night when all the office workers left their tall towers. Yet it was also home to the Overtown area, previously called "colored town," which contained desperately poor people of African American descent.[5]

The Shape of Miami's Public Space for African Americans

Beginning in the 1880s, if not before, blacks were a major labor force in clearing the land, working the fields, and cleaning whites' homes in the Miami area. They helped transform a wilderness into settlements within a startlingly short period of time, yet many were forced to live in unsanitary shantytowns and were disenfranchised by the late 1890s. Miami possessed a unique mix of migrants—blacks from Georgia interacted with northern tourists, thousands of Bahamian immigrants, and, in later years, large numbers of northern Jews, retirees, and union activists—all slowly heightening Miami's sensitivity to the plight of African Americans, notably by the end of the New Deal era. The presence of numerous members of the Ku Klux Klan in the city police force ensured the harsh enforcement of the color line that constrained so many uses of public space. The tension was played out in ways that constrained use of public streets, parks, schools, and other places.

Notions of how to act in stores and streets were often defined by ever-changing conflict zones brought about by new technologies, notably the car. A major issue for several years following the opening of the Dixie Highway in 1915, for example, revolved around the ability of African Americans to drive cars on city streets. The uniformed chauffeurs (often from the North), representing class hierarchies, and African American residents driving their own cars, representing equality, were offensive to many whites. Eventually the issue died when it became clear that the city did not want to drive away northern tourist dollars from the local economy.[6]

Parks had been segregated, and most were off-limits for blacks from the time that John D. Rockefeller's partner, Henry Flagler, who bankrolled the creation of Miami in 1896, acceded to local customs in strengthening the racial barriers in the new city. The city made no provision for parks for blacks in the early years. As late as 1919, one editorial in the *Miami Metropolis* underscored the sad lack of parks faced by African Americans: "Several years ago it was generally understood that . . . a park was to be provided. . . . . The citizens of colored town are quite as entitled to their share of the public tax money as are the citizens of white town. They are entitled to a park. They are entitled to a decent school house and to well-kept playgrounds." The paper expressed hope that the "promises of a park for colored town are fulfilled."[7]

The next year, the *Miami Metropolis* reported on conditions in the black community, including the "unpardonably crowded housing where 100 families lived in one block with four and five individuals in one room," laying the blame on both white and block speculators. "In one case," the paper reported, "there are nine cottages on one 50 foot lot." Regular collection of garbage was asked; also a day nursery and playgrounds. In one black neighborhood, it was found that there were 63 children locked up in the houses for safe keeping all day long while the mothers are working in hotels and homes in white town. Parks were "badly needed," one man reported, adding that he had sent a complete baseball outfit to the colored branch of the YMCA several weeks before, but "they haven't yet been able to find a place to play."[8]

Eventually, the city created two parks for use by blacks, Dixie Park and Dorsey Park, which was primarily a sports field. Yet funds to improve and expand Dixie Park, located at Northwest Fourth Avenue between 12th and 13th Streets, was interminable, as reflected in newspaper accounts. In 1957, the pool at the park was closed for repairs for ten months for a three-month repair job, prompting numerous phone calls from angry residents. In later years, from the 1968 riots through the 1980 McDuffie riots, funding for parks in black areas was increased, but primarily as a form of social control of youth.[9]

While the basic necessities of food, housing, jobs, education, and safety were paramount for most African Americans, a black middle class was slowly emerging in the Miami area, asserting its right to freedom. These African Americans gathered in the safety of churches and private homes, formed new associations, learned about their constitutional rights, and developed forms of social etiquette as well as symbols of rebellion. Black religious institutions, beginning with the Greater Bethel AME Church established in 1896, were central gathering places. Booker T. Washington High School, established in 1929, possessed a meeting room for community groups. The black-owned Lyric Theater opened in 1913 on 2nd Avenue in the heart of colored town, and numerous nightclubs brought a musical joy to the area as well as white late-night jazz aficionados.

Enid Pinkney, an African American educator and the president of Dade Heritage Trust, shed invaluable insight into the limitations of public space in the Overtown area during the summer of 1999. She described how, as a child, she could not visit a local museum or the public library. She remembered that the "YMCA was housed in Dixie Park . . . but I didn't go there much as a child because it was on 13th Street. My parents were so strict; they didn't want me going that far to go someplace, so I didn't go to Dixie Park. The kids in our neighborhood played in the street."[10]

Expressions of resistance to racism by African Americans were also carried out collectively in the streets, which sometimes functioned as contested territory. By the early 1920s, the Universal Negro Improvement Association (UNIA) held marches to show their power and solidarity in the face of white lynchings and other degradations. At one point UNIA allegedly massed several thousand people with wooden rifles in the streets of colored town. Police had informants and induced fear in many who wanted to attend meetings indoors. One Bahamian migrant, James Nimmo, told an interviewer that around a thousand people were financially supporting UNIA but hundreds of them would not attend the meetings because "they were afraid, and police would frequently attend the meeting and in those days in the '20s, and early '30s, this was a tough challenge. Police called you niggers, and bossed you around, treat you with such disrespect. We had a number of visitors who were ran out of town here, and they lost their business, gave it up, they were afraid of the policeman." The streets involved visible contests of power by the KKK; its members were seen in numerous public parades and had a strong presence within the police department. One witness from the 1920s said later that the KKK marched down Grand Avenue in the nearby West Grove area on many Saturdays during the 1920s.[11]

By the 1930s, federal assistance helped Miami-area blacks in limited ways, fostering new public housing and support for black culture while simultaneously reinforcing forms of residential discrimination. One product of the Works Progress Administration, the St Agnes Marching Band, became a familiar galvanizing force in the community through its participation in religious holidays, funerals, and street life. Eleanor Roosevelt came to Miami and was photographed with black leaders. The Federal Writers Project, led by Stetson Kennedy, compiled the oral traditions of local blacks while Farm Security Administration photographers caught some of the stark living conditions, as did the *Miami Herald* in a 1934 series of articles that led to the creation of the Liberty Square Housing project. Yet as historian Raymond Mohl's work illustrates, federal housing policies reinforced redlining and poor housing in urban areas.

The county commission, responding to complaints by whites, passed a resolution in 1935 prohibiting a "colored CCC work camp" near Matheson Hammock Park (the first county park created in 1929 and located south of Miami) because African Americans "would come constantly in contact with people enjoying park facilities." Thus the rigidity of segregation in most public spaces was seldom breached. The conflict over black voting rights and safe access to the street came to an important juncture in May 1939, after an evening when the KKK rode through the downtown area, placing burning effigies on telephone poles and passing out cards attempting to intimidate blacks from voting in the next day's local election. In response, black voters tripled their normal voting numbers to assert their right to vote and sent a powerful message about the failure of the KKK's tactic.[12]

There were few moments of optimism for African Americans following World War II as they sought to expand their rights and their sense of community in the face of pervasive white repression. After a demonstration in May 1945, they were able to secure their first access to a public waterfront park at Virginia Key. Over the next decade and more, civil rights advocates were increasingly associated with communism and harassed by local police, the FBI, and the infamous Florida Legislative Investigation Committee, or Johns Committee. Integration of schools did not begin in Miami until 1960, although the issue of equal access to bus transportation had been championed earlier by Father Theodore Gibson of the West Grove, who himself later became a city commissioner.

By the 1970s, the history of the African American experience in Miami was championed by historian and archivist Dorothy Fields, who created the Black Archives Research and Study Center and subsequently sought to preserve the Lyric Theater and the Overtown Folklife Village. Other scholars, from Mohl to Paul George helped uncover bits and pieces of the complex history of the impact of segregationist strategies. Then in 1999, Professor Marvin Dunn published his *Black Miami in the Twentieth Century,* the first comprehensive study. With Florida International University students, Dunn also started his own community garden project in an area of Overtown next to I-395, which had been decimated by highway building when it was built in the early 1960s.

The nearby waterfront in Miami and Miami Beach had long been a zone of conflict. From the early days when Miami was incorporated, blacks had been forbidden to swim in the bay, although a few were informally allowed to do so by their white employers. All sorts of strategies were used to circumvent the ban on waterfront bathing. The question of prohibiting black access to the waterfront became acute after World War I because an increase in cars brought about a certain amount of spatial democratization. Thomas Pancoast, a prominent realtor in Miami Beach, wrote a letter to Carl Fisher, who is generally considered to be the guiding genius in founding Miami Beach, in which Pancoast said: "About two years ago, the negro in Miami had very few liberties, and as you know, they were not allowed to drive an automobile. The tourists who came to Miami with their negro drivers resented this very much, and as we didn't want to keep the tourists away we finally opened the door to the negro driver. Then the negroes of the town commenced to buy cars and now on Thursdays and Sundays especially, the negroes come over to the Beach car load after car load. Just this afternoon inside of an hour there have perhaps been twenty-five cars go by our office, everyone loaded to full capacity with Negroes." Responding to Pancoast, Fisher wrote back: "the negroes should have a place of their own to bathe . . . same as white people, and if I knew where we could build such a place for them at not too prohibitive a cost, it would be to our advantage to build it." Black realtor Dana Dorsey had earlier attempted to secure what is now Fisher Island directly south of Miami Beach to be a place for blacks to bathe in the bay, but boat transportation was a problem and he sold the land. Fisher then proposed to find funds to build a bridge to Fisher Island, adding: "the best way to keep them off our Beach is to get rid of the road up the Beach and then give them a place of their own."[13] Yet no bridge was ever built.

African Americans still had to face twenty-five more years without any place where they could legally bathe in the sea. The park they were finally given by the county commission in 1945 included a few dozen acres of Virginia Key, accessible only by boat over dangerous currents that were to kill many swimmers in future years.

Who's Afraid of Virginia Key?

As a large uninhabited parcel of waterfront land, Virginia Key had long been a major development challenge for area leaders. Formed in the aftermath of a hurricane in 1835 a mile or so out into the bay, the key possessed a fragile ecosystem, reflecting the constant shift of sand and sea due to hurricanes and the swift currents of the bay and ocean. Studied along with Key Biscayne and other islands further south in the early days of oceanography, Louis Agassiz included it in his coast survey in 1851. Over the years, the key and its surrounding submerged lands included a complex array of government owners: federal, state, county, and the cities of Coral Gables and Miami. Title to the land had been in dispute during World War I after it had been taken over briefly by the military in the Spanish-American War by executive order. By the 1990s it was coveted by the nearby city of Key Biscayne.

Home to nesting sea turtles and numerous bird populations, Virginia Key, for many, was a barely noticed stopover on the way to the upscale resort island and public parkland of Key Biscayne. In the early twentieth century, the wealthy Matheson family had a home on Virginia Key and owned most of its land. In later years, it would become a recurrent object of desire.

Countless schemes had been proposed for the island over the years. The military took it over and planned to build an airport and seaport there during World War II, but those plans were never realized. The city bought hundreds of acres in the postwar years and, along with private developers, dreamed up plans to develop the island.

In 1961, a group of New York investors sought a thirty-year lease to develop a high-class interracial hotel, convention hall, and golf course. The commission eventually turned the idea down because of deed restrictions. One county government planning report in 1962 opposed private development on the key until the government had exhausted every means to develop it. The report called Virginia Key "the last untapped frontier in the City of Miami" and said "its use should be judiciously determined." The planner warned about moving too fast to build a marine stadium; nevertheless, such a structure was subsequently built and then left to deteriorate by the 1980s. By 1989, the Miami Rowing Club had leased out prime waterfront land on the key for its clubhouse at one hundred dollars per year, and later made thousands of dollars in rental fees from the space. Many movers and shakers gathered there, including City Manager Cesar Odio, who was a life member.[14]

Virginia Key includes a bewildering array of land parcels and zoning classifications but no residents. The famous but fading Seaquarium, educational facilities such as the University of Miami's Rosenstiel School of Marine Science (a facility of the National Oceanic and Atmospheric Administration), the public magnet school Mast Academy, and the large, poorly situated county sewage treatment plant, built in the 1950s, are all located on parts of the island. The Bill Sadowski Critical Wildlife Area includes protected land and submerged lands that border the port of Miami to the north on Watson Island. There are also several famous restaurants, marinas, and Duck Lake, an uncontrolled landfill that is now closed. Then there is the well-known bar complex called Jimbo's Place, a curious remnant of old Miami with bocce ball courts and smoked fish, where Jim Luzner, a shrimper since the 1950s, holds court. There is a north beach area as well as the old, so-called black beach. Overall, it is a hodgepodge of land uses that had never been well planned.

The county conveyed the so-called colored beach to the city of Miami in 1982 through an interlocal agreement. A deed restriction stated: "the City utilizes the said property for public park purposes only." The city agreed to keep the property open to the public, provide maintenance and a level of services equal to or exceeding that which was provided by the County or it would "revert back to the County." It was subsequently learned that the county never oversaw that its own deed restrictions were enforced.

The city of Miami's master plan, created in 1987, contained rather a clear strategy to sell off waterfront parkland. The former segregated beach was to become an "Ecotourism campground" with four hundred to five hundred campsites. Later attempts in 1994 by Miami's planning director to create a waterpark had been rebuffed by the chief of the county's Department of Environmental Resource Management, due to its impact on the hardwood hammock on the island and on endangered species, notably the manatee. Then in 1995, the city administration attempted to develop the land as an RV park, but a referendum to that effect was defeated at the polls. City administrators continued to seek uses of Virginia Key Beach for commercial purposes as the financial condition of the city got worse. Developers remained interested, and the Seaquarium sought land to expand its operations, so city staff were instructed to lease off unused waterfront land, and city commissioners remained largely passive or informally encouraging to private development.[15]

Commenting on the sad fate of the key in 1997, *Miami Herald* columnist and best-selling novelist Carl Hiaasen wrote: "the stewardship of Virginia Key has been one of bungling, neglect and political favoritism. Practically everything the city touched has turned to failure. It's as if Miami purposely abandoned Virginia Key and let it crumble, in order to stir support for development." City staff, led by planner Jack Luft and armed with his award-winning 1987 Virginia Key master plan, sought to rezone parts of the key by removing the "conservation" designation. "Ironically," Hiassen continued, "Miami wouldn't be broke today if it hadn't mismanaged city holdings and given away so many costly favors; if it had collected reasonable rents and leases (not to mention a few debts)."[16]

From Ecotourism to Civil Rights

In the midst of the city's financial crisis, officials grew increasingly impatient to accede to the voices of developers. City Manager Donald Warshaw wrote to the county director of planning on September 3, 1998, reasserting the city's desire to lift "Public Purpose and Park Purpose" in order to modify deed restrictions for the Old County Park area as well as the Marine Stadium area. County Manager Merrett Stierheim sought more specifics about how the land would be used with the proposed zoning changes and lifting of deed restrictions. Although city officials were never publicly clear about their intentions, their goal was to lift deed restrictions in order to accommodate hotels, restaurants, and perhaps larger attractions. Notably, City of Miami park officials were seldom involved in discussions about the fate of their own parks. Most of the initiative was in the hands of the Economic Development Department of the city, which was seeking to lease out dozens of city properties to augment the tax rolls.[17]

Late in 1998, UEL member and longtime activist Mabel Miller informed me that a city committee had been formed to plan for the future of several parcels on Virginia Key including the colored beach and the Marine Stadium site. She had come to a UEL meeting to set up a public parks coalition to try and advocate for parks countywide. A longtime friend of the famed environmentalist Marjorie Stoneman Douglas's and an environmental educator of long standing, Miller's trademark was a wide-brimmed straw hat with long gray braids peeking out. She had a sweet southern accent that belied her tenacity on behalf of the natural areas of the key. She belonged to a group called "Friends of Virginia Key," which had dwindled from a group of at least forty in the late 1970s to three or four active members. She attended numerous meetings, was familiar with the political process and provided valuable advice in her twofold quest to retain the natural features of the key as well as to create a campground for kids.

The city begrudgingly formed an ad hoc group called the Virginia Key Task Force to make recommendations for land use changes and to quell Mabel Miller as well as voices from the Sierra Club and the Tropical Audubon Society, groups interested in conserving the natural areas, and a vocal group of windsurfers. Many of the participants lacked sensitivity to the island's history—including the environmentalists who sought to preserve the land from development. Those on the task force included a garrulous man, Jim Courbier, appointed by the City Waterfront Board, who was ostensibly close to Mayor Joe Carollo and who dominated the group. Courbier was also a friend of Commissioner J. L. Plummer's and part of a clique that met at Taurus Restaurant to promote various development schemes. He had been around town for many years and was widely known in the area. He knew the political process and clearly wanted the woebegone beach to be developed to provide a revenue source to the city (and perhaps to his friends).

The questions of what to do with Virginia Key involved an enormously complex set of issues. Due to pervasive fiscal mismanagement and corruption, by 1997, Miami's financial affairs were overseen by a state oversight board, which reviewed all of the city's financial decisions. In the city's proposed recovery plan to the state, Virginia Key development schemes figured as part of their economic recovery strategy. Ads had already gone out to developers for two parcels: the former Marine Stadium areas as well as the old county beach, sometimes called the black beach—even though the ad hoc committee had not even made its recommendations. One central actor in the evolving drama was the Miami Seaquarium, which sought to build a new theme park in some of the largely unused land. That proposal unleashed the anger of Key Biscayne officials and residents who focused on potential traffic problems stemming from overdevelopment. To address those issues, the Florida Department of Community Affairs created a Virginia Key–Key Biscayne working group to find a settlement, although no agreement emerged from this group before its life span ended.

At the first meeting of the Virginia Key Task Force that I attended in January 1999, those attending included Jonathan Ullman of the Sierra Club, Mabel Miller, Bob Weinreb and Nancy Lee of the South Florida Board Sailboard Association, Dick Townsend of the Tropical Audubon Society, and Jim McMaster of Friends of the Everglades. All of them were white and appeared knowledgeable about the Virginia Key master plan and the legal status of the diverse parcels under review. All were outspoken proponents of keeping the land in public hands and firmly against private lease arrangements that the city staff seemed to favor.

It quickly became clear that the ad hoc committee, dominated by Courbier, was in support of leasing the land for an eco-campground and finally bringing definitional closure to the park areas. The group was strongly guided by city development staff member Diane Johnson, who said: "Eco-campground is not a dirty word." Wendell Collins, a member of the state's commission on heritage tourism and ecotourism and president of Eco-Experience, a Florida-based company, also gave a presentation. Eco-Experience was owned by Arthur Hertz, who also owned the Miami Seaquarium. Capitalizing on his state credentials and not mentioning the Seaquarium connection, Collins made a presentation showing a model of simple and beautiful cabins in the Maho Bay area of the Virgin Islands. Those who wanted to preserve the land as a park became increasingly skeptical of the business of ecotourism that was promoted by Collins and others, and later learned that room rates at such a place might range up to two hundred dollars or more per night.[18]

The crucial parcel under consideration by the ad hoc committee was the former segregated beach, seventy-seven acres of prime waterfront land on the east side of the key. Designated as a "colored beach" by the county commission in 1945 after demonstrations at Haulover Beach north of Miami, the location on Virginia Key had long been a vibrant place for African Americans. Later it was learned that blacks had gone there for years before the official designation. A 1918 map of Virginia Key supplied to Nancy Lee by the Florida Department of Environmental Protection showed that the key had a "negro dancing pavil- ion," so it had a long and largely unknown history with the black community. Former city commissioner Athalie Range recalled going there—to what they then called Bear's Cut—for 1930s outings. Virginia Key was also one of the most dangerous locations for swimming, containing currents that drowned numerous people in the coming years. Athalie Range remembered it well: "We went over on small boats over to an Island that was known as Bear's Cut, and that is where we swam. Now this was a very, very dangerous circumstance, because it was not really a swimming beach, and the men in our company would stand around so that the youngsters would not get away from the shoreline." In fact, the Request for Proposals for Virginia Key (put out by the city of Miami in 1995) said ". . . it will be necessary to provide a flotation barrier off-shore to separate and protect swimmers from dangerous channel currents."[19]

Even though swimming was dangerous, the park became enormously popular. In the decade after 1945, a carousel, bathhouse, and several cottages for staff were built, as was a large parking lot. It was a major social gathering spot for the African American community and a symbol of religious commu- nity. Churches held baptisms there, remembered Enid Pinkney. After the beach was opened in the 1940s, she watched her father, Henry Curtis, a min- ister at the Church of God, dunk white-robed adult members of his congrega- tion in the sea: "They would sing songs like 'Take me to the water! / Take me to the water! / Take me to the water, to be baptized,'" she recalls. "They'd duck you under the water, all the way under the water, and bring you back up. There'd be somebody there with a towel or whatever to wipe your face. And people would come back up with the spirit of the Lord and they'd be hollering and shouting and crying. It would be a very emotional experience!"[20]

As desegregation increased in the 1960s, the special feelings associated with the black beach area started to erode. Memories of its meaning dimmed as access to other parks broadened, notably at nearby Crandon Park on Key Biscayne. Ironically, integration proved to be the downfall of Virginia Key Beach. Blacks could and did go to other beaches with better facilities. Nudists increasingly gathered to informally claim parts of Virginia Key Beach. By 1975, as attendance had fallen off, county officials closed the park on winter weekdays, further discouraging regular use. This angered at least a few African Americans who remembered its importance in their lives. The head lifeguard of the beach, Johnny Robinson, was part of a group calling for the preservation of the park, noting: "the beaches belong to the public and this order constitutes a direct affront to the democratic rights of citizens and taxpayers of Dade County. Virginia Key used to be the 'Colored Beach' in Dade County and during the past years has experienced a gradual abandonment by Dade County parks," citing such specifics as "cabanas destroyed by a hurricane in 1965 [that] weren't rebuilt. The refreshment stand has remained unopened since 1969 . . . a miniature train and carousel were removed."[21]

Miami Herald columnist Bea Hines wrote: "It's ridiculous to those of us who grew up here and remember the good times, the beach parties, the long walks along the shores and the dreams of faraway places—that our beach has reportedly become a haunt for undesirables. Back then, going to Virginia Key beach was the next best thing to Christmas. . . . It was our beach and we were proud of it." Hines noted that she took a nostalgic walk back to the beach: "The swaying palm trees whispering in the breeze had an eerie appearance. I walked over to the 'dancing circle' (a concrete platform where we used to go to dance to the music of a jukebox nailed to a post) and saw that the sand had all but covered it. I turned and walked away. The times have changed. People have changed. My children have no special feelings about Virginia Key beach. To them, a beach is a beach." Many looked back at the segregated beach as a relic of the bad old past and stayed away. Athalie Range noted that Virginia Key Beach "began to deteriorate and nobody was doing anything about it. People began going over to Crandon. But [Crandon] was never the same. Because the folks you'd meet at Virginia Beach were your good friends, your neighbors, your church people."[22]

In January 1999, at the first ad hoc committee meeting I attended, and after listening to the environmental advocates, I stood up and said that what was being overlooked was the historical significance of the park to the black community. I asked: Why shouldn't the whole park be designated to honor the meaning of the civil rights struggle within the history of Miami? That would be a perfectly valid reason to deny the privatization of that land. I was conscious that galvanizing a black constituency was probably the only way to save the land from development and that other civil rights museums were being created in the south.

Courbier was immediately dismissive of using the Virginia Key site in such a manner and said a plaque could be erected to honor civil rights on the site as a commemoration. Many took offense at this trivialization, provoking further definition of a public purpose for the land. No one that I knew of had thought to have a beach commemorated in the civil rights struggle. The historic officer for the city of Miami said she had never heard of land itself getting historic designation. As events turned out, promoting the historical association of the beach to the black community proved a strategically important component in saving the land.[23]

After reading the older (inadequate) set of land use principles from the 1987 master plan, I drafted a set of the "Principles and Possibilities for the Future of Virginia Key" and subsequently presented them at the next meeting of the task force on February 3, 1999. Many of the sixteen tenets promoted notions of abiding by deed restrictions and reopening the land for the public. I also advocated the need for a public charrette (a public planning meeting) to determine the fate of the key. Several members of the ad hoc committee scoffed at the cost of that to a city that was bankrupt, saying that it would cost a minimum of seventy thousand dollars. That figure sounded intimidating, and the idea that it could be done for less seemed impossible to many.

Nancy Lee and I, two middle-class white people, then collaborated in dreaming up the idea of a civil rights park for the site. Nancy and her husband Bob Weinreb had done extensive research on Virginia Key and exuded deep skepticism about the evasiveness of city staff and administrators. They were largely marginalized by city staff for their outspoken advocacy. As events turned out, their perceptions were usually on the mark. Nancy suggested adopting the outdoor FDR Memorial in Washington as a model for the beach and sketched a largely open-air site along the bay. This stirred memories of Yad Vashem, the Holocaust Memorial in Israel, which I had recently visited. But we knew that the attempt to make the land into a civil rights park would be a failure unless it was led by African Americans. To this end, with the permission of Dr. Dorothy Fields, I spoke in front of a panel of African Americans at the downtown public library calling for a charrette to redesign the park.

Yet the struggle for Virginia Key Beach was about more than memorializing segregation; it was also about the costs of forgetting to both the community and the land. Only a century before, Miami had been a vast wilderness. It had rapidly turned into a great tropical resort, a vast market for waterfront land, and the largest cruise ship port in the world. But alongside the push for economic development, there was a parallel emotional and spiritual connection between the black community and Virginia Key that had been dormant and gradually surfaced through the use of oral history.

The decision was quickly made to campaign hard for a civil rights park, and efforts were made to enlist the aid of numerous African American leaders to save the historic beach. One of the first people contacted was Dinizulu Gene Tinnie, an artist, writer, and profound thinker who had recently been involved in the Miami Circle demonstrations. He later said of Virginia Key: "One of the strategies that we have to have is looking at our sacred sites, places that have been consecrated by, labored by, the struggle. There are too many people with too many fond memories, too many people who have been baptized out there; had their honeymoons out there, had their first love affair out there. I said that was a place that brought together an entire black community. It was the only place we could go."[24]

Enid Pinkney also became an outspoken advocate passionate about historic preservation, including her own home in the Bahamas. She wrote Mayor Joe Carollo:

> As a person who was born in Miami and having to live under segregated laws, in a segregated community and world, Virginia Beach was the only beach that I was allowed to go to by law. Virginia Beach is a part of Miami History, and I feel that it should remain as a public beach. Many African Americans made sacrifices and put much time and effort into asking for and getting a beach where African Americans could have an experience at the beach. Keeping Virginia Beach as a public beach could be a memorial to those brave African Americans who stood up for the right to enjoy God's ocean, sand, and sun in a beach setting.[25]

Support began to pick up from within parts of the black community. While never a deafening roar, it was enough to make a difference. Central to the overall success was the input from Tinnie, who continues his work even up to the time of this publication. Tinnie writes columns tracking relevant events for the *Miami Times,* published by Garth Reeves, who had originally been one of the demonstrators desegregating Crandon Park in the late 1950s. In his articles, Tinnie criticized the "'back room" decision making in meetings that are technically open to the public but which, in reality, are generally unknown to ordinary citizens and often scheduled during working hours. He also raised concern about the (non)workings of the democratic process in the city of Miami. When Tinnie subsequently showed up to speak at the ad hoc committee in February 1999 about the history of the park, Courbier was furious. He said, "this is never going to fly."[26]

The ad hoc committee's work had not adequately looked at the history of the site as a failed park; its focus and agenda had been narrowly conceived, it lacked any sense of principles for park management or purpose, and its activities had been shoddily handled, mostly by city staff who were expert at marginalizing public input. For its part, the UEL board endorsed a resolution written to reopen the park and promote a public design process, noting that "the rights of citizens are eroded when they have inadequate access to public parkland" and concluded that "in the event that the City of Miami fails to enhance the public land, we request that the County consider reversion of the title to the land back to its control or to state control so that the public can benefit from it."[27]

The narrow scope of the committee's work aroused anger in park advocates. On February 18, 1999, I sent a letter to Virginia Newell, chair of the committee, an assistant dean of the Rosenstiel School of Marine and Atmospheric Science, and a marine biologist. The letter criticized the committee for its lack of black representation and other factors related to weak public inclusion in the process:

> As a result of these questionable procedures, the proposal for an African American Memorial/Civil Rights Park that was brought forward in prior weeks, the notion of preserving this historic beach as public parkland with a major Civil Rights/Memorial Park, was blatantly ignored by a committee that is totally unrepresentative of the diversity of the city of Miami. The heritage of the African American community has been given short shrift—again—in considering what to do with public land. What an affront to those engaged in the heroic struggle for civil disobedience at Haulover Beach in 1945, those who demanded access to waterfront beach which had for so long been denied to people of color. This is an issue that should interest people of all backgrounds because the struggle for civil rights continues, is central to all our lives and is broadening its scope in this day and age to include such issues as the right to adequate public space for ALL OUR PEOPLE.

A number of people, including members of the Sierra Club, the UEL, Friends of the Everglades and Tinnie, spent dozens of hours organizing the proposal presented before the city's Waterfront Board on March 10. As Tinnie recalled:

> When it came to light that [Virginia Key Beach] was very much in the pipeline for private development to come in . . . a few of us attended . . . meetings and began to articulate an alternative . . . to say well, no, we really aren't interested in how far down the pipeline you've gone with this presumed development. No, we cannot be satisfied with a monument that says this was once a black beach. There are much greater issues at stake here, environmental ones, social, and the like. We did a history gathering session where we actually had audio and video taping of elders sharing their experiences and there was news coverage. We knew . . . this was [a] city owned, citizen owned, we like to emphasize that, piece of property. We do not want to be a self-appointed watchdog group on the outside that they could listen to or dismiss as they saw fit.

Even with the growing list of prominent African American leaders testifying to the importance of the beach as a memorial spot, the ad hoc committee finally made its recommendation to the Waterfront Board in March. It obfuscated the decisions to develop both the Marine Stadium and the black beach under a vague go-ahead for an RFP (Request for Proposal) "as one economic engine for developing the park." The committee also advocated the establishment of a Virginia Key Foundation "for oversight of the holistic financial and environmental reconstruction of the park." Buried beneath the formal language was the tacit approval to lease part of the park for an eco-campground. Yet by March the committee was losing its legitimacy and it subsequently disbanded. The Waterfront Board was confused as to which proposal even represented the city's presentation: For example, Chair John Brennan held up a white book with an aerial photo of the park on the cover, which had been produced by Nancy Lee for the advocates of the civil rights park, and asked: "Is this the city's proposal?"

The *Miami Herald* totally ignored coverage of lower-level committee activities early in 1999. We learned how to play members of the press against each other to get more exposure for the issues we thought so important, never relying on the *Miami Herald* or television news to cover the story. A helpful outlet was the *Miami New Times,* a brash weekly paper whose editor, Jim Mullin, loved a good fight about public space—especially if the *Herald* was not covering the issue. One of Mullin's stories on our efforts quoted me as saying that this was nothing less than a battle to "reclaim Miami's forgotten past." The article continued:

> The once segregated Virginia Beach may not hold the archaeological import that rallied thousands to save the mysterious Miami Circle, but with the same newfound respect for history, it has inspired its own circle of impassioned advocates. As this movement has gained momentum, the wider planning process for Virginia Key has virtually ground to a halt, an unexpected turn of events that has pleased environmentalists and park advocates who long have fought to protect the island from commercial development. For those who have sought to exploit the key as a revenue source for the financially beleaguered city of Miami, the injection of race relations into the debate has changed everything.

Mullin noted that city staff "now found themselves in the precarious position of appearing bigoted if they raised objections. . . . And in an ironic twist to a tale that is full of them, all this drama surrounding the fate of Virginia Key has been orchestrated not by concerned black Miamians, but by a small cadre of white activists."

Although helpful to us, Mullin's story concluded by trying to stoke contro-versy, relaying comments that appeared to characterize Nancy and me as in-sensitive to blacks because the idea for the civil rights park had not originated with African Americans. Mullin, nonetheless, quoted my statement: "Here's a city that has had Lummus Park [downtown along the Miami River] closed since 1992. . . . Bicentennial Park is closed. Virginia Key has been closed how many years? Is there a pattern here?"[28]

History was coming to the rescue of the beach through both local and na-tional publications. *Miami New Times* reporter Kirk Nielson wrote: "Today the long-closed beach on Virginia Key is a symbol of racial segregation, the black struggle against it, and the need to preserve history." Athalie Range told re-porter Teresa Mears of the *San Francisco Chronicle:* "the struggle, the civil rights issues that have been part of Miami for now over 50 years, needs to be remembered . . . I can think of no better way to remember it than by opening this park and doing what needs to be done to bring the citizens back." Rick Bragg of the *New York Times* wrote an article focused on the memories of Af-rican Americans rather than the relative value of developing the park into an eco-campground. Drawing on the meaning of the memories black residents had of the beach, he also quoted Range, who said: "we forget about these things and when it comes to a point when someone wants to do something else, you remember."[29]

Attracting the interest of eighty-three-year old former city commissioner Athalie Range had proved pivotal. As the first black woman elected city com-missioner and the first head of the State Department of Community Affairs, Range held commanding stature in the black community. For decades, she had run the most prominent black funeral home in Miami. In 2000, she de-scribed Virginia Key as: "Important to me as a citizen of the community. I like to think of Miami as I have always known it. And as a very small child, I re-member Virginia Beach as the only beach where blacks would go to have some entertainment or refreshment as far as water sports were concerned, and this came about because of the terrible segregation that we've always had here in Miami."[30]

Determined women—Nancy Lee, Mabel Miller, Athalie Range, Enid Pink-ney, and Blanca Mesa of the Sierra Club—were showing how to work the sys-tem from the bottom up: show up at meetings and get known at many levels of city administration and boards and never personalize a problem with a staff person. Officials need to know an advocate's face and gain some trust in his or her motives, even if they substantially disagree on some issues. A great deal of work went into creating a bold, thoughtful, and complete presentation to the

Waterfront Board. The group researched the historical record and handed out a clear and concise proposal citing past ordinances and the train of official neglect. The Waterfront Board endorsed the proposal for the civil rights beach.

The next step was to apply pressure to the city commission, the mayor, and the city manager. A small delegation, including me, Athalie Range, Gene Tinnie, and Nancy Lee and Bob Weinreb met with Arthur Teele, the lone African American commissioner, in his office at the Dupont Plaza Hotel overlooking the Miami Circle site. He seemed sympathetic, decried the state of corruption in the city, and warned us that lobbyists were lining up to develop hotels on Virginia Key. A small delegation also met with City Manager Donald Warshaw that spring. He denied requesting that existing deed restrictions be lifted on the park, something Nancy Lee corrected when she showed him a copy of his own letter to the county manager, proving that he had just lied to us.

At one point in the spring of 1999, Mayor Joe Carollo cleverly outflanked the groups' efforts by peremptorily getting an adjacent parcel of beachfront land opened that had been closed for years. The *Herald* pictured him romping in the surf with black kids, a publicity home run in his attempt to secure re-election coming up in a year. Most of the Virginia Key advocates felt it had been a cynical ploy to deflect attention from the revival of the black beach itself. Eventually, the debate on the eco-campground versus the civil rights memorial park went to the city commission. City staff hired a black woman to extol the virtues of eco-campgrounds. The *Herald*'s editorial board finally came through with a strongly supportive statement that "nothing could be more fitting or astute than for commissioners today to agree to turn the beach on the southern portion of Virginia Key into a park free of development, mindful of history and open to the public."[31]

The city administration finally created a temporary task force that later turned into the Virginia Key Park Beach Trust, and helped pay for a charrette (or design workshop for the public) that was held in January 2000 at the University of Miami's Rosenstiel School. The Commission appropriated twenty-five thousand dollars for the job, a pittance in standard terms yet nonetheless a sign of support. The charrette sent an important message about new opportunities for public involvement. Many community members—black and white—came out to speak about what they wanted for the site. Numerous architects donated their time, led by Clyde Judson, the African American architect and vice president of the UEL. Professor Juan Bueno of Florida International University's School of Design came up with the notion of having an aqua necklace of parks and waterways around Biscayne Bay, a brilliant spin off of Frederick Law Olmsted's emerald necklace vision for Boston. The park would recreate the carousel, the concession stand, nature trails, the railroad, environmental exhibits, and a Civil Rights Historical Museum.

Tinnie recalled:

> The beauty of [the charrette] was that . . . many of the leaders, county commissioners, [and] Congresswoman [Carrie] Meek's representatives show[ed] up there to kind of underscore how important it was and how supportive they were. But a lot of us went into that process a little bit weary that well, you know if everybody w[as] heard on an equal basis, wouldn't the guys with the big money and interests and the lawyers carry the thing. And to everybody's surprise that's not what really happened. While a lot of us went in there with maybe some visions of what this could be, what came out of it was a real consensus. Everybody got a chance to hear other ideas, other concerns, reasons why this in the real world may or may not work.
>
> . . . We knew this charrette was not going to answer all questions. But, what we do is raise the right questions and set the groundwork for the next detailed plan. So we are looking at a Museum complex. I say complex because we are looking at some kind of an indoor, outdoor [design], maybe along with a building that would have exhibition space, meeting space. We are looking at restoring and preserving the historic site the way it used to be. We're looking at environmental excavations, at even a regional linkage of VK [Virginia Key] to other waterfront parks. Also, to other historic sites like Overtown, the New African American Research Cultural Center in Broward. So that as you go to VK some way you become aware of these other places and even the transportation links to them. We are looking at the environmental nature trails, wildlife observation platforms and so forth so that it actually does become this natural experience that's not so intrusive and disturbing. That's the bright vision for the future.

Eventually the city commission passed an ordinance creating the Virginia Key Park Beach Trust to oversee fundraising, events, and planning for the revitalization of the seventy-seven acres of the old "colored beach." Athalie Range was and remains chair as of 2005, with Gene Tinnie serving as vice chair. The trust has been dominated by African Americans. Congresswoman Carrie Meek proved instrumental in getting millions of dollars of federal funds for beach restoration as mitigation, and Senator Bob Graham's office started exploring the feasibility of the park becoming part of Biscayne National Park, along with the Miami Circle site. Contrary to conventional wis-

dom, Virginia Key now has a state historical designation—and its own substantial city budget.

〜

With enormous effort, including the work of a number of dedicated
people over several years, the park was saved. The monstrous wrong of deny-
ing so many people the right to refresh themselves in the sea had fully legiti-
mized the politicization of cultural memory into a strategy that challenged the
prevailing and exclusivist development ethos of city officials. A broader constituency had been formed, a new tool of modern democracy tried, and those
who remained committed to the process or who cared, by and large, worked
effectively together. A wonderful plan for the park had emerged, but the process continues to find pitfalls, and vigilance is needed to retain the park "for
public park purposes only."

Since 2000, as the focus has shifted to other park and planning issues, primarily along Miami's waterfront, serious reservations about how charrettes
could be misused have arisen. There are new attempts to commercialize the
Marine Stadium area, an issue that interests members of the Virginia Key Park
Beach Trust. The city has also initiated a new master plan process for the entire key. Many will never forget the sense of triumph felt by the audience that
first day of the charrette when the splendid restoration plan for Virginia Key
Beach was announced. Yet forms of power remain hard to grasp and resistance
to them is consequently difficult to define, notably in our era of academic,
economic, and legalistic specialization.

Confronting an apathetic public, inadequate concern for the cultural heritage of African Americans, and a bureaucratized growth mentality that saw
the land as little more than economic potential, Miami made great strides in
coming to grips with the past abuse of its people and its public lands. However, ours was more than a quest for preservation. Engaging the public in the
process of envisioning the landscape that they might want was an exciting
adventure for all of us. Parks were levers of power, tests of local democracy,
evoking memories and a community focus, and signifying larger issues such
as fair standards for public inclusion in growth issues, and their relationship
to environmental justice.

Gene Tinnie recently wrote an e-mail, in which he explained:

In the 21st century, two things will be recognized that will change the
paradigms of our traditional thinking. One is that all political questions
will need to be reduced to the single question of Land Use; the old pa-
rameters of income, social class, race and ethnicity, education levels as
determinants of political decisions (Politics is nothing more or less than

the art and science of determining who gets what, where, when, how and why) are outdated, divisive and dysfunctional for today's needs. The second sea change in thinking is directly related to this one, which is that history and land are one and the same thing. No human history has ever occurred anywhere but on a land base. (Even our adventures at sea or in space must take place aboard structures manufactured from land-based materials, with land-based methods). Because land is the embodiment of its natural history (volcanic eruptions, glacial movements, sedimentary rock, wave action, etc.), and humans—whether we admit it or not—are a part of nature ("we're all made of stardust"), not apart from nature, then human and natural history are fused.

❧ 13

Black Environmental Liberation Theology

DIANNE D. GLAVE

> We, African-American Church leaders, historically committed to justice issues, affirm the unitary nature of life and commit ourselves to the ministry of converging justice and environmental issues that are critical matters of life and death for our Church and for our community.
>
> —"National Black Church Environmental and Economic Justice Summit,"
>   1993

> A new generation of Rosa Parks and Martin Luther Kings, Jrs. are meeting in churches to pray and plan and then heading out to work for the health of their communities.
>
> —"African American Denominational Leaders Pledge Their Support to the Struggle Against Environmental Racism," *AME Christian Recorder,* 1998

In the United States, the government and corporations have long targeted people of color and the poor—including African Americans—by dumping toxins and garbage into marginalized neighborhoods. Some African Americans who are working to remedy these injustices to the African American community have applied a Christian framework to their activism. This model of Christian self-empowerment for environmental justice owes much to Martin Luther King Jr. In 1955, King transformed Rosa Parks's refusal to sit in the back of the bus into a church-based movement igniting the mid-twentieth-century civil rights movement. Throughout his ministry of nonviolent activism, King defined social justice through a biblical lens, agitating for civil rights, condemning the Vietnam War, and, in his final act before he was assassinated, advocating for sanitation workers. His historical and theological legacy has endured and is now a cornerstone of environmental justice. This article introduces a working model for a black environmental liberation theology (BELT), a strand of black liberation theology; describes the recent history of environmental justice by the African American church and Christian organizations; and proposes an environmental justice agenda for change based on this theology and history.

Members of the African American church and Christian grassroots organizations launched the environmental justice movement out of a confluence of religious beliefs and civil rights social thought and action. In 1970, James H. Cone articulated and formalized a black liberation theology or a biblical interpretation of civil rights activism by the African American church through a scholarly lens. Black liberation theology, which decries the oppression of Africans Americans based on biblical principles—is the foundation of BELT, a nascent theology based on environmental justice history and activism by African American Christians. Like black liberation theology, BELT is both a theology and an ideology that is actualized by shielding contemporary African Americans exposed to toxins and pollution from landfills, garbage dumps, auto mechanics' shops, and sewage plants.[1]

Theology, Civil Rights, and Black Liberation

How can the language of environmental racism, justice, and liberation theology begin to define BELT? Environmental justice scholars, including Robert Bullard, have documented that some in the public and private sectors have deliberately or passively threatened the lives of Native Americans, African Americans, and Latinos through social, economic, and political policies in the form of environmental racism—the inequitable exposure of people of color to air, water, and noise pollution on a scale sufficient to trigger birth defects, miscarriages, stillbirths, cancer, and stress-related illnesses documented since the 1980s. Environmental justice seeks to eliminate such racism by demanding the equitable treatment for people of color and the poor through government policy, legislation, regulation, and law enforcement. Environmental justice activists have employed many strategies, including lobbying, legislation, law enforcement, and protest, which were modeled upon civil rights initiatives to counter environmental racism.

The language of theology is a means of combating environmental racism. Black liberation theology is based on scriptures, especially from the New Testament, that hold the promise of environmental equity and justice for African Americans. Galatians 3:28 is one such scripture of equity: "There is neither Jew nor Greek, there is neither slave nor free, there is neither male nor female; for you are all one in Christ Jesus." Psalm 82:3–4 advocates justice for the oppressed: "Defend the poor and fatherless; Do justice to the afflicted and needy. Deliver the poor and needy; Free them from the hand of the wicked." In Luke 10:25–37, Jesus tells the Good Samaritan parable, modeling diversity and social justice. A Jewish man was waylaid and beaten by thieves as he traveled from Jerusalem to Jericho. Two Jewish religious leaders passed without assisting the beaten man. Although Samaritans were excluded from Jewish society, a passing Samaritan stopped to bandage the traveler's wounds, then took him to an inn, cared for him, and left money for his expenses. The parable models caretaking and righting injustice. In this same manner, the modern African American church has sought justice for the African American community who are inequitably exposed to water, air, and noise pollution.[2]

According to Cone in *A Black Theology of Liberation* (1970), black liberation theology commissioned the African American church to continue to eliminate oppression against African Americans after the civil rights movement. Cone expanded his theological interpretation of black liberation theology to include environmentalism in his article "Whose Earth Is It Anyway?" in which he argued that mainstream theologians "often include a token black or Indian in anthologies on ecotheology, ecojustice, and ecofeminism, . . . But people of color are not treated *seriously,* that is, as if they have something *essential* to contribute to the conversation. Environmental justice concerns of poor people of color hardly ever merit serious attention, not to mention organized resistance."[3] At the 1993 National Black Church Environmental and Economic Justice Summit, Reverend Eugene F. Rivers III, the cofounder of the Azusa Christian Community, concurred: "And what we've done in connecting the issue of environmental justice and racism is we've drawn the connection between environmental racism as an expression of white supremacy."[4]

Resistance was not new to African Americans, typical of civil rights activism of the early twentieth century. For example, during the 1917 New York City Silent Protest Parade, approximately ten thousand African Americans marched peacefully with banners against racism. Founded upon this early twentieth-century history, African Americans and their supporters of the 1950s and 1960s organized boycotts, marches, freedom rides, sit-ins, and protests, which shamed the United States government and citizens who harbored racism. As a result of the scrutiny and, more importantly, the dedication of civil rights leaders and volunteers, this activism culminated with the Civil Rights Act of 1964, which legally banned discrimination in public places, and the Voting Rights Act of 1965, which authorized federal employees to register African Americans to vote and suspended discriminatory literacy tests and poll taxes.

Against this backdrop, African American ministers and civil rights activists were catalysts for social change, leading peaceful demonstrations and ultimately influencing a theology much like environmental activists of the African American church and Christian grassroots organizations. Dwight N. Hopkins says that Christian leaders of the civil rights era "religiously told white officials to stick to Christian love and nonviolence . . . preached funerals for nonviolent civil rights workers. And they experienced the pain of having their churches dynamited in the early morning hours."[5] As president of the Southern Christian Leadership Conference (SCLC), a civil rights protest organization led by African American ministers, Martin Luther King helped to define civil rights activism by knitting together social justice and a theology. In his "Letter from a Birmingham Jail," written to his fellow clergy in 1963, he said: "Just as the prophets of the eighth century B.C. left their villages and carried their 'thus saith the Lord' far beyond the boundaries of their home towns, and just as the Apostle Paul left his village of Tarsus and carried the gospel of Jesus Christ to the far corners of the Greco-Roman world, so am I compelled to carry the gospel of freedom beyond my own home town."[6]

Environmental Racism, Environmental Justice

Environmental racism by whites has biblical, historical, and contemporary origins. Some Christians have ignored or distorted biblical directives, instead emphasizing the authority granted by God to rule the earth. In the book of Genesis, Adam and Eve named the flora and fauna based on a covenant of stewardship in which God gave humankind control of nature. In return, Adam and Eve cared for the land, plants, and animals. Unfortunately, something went awry in the interpretation of this portion of scripture by some Christians. Lynn White Jr. argues that Christians embraced dominion of nature, ignoring their caretaking responsibilities in this covenant with God: "No new set of basic values has been accepted in our society to displace those of Christianity. Hence we shall continue to have a worsening ecologic crisis until we reject the Christian axiom that nature has no reason for existence save to serve man."[7] Biblical dominion, though subverted, remains the foundation of modern interactions of people with nature in Christian and even secular circles in the United States.[8]

Christian or not, this biblical interpretation of self-entitlement toward nature has seeped into contemporary environmentalism, often rejecting the rights of grassroots activism organized by and for lower-income groups and people of color to ensure a safe environment. Cone wrote: "Blacks and other minorities are often asked why they are not involved in the mainstream ecological movement. To white theologians and ethicists, I ask, why are you not involved in the dialogue on race?"[9] Mainstream activists, much like the Christians described by White, focus on conserving resources and preserving wildlife, often ignoring the concerns and role of people of color including African Americans. They rely on tokenism to diversify their staff; they are, as Robert Gottlieb has stated, "caught up in the terrain and action that placed their groups apart from the new kinds of environmental politics being influenced by ethnicity, gender, and class factors."[10]

Another aspect of BELT—a strand of black liberation theology—is the history of environmental justice by the African American church and Christian organizations. Church environmental justice activists, part of the long history of civil rights in the African American community and an underpinning of BELT, struggled to reverse twentieth-century environmental racism. Bullard, in *Unequal Protection: Environmental Justice and Communities of Color* (1994), refers briefly to King's role in the 1968 sanitation workers' strike, in Memphis, Tennessee, which precursored late twentieth- and twenty-first-century environmental justice activism.[11] This strike deserves a closer look. On February 12, 1968, the Memphis sanitation workers went on strike to improve wages, hours, and vacations, with an unhealthy work environment as a subtext. Sanitation workers handling the city's trash were exposed to hospital waste and rotting food, which drew rodents, roaches, and birds, creating a petri dish for rashes and disease. In the words of Leroy Bonner, a sanitation worker: "[One time there were] two maggots right around my navel. I took a bath and they stretched out and they fell off in the tub. And my wife said, 'Lord have mercy, Leroy, wait a minute and let me run that water out' . . . She ran it out and she came in and washed my head and everything, and [she] was pulling them out of my head. You see, that was summertime. I said, 'Well, I can't help it . . . We got to try to make it.'"[12] Bonner's exposure to rotting trash and maggots signified how race and poverty defined the status and treatment of African Americans in the 1960s. As a poor African American man who had limited choices for employment, his work environment was a hostile place.

African American ministers, local leaders, and church members joined sanitation workers like Bonner who organized a citywide strike and boycott on February 24. A day later, the ministers urged their congregations to support the sanitation boycott and march on behalf of the workers. Throughout March, Memphis mayor Henry Loeb met with the ministers, who continued to lead marches, while their congregations raised money by holding a gospel music marathon. The strike drew national attention when King led a rally on March 18. Later, on April 3, King spoke at the Mason Temple in Memphis, Tennessee, supporting the sanitation workers in his famous speech "I've Been to the Mountaintop," a template for the justice of black liberation theology and BELT:

> There are thirteen hundred of God's children here suffering, sometimes going hungry, going through dark and dreary nights wondering how this thing is going to come out. . . It's all right to talk about streets flowing with milk and honey, but God has commanded us to be concerned about the slums down here and his children who can't eat three square meals a

day. It's all right to talk about the new Jerusalem, but one day God's preacher must talk about the new New York, the new Atlanta, the new Philadelphia, the new Los Angeles, the new Memphis, Tennessee.[13]

King's vision for improving the living conditions of poor African Americans was inherently environmental. He addressed the complexities of wages, safety, and health and gave the plight of sanitation workers context, mindful of the environmental problems in the inner city during the civil rights era. King's speech also evoked something broader—"a moral geography of social and political progress"—and constituted an implicit environmental manifesto decrying and dismantling everything from slavery to segregation set against nature.[14]

After the 1960s, Benjamin F. Chavis Jr., a one-time reverend and the president of the National Association for the Advancement of Colored People (NAACP), advocated for African Americans in a way that was critical to environmental justice as a national movement. At the 1993 National Black Church Environmental and Economic Summit, he described in biblical language—responsibility, creation, and sin—the foundation of BELT as he described an implicit and explicit culpability of whites and African Americans respectively concerning the environment: "The fact that we [African Americans] are disproportionately dumped on is just consistent with being in America. . . . And the demand that God puts on us is that we will face up to the contemporary responsibility that God has given us to not let God's creation be destroyed by sin. . . . Environmental injustice is sin before God."[15]

Chavis's previous historical and activist role in Warren County, North Carolina, had been one of the modern catalysts of the national environmental justice movement. In 1978, liquid tank drivers hired by the Ward Transformer Company secretly poured toxic manmade polychlorinated biphenyls (PCBs) along roads across thirteen North Carolina counties. In an attempt to dispose of the tainted soil, the state of North Carolina constructed a landfill in Warren County, which was predominantly African American. In 1984, Christian African American leaders like Chavis joined Warren County citizens to demonstrate against the government's attempt to collect and then dump the soil in the county. Other church leaders, including Reverend Joseph Lowery of the Southern Christian Leadership Conference and Walter Fauntroy, a Progressive National Baptist minister, united with locals to peacefully protest the dumping. The protesters were concerned about the correlation of PCBs with various illnesses including skin disorders, reproductive problems, liver disease, and cancer. African American women mixed prayer and supplication with activism in a rural Baptist church, an underpinning of BELT. As it was later described, these women "got on their knees and prayed to God to give them the strength to lay down in the street in front of those trucks. . . . But thank goodness these women said, 'You're not going to dump in my church, you're not going to dump in my community.' And out of that vigilance, out of that resistance, it helped energize a movement that was building in many different places; God helped put it right; it wasn't just the black community."[16] Though these women were arrested, along with other protesters, they succeeded in igniting the national environmental justice movement.

The Commission for Racial Justice of the United Church of Christ (UCC) also sought social justice for African Americans—later including other people of color—by picketing with the Student Nonviolent Coordinating Committee during the civil rights era and participating in the 1972 National Black Political Convention in Gary, Indiana. The commission continued its commitment to justice and environmental justice, through their landmark study *Toxic Wastes and Race in the United States: A National Report on the Racial and Socio-Economic Characteristics of Communities with Hazardous Waste Sites* (1987). Chavis said of the UCC's decision to produce this publication: "We believe that the time has come for all church and civil rights organizations to take the issues seriously. We realized that the involvement in this type of research is a departure from our traditional protest methodology. However, if we are to advance our struggle in the future, it will depend largely on the availability of timely and reliable information."[17] This report by a Protestant organization remains a critical source for studying and further developing the environmental justice movement. Later in 1994, the UCC also responded when the Shintech Company planned—but never succeeded—to construct a polyvinyl chloride (PVC) manufacturing plant in Convent, Louisiana.

The activism of local grassroots organizations against environmental racism defines BELT. In 1977, the Reichold Chemical Company located in Columbia, Mississippi, was accused of exposing two hundred cattle to dioxins and exploding Agent Orange, a defoliant herbicide and dioxin. In addition, the company allegedly poured chemicals downstream into Jingling Creek, past a recreational facility and high school frequented by African Americans. Four floods also exposed toxins that Reichold had buried off-site at what is now a Superfund site. In 1992, the Jesus People Against Pollution (JPAP) established a grassroots environmental justice organization, responding to years of toxic dumping by Reichold. JPAP exposed Reichold's disregard for the community and the resulting health problems and increased mortality among African Americans.

During the 1990s, Helping Other People Emerge (HOPE), established by Reverend Buck Jones in East St. Louis, drew upon environmental activism and

Christian faith, to battle local problems. Residents approached HOPE because they were being shaken out of bed at 3 a.m., having their windows and dishes broken, and finding the foundations of their homes cracked. This damage was caused by a company that was shredding cars, including contaminated vehicles, and their gasoline tanks, creating explosions. According to Jones, "We marched, we prayed, we threatened to file a lawsuit, we blocked the entranceway to the plant, and we won. They (the shredder company) hired residents to check and inspect the cars; in addition, they also gave a cash settlement." He organized projects reducing lead poisoning among children, cleaning up of Dead Creek, and a rallying against Onyx Environmental Services, which planned to incinerate neutralized nerve gas for the United States Army at the expense of local African Americans.[18] Before Jones's death, he organized toxic tours of East St. Louis, exposing toxic hotspots and the role of the government and corporations in environmental racism in East St. Louis.[19]

Jones based his final initiatives upon the efforts of the National Council of Churches (NCC), which consolidated grassroots into a national effort in December 1993. Leaders of the major African American churches, including the African Methodist Episcopal, African Methodist Episcopal Zion, National Baptist Convention, USA, National Baptist Convention of America, Progressive National Baptist Convention, and the Church of God in Christ met for two days at the National Black Church Environmental and Economic Justice Summit in Washington DC. The attendees emphasized quality of life and health in the African American community, focusing on pollution and dumping rather than the mainstream interests of eliminating global ozone depletion and protecting endangered species. Reverend Franklyn Richardson, the general secretary of the National Baptist Convention, USA, presented the NCC report, containing six specific demands, to Vice President Al Gore. These demands included a presidential executive order on environmental justice and regulation of corporations, the identification of a church representative for the Sustainable Communities Task Force of the President's Council on Sustainable Development, and the involvement of local churches in key environmental decisions by the government.[20] These items suggested ways African Americans could influence government policy from a Christian perspective.

As a result of the NCC Summit, on March 13 and 14, 1998, approximately twelve African American church leaders toured toxic sites in Louisiana communities, including Convent, Oakville, and New Sarpy/Norco. The NCC Eco-Justice Working Group and Black Church Liaison Committee and the United States Conference of World Council of Churches sponsored the tours. The leaders traveled around communities polluted by PVC, a toxic dump, and "fumes, explosions, and fires" from twenty-seven oil refineries. They scheduled a meeting with Gore, which was ultimately canceled, to plead the case of the Louisiana communities.[21]

Agenda for Action

An agenda for action for environmental justice by the African American church is based on this theology and history of BELT. Dorceta Taylor outlines three options for environmental justice nonprofits: (a) join established mainstream organizations, (b) create their own organizations, rejecting any collaboration or coalitions with the mainstream, or (c) start new organizations, using the resources available from mainstream organizations.[22] Based on Taylor's recommendations, biblical mandates, and the realities of environmental racism, the third option best suits the African American church and the community. African Americans in the church are called to operate and serve in a multicultural world that includes whites. In addition, African Americans are not isolated and are part of a community that includes whites —some of whom are racist—that wield great economic, social, and political power. The African American church must be practical while resolving environmental racism, even when biblical beliefs including unconditional love and the realities of mainstream racism collide.

The following fifteen-point environmental justice agenda for action is based on a theology and history of social and environmental justice, grassroots activism, spirituality, and organization in the African American church:

(1) Establish goals of self-sufficiency and autonomy in the African American community to eradicate environmental racism, applying the language, along with the theological and historical framework of BELT;

(2) Teach the interrelated history of the African American church, civil rights, and environmental justice to the African American community as a foundation for meeting these goals;

(3) Co-opt organizational, strategic planning, and management tools from mainstream or white environmentalists, including networking, tailoring them to the needs of the African American church and community;

(4) Reverse the political apathy in the African community by modeling and combining historical civil rights activism—sit-ins and marches—with modern twenty-first-century lobbying, legislation, and law enforcement;

(5) Focus narrowly on critical environmental problems, at least temporarily, that have threatened and diminished the health and longevity of African Americans, including solid waste management, incineration, pollution,

and toxins, avoiding—for now—a drift toward the mainstream issues of wilderness and conservation, even if coalition-building remains limited among ethnic groups with conflicting agendas;

(6) Create coalitions with other ethnic churches, including Native Americans and Latinos, without losing autonomy—in turn gaining power through increased numbers;

(7) Acknowledge that coalitions with mainstream and other ethnic organizations are short- to midterm tools that ebb and flow depending on the needs of the African American church and the community, and on existing relationships with other ethnic groups;

(8) Model and teach selfless Christian service for environmental justice in the African American community, as described in Galatians 5:13: "For you, brethren, have been called to liberty; only do not use liberty as an opportunity for the flesh, but through love serve one another";

(12) Limit the role of mainstream environmentalists until they develop a more holistic and equitable understanding of environmentalism pertinent to the African American community;

(13) Discard the historical model in which the African American church relies on one or two charismatic religious leaders like King to maintain a cohesive movement; instead train many new leaders to develop management, coalition building, facilitation, and collaborative skills for environmental justice;

(14) Organize church and community members, mixing traditional and modern activism, including fliers, telephones, letters, e-mails, cellular phones, and the Internet; and

(15) Develop the growing national movement further, always remembering the importance of the first grassroots initiatives, the foundation of environmental justice activism.

This agenda is the next step that can transform BELT, the genesis of which was in black liberation theology and a history of civil right activism by African Americans, into a theology that incorporates twenty-first-century action.

Since the end of slavery, the vision for racial equality has been deferred in the United States. In 1865, Alexander Crummell, an African American theologian, said, "The trials and suffering of this race have been great for centuries. They have not yet ceased. They are not likely to cease for a long time. It may take two to three generations for the race to get a firm and assured status in the land."[23] Crummell would be alarmed at the tenuous standing of third-generation African Americans undermined by environmental racism in the twenty-first century. In response to African Americans being inequitably exposed to toxic chemicals and waste, the church is called to further expand grassroots and national reform looking to BELT—justice, grassroots activism, spirituality, and organization—all based on the Bible. Combined, the history and theology can be a "spearhead for reform" for African Americans embattled by environmental racism in the future.[24]

14

Reflections on the Purposes and Meanings of African American Environmental History

CARL ANTHONY

This book provides a foundation for a deeper understanding of contemporary struggles for sustainability and justice. It addresses some of the ruptures that African Americans have experienced in their relationship to the natural world. This volume contains many surprises, forcing us to think more carefully about what we mean by our relationship to the environment. More fundamentally, it is an invitation to think differently about who we are as a people.

Much of environmental history has been written out of concerns for the fate of nature in Western culture—the destruction of the forests; the degradation of landscapes; the loss of wolves, bears, cats, and birds; the uprooting of indigenous people. These concerns should and will continue to have force. Yet environmental history from an African American must incorporate an additional theme that is typically overlooked: the importance of inclusion of the stories of African Americans who helped to lay the foundations of the nation, in the face of an atmosphere of hostility and disregard.

❧

Twenty years ago I was working in a small architecture and planning office in Oakland at a time when Berkeley faced major decisions in planning its waterfront. The whole western end of the city had been, essentially, a dump. People brought their garbage there and dumped it at the waterfront.

Eventually this process created 170 acres of new waterfront land. Since the land was unzoned, the city was unsure what to do with it. The Santa Fe Realty

200

Company, which owned the property, wanted to build a whole new downtown on the Berkeley waterfront. It maintained that since the land was unzoned, the city had no right to use it and the city's efforts to do so would amount to a "taking," an unlawful use of private property.

I was hired, along with a number of consultants, to come up with a waterfront plan. We held a number of public meetings to address this issue. The first meeting in the Berkeley City Council chambers drew about three hundred people, all of whom were opposed to the Santa Fe Realty plan. Virtually everyone in the room held some version of the position, "Save our waterfront; protect the land from the greedy developers."

About three-fourths of the way through a public hearing, a well-dressed African American man came to the microphone and said, "I want to speak in favor of this plan. I am from South Berkeley. The young people who live in South Berkeley don't have any jobs. If we build this new downtown, the company has promised twelve thousand jobs. You can't eat open space. You can't eat the environment." What happened next disturbed me greatly. All these people who opposed the waterfront development began booing him, saying, "Go back to South Berkeley."

I was unsettled by this and didn't know what to make of it. Here was one of the few African Americans in the room—the only one who actually got up to say anything—being booed. I felt that this was inappropriate and disrespectful. I had to consider the question: Who am I, in this situation, and what am I supposed to be doing?

The large body of environmentalists in that room shared a sense of history and purpose, a frame of reference, that was different from the history and purpose of this African American man. I began to wrestle with the question of how to integrate these two perspectives.

The decision about the waterfront was a moment in time in which a decision was being made about how to build part of a metropolitan region. This moment changed the course of my life and set me forth on a whole different path, leading ultimately to my current efforts to help build sustainable metropolitan communities. The seed of my involvement in the movement for metropolitan regional equity—incorporating concern for the earth, concern for the city, and concern about race—was planted that day.

Not long after the public hearing, at the end of a long week, I went home and settled in for a pleasant evening. I poured myself a glass of sherry, reached for a slim volume of poetry on the shelf, and made myself comfortable in my easy chair. The volume I picked was Alexander Pope's long poem, *An Essay on Man*, written in the late-eighteenth century. It was based on a hierarchical concept called the Great Chain of Being. In this hierarchy, the angels are at the top and the grass and bugs are at the bottom. Man is in between, struggling to reconcile his beastly nature and his divine nature.

In a contemplative mood, I reflected on where I, as an African American, might fit in this Great Chain of Being. To my surprise, *I placed myself just below the white people.*

Isn't that amazing? At that point I was forty-five years of age and had been actively engaged in the struggle for racial and economic justice for twenty-five years. As I sat there, no slave traders were holding my arms and legs in chains, no plantation owners were restricting when and where I could go, no patrolling vigilantes with hound dogs were lurking to keep me in my place, no Ku Klux Klan members were burning crosses on my front lawn, no admissions officers were telling me I was unqualified, and no policemen were eyeing me suspiciously as an intruder in the neighborhood. Here, by myself, in my own living room, I placed myself just below the white people.

Putting this experience alongside my experience at the Berkeley City Council hearing, I tried to make sense of my deep commitment to the struggle for racial justice, my history, my sense of self—and this other view of "the environment" that didn't seem to include me. At that point I had another vital insight that has sustained me over the succeeding twenty years. As I thought about my own history and who I am, I realized that I am an end product of fourteen billion years of life in the universe. I saw that even as humans have a conscious and expanding role in shaping life on planet earth, the forces of the universe are much larger. Only through reclaiming my sense of who I am, in that largest sense, could I make sense out these two stories—the story of the environment and the story of the struggle for racial justice.

Although I had inherited the legacy of oppression and had struggled mightily against it, I vowed that, from that moment on, I would no longer think of myself as white people had defined me. I would no longer be constrained in my sense of self by the five hundred years of oppression that had helped to shape my consciousness. I had managed to extract something useful from those years—for myself, for African Americans, for other people of color, for the community at large. But with this newfound larger awareness, I would no longer define myself centrally by this unthinkably brutal experience. Instead, I knew myself to be the end product of four billion years of evolution of life on the planet. In that moment, I claimed this as my heritage.

The earth is the ground we walk on, the sea and air, the soil that nourishes us, the sphere of mortal life, the third planet in order from the sun, near the center of the Milky Way galaxy. Everything that we do, or aim to do, is governed by our relationship with the earth—to its inspiration and resources, to our consciousness of its relationship to the cosmos, to our affinity with human and other-than-human life. Our knowledge and affinity with the earth, in all of its richness of life and diversity, stretches from the tiniest particles, waves and cells, to its plant forms and ecosystems, its rivers, mountains, and seas, to the majesty of our solar system, galaxies, and outer edges of the universe. The knowledge of the earth, and of our place in its long evolution, can give us a sense of identity and belonging that can act as a corrective to the hubris and pride that have been weapons of our oppressors.

What follows from this realization? I began to conduct a little internal audit, a quick survey to think of how this fourteen-billion-year framework could help me to be clearer about my own being. What sort of orientation do I need to have toward these fourteen billion years of life in order to do what I need to be doing in my daily life and my practice?

Around that time I came across a very important book by Thomas Berry, called *The Dream of the Earth*. Berry proposed that, in order to get our bearings in terms of our current ecological crisis, we need a new story about who human beings are in relationship to the story of the earth. Berry outlines the story of the earth and the place of human beings in it. I really liked that. It gave me a starting point for working through these issues.

At the same time, I found I had an uneasy feeling about the book because it didn't appear to include black people at all. There was wonderful talk of Native Americans—the ecumenical spirit, the struggle against patriarchy, etc., were reflected—but where were the black people? In fact, African Americans' experiences were not included in *any* of the environmental literature I could get my hands on about people's relationship to the land. Thoreau, David Brower . . . none of them reflected black people's experience.

How could this be? What was I to do with this?

One day, while reading a Civil War book, I came across a map of North America showing where black people lived on the eve of the Civil War. There is a coastal belt that stretches from the tidewaters of Virginia to the Atlantic coast, to middle Georgia, Alabama, Mississippi, Louisiana, and Texas. Along this particular belt were counties that were 50 to 75 percent black.

At the same time, while reading about the earth's evolution, I found a map of the North American continent as it was shaped fifty million years ago. The continent was the same shape then as it is today, with one exception: the areas where black people lived just prior to the Civil War were underwater.

As I read more and more about the evolution of the planet, I came across writings about plate tectonics. Around three hundred million years ago, only one huge continent existed. We now call this supercontinent Pangaea. Something caused Pangaea to break up, after which the continents began drifting apart. About one hundred million years ago, there was a reversal that led to a huge collision between Africa and North America. This produced the Appalachian Mountains, from Maine all the way to Georgia. If you look at the map, you can see how the western bulge of Africa and eastern part of the United States coast, around South Carolina coast, used to fit together. The fossils and the geological strata from both places were the same—they match exactly. And, as it happens, the foothills of the Appalachians are one of the major regions where black people lived in the Civil War era.

What does all this mean? How does this set of facts illuminate anything of significance? What I concluded was that there is a much bigger story about my relationship to North America than the story I was carrying in my head. The story in my head was that black people were brought here in 1619 by some pirating Dutchmen and then forced to work as slaves for hundreds of years. By no means am I saying that this is not a central part of the story. Yet there is also a much bigger story. It has been a relief to free myself from being trapped solely in the limited perspective that I had carried around all my life.

As I began to think about the origins of some of my African ancestors, I came to realize what should be obvious to everyone: In some sense, we are all African American. Everyone has African heritage. What happened to that part of the story? What about the first million years of human evolution? The dominant theory of the history of how the human race emerged, in the rainforest and savannah regions of Africa, is a central part of the narrative that needs to be articulated.

ᨘ

If you look at a map from the height of European expansion and the slave trade, around the sixteenth and seventeenth centuries, you can see that in Europe—in the British Isles, France, the coast of Spain—in West Africa, all along the coast of South America, in the Caribbean, and in North America, about fifty towns were built as a direct consequence of the slave trade. The whole town of Liverpool, for example, was built on the wealth that came from the slave trade. Every street in town was named after a slave trader. (No one ever told me about this version of city building when I learned about urban planning in school!)

City building in such places was based geopolitics that had at its core an explicit desire to take advantage of the slave trade. Slave traders that went to Africa exchanged England's merchandise for black people at a profit. Then they took the black people across the ocean and traded them for a profit to colonists and merchants in North America, the Caribbean, and South America. Then they took the raw materials accumulating from the labor of African American slaves—sugarcane, rice, and tobacco—and took them back to England at yet another profit. New towns were funded by the huge accumulation of capital produced by this process.

Raw materials from the new world built wealth in Europe and the colonies. In the American South, descendents of African people worked the land, in some places as many as twelve generations, without receiving the benefit of their labor. Slaving under the hot sun, they cleared the forests, drained the swamps, planted and harvested sugar, rice, tobacco, and cotton. These resources were shipped and processed in Portugal, Spain, the Netherlands, and England, and later in the northern colonies. Profits from molasses, rum, and tobacco were plowed into maritime enterprises and factories in Liverpool, Manchester, and Bristol—cities of the industrial revolution.

A racially blended environmental narrative ignores these crucial relationships. Such a narrative, part of an expansionist cosmology, tends to ignore as well the diversity of European experiences with the land—the exploitation of the Irish, Jewish, or Italian populations, for example.

Historically, in some instances, people of European heritage in the United States tend to think of themselves as a uniform population, naturally superior to people of non-European heritage. This sense of natural superiority provides the basis for white supremacy—solidarity among people of European heritage to dominate, marginalize, and exploit people of non-European heritage.

The dominant culture has rejected a vision of community that embraces African Americans as central to the life of the human community in the United States. We must reject such a vision of community that systematically (consciously or unconsciously; intentionally or unintentionally) overlooks, minimizes, marginalizes, or otherwise devalues the experience and contribution of African Americans in the United States. Such a vision is racially biased, if not racist.

⚘

This reflection on the elements of African American environmental history calls attention to much that has been missing in the conventional story about people and the land in North America. The hidden narrative of race is more than a collection of episodes and facts that have been overlooked. The lesson that comes out of this ensemble of facts has to do with the fragmentation and disruption of personal and community life, and therefore, the quest for wholeness.

African Americans have a long, if not well-understood, relationship to the land in North America. The ancestors of African Americans were uprooted from the land in Africa, transported thousands of miles away, and forced to work the land without remuneration for the benefit of another people. But

African Americans survived, and they now live in the cities. The future of our urban, suburban, and rural communities depends in part upon our willingness to face this terrible history and consciously make something of it.

The city, in its multiple manifestations, is the largest human invention on the planet. The roots of city building go way back. As the famous historian Lewis Mumford wrote about in *The City in History*, if we want to find out the roots of the idea of a city, we have to look at the prehuman origins of this impulse toward community. This impulse of species to come together has a deeply rooted biological basis, as evidenced by schools of fish, flocks of birds, etc. We are following a deep-seated trait that is grounded in all of these other species.

The city is also the largest intervention of humans in relationship to the natural world. We shape the cities, and the cities in turn shape us. An inquiry into the character of this relationship necessarily involves an understanding of ecological dependence of urban populations upon the hinterlands for food, building materials, energy, and disposal of wastes.

The connection between the city and the rural environment has always been historically clear. What hasn't been clear is the relationship of this process to the people who lived in those places. You could never live in the cities if the food, the drinking water, the forests that make paper and buildings, the natural resources to produce electricity, weren't coming from somewhere. City building has been based on extracting resources from the surrounding areas, and on exploiting the people who are making these resources available without giving them anything back, without honoring them or their story.

We need a new story about race and place in America. This new story is not only about toxic waste dumps and hazardous materials; it is about the fundamental right of a people to have a relationship with all of creation.

So what ever happened with the Berkeley waterfront? Although the African American man who voiced opposition to this plan never returned to the public meetings, he—and others who shared his views—made an impact. After a long and protracted participation process, the city decided to protect the open space along the bay. The Santa Fe Realty Company, donated the land to the city to build a waterfront park. The city made a commitment to replan its industrial edge to protect and expand manufacturing jobs in 160 blocks of its industrial corridor. Hammered out over a three-year process, this plan involved residents, workers, industrial business owners, and city staff working together to expand West Berkeley as a manufacturing and industrial base, while improving West Berkeley's environment. The city worked closely with local businesses to reduce the production, transport, and handling of toxic and hazardous materials in the area. First-source hiring agreements ensured that jobs would be filled by Berkeley residents, with the additional environmental benefit of reducing the commuter traffic.

Ultimately it became clear to me that the African American man at the hearing was actually representing his people's quest to be acknowledged, to be part of the picture. The deep meaning of this journey has to do with the quest of his people to belong, to be full participants in society. In short, he was voicing a quest for justice, which was every bit as important as saving the waterfront. I'm not saying it was more important. I am saying that our task is to reconcile these two aspects in a way that includes the human aspect. The challenge of building sustainable communities is to resolve the conflict between these two potentially competing goals, to synthesize, and to meld these important impulses over a period of time.

I had spent nine years at Columbia University getting my professional degree in architecture, and then ten years teaching architecture and urban planning at the department of environmental planning and design at University of California, Berkeley. Still, I realized that I had to start over. How to proceed? No one had ever taught me about these things. In that moment, I decided to start Urban Habitat, a nonprofit organization.

*

The mission of Urban Habitat is to build multicultural environmental leadership for sustainable communities in the Bay Area. At the time we founded Urban Habitat, most environmental groups were ignoring cities. Urban Habitat was the first environmental justice group to embrace the idea of regional equity. We incorporated this idea in our mission statement from the beginning.

We introduced the idea that people of color should provide leadership, not only of their own communities, but also of the whole society. By leadership we understood that people of color were obligated to develop a vision of what we were for as well as what we were against.

The first thing that Urban Habitat did was to treat the city as a whole, as a part of the larger ecosystem or watershed. This means viewing the inner city, the downtown, the suburbs, the surrounding rural areas, and the wilderness— the whole metropolitan region—as interconnected, not as fragmented parts.

Second, we understood that in thinking about cities, we had to think about the more-than-human world. We had to learn about housing and transportation, workplaces, schools, and churches. But we also had to learn about land, air, water, biological resources, and patterns of energy consumption and waste. These ideas were embraced in the idea of "habitat."

Urban Habitat is multicultural and consciously and deliberately gender-

balanced. It was the first environmental organization in the Bay Area to incorporate, systematically and consciously, contributions from Asian Americans,
African Americans, European Americans, Latinos, and Native Americans. We
also helped to found or support dozens of environmental justice organizations in the San Francisco Bay Area.

The *Race, Poverty & Environment Journal,* which we cofounded with the
California Rural Legal Assistance Project, introduced a broader definition of
environmental justice beyond toxics to include such issues as water conservation, transportation, population and immigration, and food security. A special issue on Asian and Pacific Islanders led to the founding of the Asian Pacific Environmental Network (APEN).

Urban Habitat was built on a solid foundation of engagement with environmental, business, and social justice groups in the Bay Area. I served for
eight years as president of Earth Island Institute, an international organization
founded by David Brower to protect the global biosphere. We were a cofounder and convener of the Bay Area Alliance for Sustainable Communities
(BAASC), which brought together the Bay Area Council (representing the two
hundred largest businesses in the Bay Area), the Sierra Club, the Bay Area Social Equity Caucus (representing labor, housing groups, and other social justice advocates), and elected officials of the Association of Bay Area Governments and the Metropolitan Transportation Commission. BAASC developed
a "sustainability compact" that was formally endorsed by over eighty Bay Area
municipal jurisdictions. We helped to inaugurate the Bay Area Footprint
Planning Process to lay out how the region as a whole should grow. We sponsored the Earth House video documentary, *Voices from the Community: Social
Equity and Smart Growth,* which presented a regional equity perspective in the
nine-county planning process. We helped establish the Community Capital
Investment Initiative, which raised $150 million to finance smart growth
projects in the San Francisco Bay Area.

᭥

All people have their story. Every people comes from a story that is
grounded in the evolution of the earth. We all need to come to terms with our
own stories, while knowing that we share a common longing and a common
struggle: everybody is struggling for a sense of feeling at home on this planet.

In my work for environmental justice, the universe has been my friend. In
this sense I feel that I am on equal footing with lots and lots of other people,
whereas when I think about the dominant discourse on the environment, I
don't feel on equal footing because of how it has been framed. Part of the
problem is that we don't have a shared narrative. The problem at the waterfront was that black people were not included in the "we." One of the purposes

of creating this narrative is to help create a "we"—to create a common language about urban spaces, rural spaces, and environmental justice. The larger frame of the universal perspective creates a form of equality. We all come from this common place.

"History is governed by those overarching movements that give shape and meaning to life by relating human ventures to the destinies of the universe," writes Thomas Berry. "Such a movement might be called the great work of a people."

The great work of human social movements is to align the purposes of our human activities with the overall purpose of the universe. I see a deeper meaning of my own work in building sustainable metropolitan communities: helping to create a fitting home for humans, in the larger context of the universe.

NOTES

Foreword

1. Rawick, *American Slave,* vol. 6, 453–55; quotations on 454, 455.

2. Roosevelt, *Wilderness Writings,* 86–106; quotations on 91.

Chapter 1: African American Environmental History

1. Regarding the use of "African American" or "black," throughout this collection, each contributor has opted to use variations in terminology according to his or her own judgment.

2. Thomas Calhoun Walker, *Honey-Pod Tree,* 232–41; quotation on 233.

3. Ibid., 239.

4. Bernal, "Race in History," 75–76.

5. Alice Walker, *In Search of,* xi.

6. See Blum, "Pink and Green."

7. Worster et al. "Roundtable," 1088–89.

8. Stewart, *"What Nature Suffers,"* 11.

9. Proctor, *Bathed in Blood,* 119 (both quotations).

10. Hurley, *Environmental Inequalities,* 13, 111.

11. Morrison, *Love,* 58.

Chapter 2: Slavery and the Origins of African American Environmentalism

I would like to thank Vongphone Luangphaxay for assisting with the research for this essay.

1. The scholarly literature that makes this argument is growing—the best recent example is Hahn, *Nation Under Our Feet.* The now abundant scholarship on the agency of African Americans in shaping their lot against the conditions imposed upon them by slavery and racism could, in general, be strengthened by more attention to the history of the relationship between African Americans and the environment—and especially the extent to which slaves used environmental knowledge as a weapon of resistance. The best recent synthesis of the "slave agency" scholarship is Berlin, *Generations of Captivity.*

2. Stewart, *"What Nature Suffers,"* 98–102, 135, 146–48; Carney, *Black Rice.*

3. Rawick, *American Slave*, vol. 13, pt. 3, 130. Slaves also used fire to blind game at night, and dogs to corner or tree game.

4. Proctor, *Bathed in Blood*, 144–68; see also the discussion of hunting and fishing to slaves by Giltner in this volume. For a vivid appreciation of the value of roasted opossum, see the account of Georgia ex-slave Rachel Adams in Rawick, *American Slave*, vol. 12, pt. 1, 3–4. Richard Laird, who had been a slave in Mississippi, claimed to another WPA interviewer that "possums" hunted at night and then cooked with sweet potatoes and coffee was one of the highest food pleasures slaves enjoyed: Rawick, *American Slave*, vol. 8, pt. 3, 1293.

5. Stewart, *"What Nature Suffers,"* 178–79. Such tales were common in the Georgia low country and ample evidence is extant for their existence in both South Carolina and Georgia. See Georgia Writers Project, *Drums and Shadows,* 79, 110–11, 160–61, 171. An older collection, with no notes on informants, is Jones Jr., *Negro Myths;* the references here to "Buh" Rabbit and his fellows come from this collection. Patricia Jones-Jackson describes the discernment of distinct features of particular animals that sea-island storytellers bring to their tales in *When Roots Die,* 16–17nn171–72.

6. On the cultural meanings of slave food: see Joyner, "Soul Food," 171–78; Moore, "'Established and Well Cultivated,'" 70–83; Morgan, *Slave Counterpoint,* 134–45. On slave property, see Penningroth, *Claims of Kinfolk,* 45–78.

7. For slaves and later for freedmen, property was always connected to family, Penningroth argues, and "was less an institution or a legal right than a social process." He connects this insight to scholarship in African studies that argues that access to resources is connected to social identity and that property ownership is more an ongoing social process than a matter of having something to the exclusion of the claims of others. *Claims of Kinfolk,* 191–92.

8. Fett, *Working Cures,* 62.

9. Porcher drew upon years of work in southern botany to compile his guide to about four hundred useful plants. He created it because of an order from the surgeon general of the Confederacy; it was designed to provide information on useful wild plants to Confederate armies in the field.

10. Fett, *Working Cures,* 69–72.

11. Morgan, *Slave Counterpoint,* 617–19.

12. Hall, *Africans in Colonial Louisiana,* 201–36. Din claims Hall overestimates the extent of *grand marronage* in colonial Louisiana, but does not deny that it happened: Din, *Spaniards, Planters, and Slaves,* 19–34; "Minutes of the Governor and Council, July 7, 1772," in Allen D. Candler, comp., *Colonial Records of the State of Georgia* (Atlanta: 1906) 14: 292–93. Aptheker, in his classic essay about maroon communities, identified about fifty in that part of North America within the present-day limits of the United States: "Maroons within the Present," 151–67. Morgan explains how recurrent patterns of running away by eighteenth-century slaves were connected to patterns of visiting: *Slave Counterpoint,* 524–30. See also Franklin and Schweninger, *Runaway Slaves;* Camp, "'I Could Not Stay There.'" Camp explains the importance of truancy (and elaborates on this in *Closer to Freedom*) but could more fully emphasize the importance of the geography of woods and swamps to slave culture in general. Slave runaways, in any case, represented only a small minority of the whole, but the

complicity of slaves who were not "truant" in the successful truancy of others made this a more significant form of resistance—as did the cultural significance of running away and the narratives it generated in the quarters. Dixon discusses how the notion of wilderness as a place of deliverance was accentuated in slave spirituals and was meant to be taken literally as well as in the Biblical sense. See *Ride Out the Wilderness*, 1–28; Rev. Charles Colcock Jones to Lt. Charles C. Jones, Jr., July 10, 1862, quoted in Myers, *Children of Pride*, 113.

13. Gutman, *Black Family*, 208–11; Faust, "Culture, Conflict, and Community," 93–94; Guthrie, "Catching Sense," 114–29; Stewart, *"What Nature Suffers,"* 179–80. The Alvord quotation is from Hahn, *Nation Under Our Feet*, 140. Many freedmen fled their old neighborhoods, no matter their sense of place, to avoid supervision by their old masters. African Americans in the South, in spite of whatever leverage they could exercise against the conditions of oppression in slavery and then in the Jim Crow South by way of the environmental knowledge they possessed, still often found themselves exploited so severely by the labor they were forced to do that opportunities for flight or migration away from those conditions overcame any loyalty to place.

14. Cashin, "Landscape and Memory," 483.

15. Stoll, *Larding the Lean Earth*, 167. The history of conservation in the South, or of the agricultural improvement movement in the United States in general, is the history of failure. Farmers and planters who sought to retard the flight to fresh westward lands and to inspire a more intricate and intimate relationship between husbandman and land were not successful, and ecological sensibilities were overcome by economic and demographic forces. But just because the history of this kind of conservation was the history of failure does not mean that it was not deeply impor- tant to the South—a region that remained profoundly agrarian until at least World War II and that has been, after all, as much conditioned and defined by defeat and failure as by success. For a discussion of leading agricultural reformer and proponent of marling, see Kirby, *Poquosin*.

16. For the history of the changing perceptions of slaves by masters from a view that saw them as less savage and more "human," but that still likened them to domestic animals and to "pets," see Jacoby, "Slaves by Nature?" 89–99.

17. For "green paternalism," see Stewart, *"What Nature Suffers,"* 186–88.

18. Aiken, *Cotton Plantation South*, 360–61. Hahn explains how rural black southern culture was transported to urban places during the Great Migration, and there became the foundation for Garveyism and other important expressions of collective action and black nationalism. *Nation Under Our Feet*, 465–78.

Chapter 3: Slave Hunting and Fishing in the Antebellum South

Throughout the notes to this chapter, the abbreviation DASC will be used for the Documenting the American South Collection, University of North Carolina at Chapel Hill Libraries.

1. Cowdrey, *This Land, This South* is perhaps the best book for tracing the general patterns of southern environmental exploitation, analyzing in detail the way that southern ecologies were transformed as human use patterns intensified over time.

2. "Hiring Negroes," *Southern Planter and Farmer* 12 (1852): 376–77.

3. The most obvious exception to this trend is the large body of scholarship on either the uses of hunting and fishing between and among different groups of Native Americans or the ways that traditional native hunting and fishing practices changed in response to contact with Europeans. See for example, Cronon, *Changes in the Land;* Jennings, *Ambiguous Iroquois Empire;* Richter, *Ordeal of the Longhouse;* and Richard White, *Roots of Dependency.*

4. For analyses of hunting and/or fishing that emphasize the intersection of such field sports and the preservation of class distinction see Hahn, "Hunting, Fishing and Foraging," which argues in part that southern elites worked to deny lower class southerners, both black and white, such common rights in order to force them to subsist within the context of the emerging integrated capitalist market. Also dealing with tension between elites and plebeians over such customary rights is Kulik, "Dams, Fish and Farmers," and Watson, "'Common Rights of Mankind." For work that places such topics within the context of changing notions of masculinity, see Herman, *Hunting and the American Imagination.* For an analysis of southern hunting and fishing that addresses the intersections of class distinctions, masculinity, and religion, see Ownby, *Subduing Satan.*

5. There are several rare exceptions to this general trend: Hahn, "Hunting, Fishing and Foraging"; Marks, *Southern Hunting in Black and White: Nature, History and Rituals in a Carolina Community;* and Rivers, *Cultural Values in the Southern Sporting Narrative.* Hahn, Marks, and Rivers argue a general connection between hunting and fishing and race relations, but none gives the topic detailed analysis or deals with the longstanding connection between race relations and the changing social, economic and cultural meanings of hunting and fishing.

6. Proctor's *Bathed in Blood* is both the best study on hunting in the antebellum South and the only study that provides comprehensive analysis of the connection between the cultural importance of such activities and the existence of slavery. Proctor does an excellent job of establishing the importance of hunting for slaves and masters, providing an excellent comparative analysis of the different ways it functioned for those two groups. Proctor stops his analysis short of hinting at any direct subversive potential of such customary activities by slaves, however, arguing that hunting helped slaves construct their own culture "from stolen moments and subversive meanings" (267). For elite white sportsmen, according to Proctor, the act of hunting an animal "dramatized the wide-ranging mastery of white patriarchy" while "participation in the hunt made them more than men, it made them a master class" (210).

7. Stewart, "*What Nature Suffers*," 245. Stewart specifically addresses the importance of swamplands as a sort of "promised land" that African Americans could reclaim for their own economic and cultural betterment. But according to Stewart, the real and symbolic importance of swampland was in fact "a story about every place in the South where undrained and unclaimed land offered a refuge for African Americans."

8. The ultimate effect of African American hunting and fishing on southern social, economic, cultural, and racial prosperity was constantly examined and debated by a variety of interested white observers in the decades following emancipation. Ultimately southern planters, sportsmen, and developers came to share the general

opinion that unrestricted African American hunting and fishing was unacceptable. Thus, when efforts to limit and restrict hunting and fishing in the South through enacting property restrictions, establishing open and closed sporting seasons, and issuing formal state and local licenses began in earnest in the 1880s and 1890s, proponents of such measures frequently invoked the dangers of an unregulated African American populace in the hopes of convincing skeptical southern voters.

9. Rawick, *American Slave,* vol. 7, pt. 2, 38; ibid., vol. 15, pt. 2, 418. Slave Joseph LeConte recounted: "There was a complete armory of [guns] up-stairs in one of the closets, besides several in the hands of the most trusty negro men to shoot game and wild animals of prey and crop-destroying birds." *The Autobiography of Joseph LeConte* (New York: D. Appleton and Company, 1903), 18. DASC, http://docsouth.unc.edu/leconte/leconte.html.

10. Susan Dabney Smedes. *Memorials of a Southern Planter* (Baltimore: Cushings & Bailey, 1887) 1, 35. DASC, http://docsouth.unc.edu/smedes/smedes/html.

11. Northup, *Twelve Years a Slave,* 153.

12. James Battle Avirett, *The Old Plantation: How We Lived in Great House and Cabin Before the War* (New York: F. Tennyson Neely Co., 1901), 59. DASC, http://docsouth.unc.edu/avirett/avirett.html. It was not uncommon for masters to pay wages or give cash or material "bonuses" to their slaves for performing overwork or specially assigned tasks. This was a way, so they believed, of guaranteeing efficient performance of certain duties and of cultivating desired ties of affection or dependence between master and slave.

13. As Proctor has demonstrated in *Bathed in Blood,* the connection between the quest for mastery, elite use of forest, field, and stream for sport, and preservation of racial dominance were inherently intertwined. Hunting and fishing for sport reinforced the planter's sense of control of the world around him; slave labor on hand to perform the menial labor required of such expeditions reinforced his sense of control over the lives of all people of color.

14. Botkin, *Lay My Burden Down,* 112; Gosse, "Possum Hunting in Alabama," 88.

15. Yetman, *Voices from Slavery,* 124; Rawick, *American Slave,* vol. 14, pt. 2, 243.

16. Osofsky, *Puttin' On Ole Massa,* 119; Bontemps, *Five Black Lives,* 70.

17. One of the biggest perils of employing sources such as the WPA narratives is the frequency with which interview subjects make claims about their lives under bondage that contradict other available evidence. Such is the case with claims made by some ex-slaves, interviewed in the 1930s, that they enjoyed ample supplies of food, clean and healthy living conditions, and exclusively benign treatment while living with their former masters. Historians have written much on this subject. For two examples, see Blassingame, "Using the Testimony," and David Thomas Bailey, "Divided Prism."

18. Mary Reynolds quotation from Rawick, *American Slave,* vol. 5, pt. 2, 240–41. Northup quotation from *Twelve Years a Slave,* 153. See also Stewart, "*What Nature Suffers,*" chap. 3. Hunting and fishing were not the only ways slaves supplemented their diets. Also common was the practice of slaves working their own gardens and/or raising their own livestock at their masters' discretion. Slaves also frequently used overwork—laboring during granted personal time at the master's request—to get

extra food, which was one way that masters compensated them for working during times when labor was not customarily required. Stealing food from the stores or the "big house" was another method used when food was scarce, though this was the most dangerous. See Hudson, *Working Toward Freedom.*

19. For examples of archeological studies of slave quarters, see Orser, *Material Basis;* Singleton, *Archaeology of Slavery;* Otto and Burns, "Black Folks." For narrative evidence of dietary habits, see Fogel, *Without Consent or Contract,* 135–36. Fogel has used the Federal Writer's Project and Fisk University narratives to construct a diffusion index for slave food consumption: it indicates that fish and game were very common, with 26 persons reporting eating fish and 49 eating game for every 100 who reported eating corn, easily the most common food for slaves.

20. Rawick, *American Slave,* vol. 15, pt. 2, 145, and vol. 16, pt. 1, 3.

21. Ibid., vol. 2, pt. 2, 215, and vol. 6, pt.1, 161.

22. Olmsted, *Cotton Kingdom,* 267. See also Wood, *Women's Work.* The advantage of trapping was particularly important for slaves who labored under a gang labor system, who generally lacked the opportunities of slaves engaged in tasking.

23. Rawick, *American Slave,* vol. 9, pt. 1, 243, 439.

24. Published recollections of southern sportsmen, as well as articles and editorials, are replete with criticism of fire hunting. William Elliott, for example, noted that "the practice of fire-hunting, forbidden by the laws, is nevertheless but too much pursued in certain parts of the country. It is the author's aim . . . to expose the dangers to property and to life, attendant on this illicit practice. It is nearer akin to poaching than to legitimate hunting; and he professes no personal acquaintance with it." *Carolina Sports,* 258. Southern state legislatures passed numerous laws banning hunting with fire throughout the antebellum period. See for example, *Laws of North Carolina* (Raleigh: State of North Carolina, 1856): chap. 134, 1821; chap. 15, 1835; and chap. 24.

25. Rawick, *American Slave,* vol. 15, pt. 2, 272. For a detailed discussion of slave ownership of dogs and white attempts to limit the practice, see John Campbell, "My Constant Companion."

26. J. Vance Lewis, *Out of the Ditch: A True Story of an Ex-Slave* (Houston: Rein & Sons Co., 1910), 17. DASC, http://docsouth.unc.edu/neh/lewisj/lewisj.html.

27. Charles Ball, *Slavery in the United States: A Narrative of the Life and Adventures of Charles Ball* (New York: John S. Taylor, 1837), 352. DASC, http://docsouth.unc.edu/ballslavery/ball.html. South Carolina law permitted slave patrols to confiscate any firearms found in a slave's quarters during searches. See Henry, *Police Control,* 36–37. Likewise, the Virginia State Legislature passed a number of statutes like this one: "Any slave who shall keep or carry any firearms, swords, or other weapon, powder or balls, or other ammunition shall be punished by stripes not exceeding thirty-nine . . ." *Laws of Virginia* (Richmond: State of Virginia, 1847), chap. 12. In some states it was required that slave owners seek written permission from state or county authorities before their slaves could hunt with a gun or purchase a bond from the state to guarantee their slaves' good behavior. For example, Northampton County, North Carolina, slave owner William B. Lockhart purchased a five-hundred-dollar bond from the county court to obtain permission for his slave Reuben to hunt with a gun on his plantation. The bond would never be paid if "the said negro slave shall be of

good and honest behavior during the time he shall so carry and use a gun, and hunt in the woods . . ." Northampton County Records, Miscellaneous Slave Records, "Bonds for Slaves to Carry Firearms" Folder, North Carolina State Archives, Raleigh, North Carolina. C.R. 071.928.12.

28. Rawick, *American Slave,* vol. 16, pt. 2, 57.

29. Northup, *Twenty Years a Slave,* 155.

30. Charles Ball, *Fifty Years in Chains, or, The Life of an American Slave* (New York: H. Dayton; Indianapolis: Asher and Co., 1859), 203–4. DASC, http://docsouth.unc .edu/ball/ball.html.

31. Edward J. Thomas, *Memoirs of a Southerner* (Savannah, GA: 1923), 10. DASC, http://docsouth.unc.edu/thomas/thomas.html.

32. Rawick, *American Slave,* vol. 16, pt. 1, 157.

33. Ibid., vol. 15, pt. 2, 222.

34. Childs, *Rice Planter and Sportsman,* 78.

35. Rawick, *American Slave,* vol. 14, pt. 1, 267.

36. Ibid., 299.

37. Ball, *Slavery in the United States,* 43.

38. Rawick, *American Slave,* vol. 15, pt. 2, 318–19.

39. There are other accounts of slaves trading with poor whites. Allen Parker explained: "There could always be found a market among the poor whites, for whatever a slave had to sell . . ." *Recollections of Slavery Times* (Worchester, MA: Chas. W. Burbank & Co., 1895), 15. DASC, http://docsouth.unc.edu/neh/parker/parker .html. James Battle Avirett recounted: "These people [poor whites] were ready, by night, to carry on a system of demoralizing barter, taking at his own price articles stolen by the servants, to wit corn, poultry, pigs; in short anything the Negro might carry in his bag, in any sense marketable." *Old Plantation,* 118. Regarding patrols, Francis Henderson asserted: "They [patrols] will take whatever the slaves steal, paying in money, whiskey, or whatever the slaves want." Drew, *North Side View,* 13.

40. William Hayden, *Narrative of William Hayden, Containing a Faithful Account of His Travels for a Number of Years, Whilst a Slave, in the South. Written by Himself* (Cincinnati, OH: William Hayden, 1846), 25–26. DASC, http://docsouth.unc.edu/neh/ hayden/hayden.html (capitalization in original).

41. Despite the power and influence of the slave family, it could not adhere to nuclear definitions. Due to the frequency with which parents were torn from children and husbands from wives, the notion of "family" in the quarter often encompassed the entire community of slaves. According to George P. Rawick, "The individual slave was never alone except when he ran away, and even then he often went from one community of slaves to the next, aided in his flight by his fellow slaves united into communities by the processes of slave production." *From Sundown to Sunup,* 11. This is why it is problematic to label slaves without mothers or fathers as parentless. Children did have role models, protectors, and providers who filled gaps left by death or distance in the form of other adult slaves, uncles, cousins, and older siblings.

42. Rawick, *American Slave,* vol. 2, pt. 2, 138, and vol. 16, pt. 3, 44. Slaves seemed to have had a fairly rigid gendered division of labor in subsistence activities. This likely resulted from the fact that women's productive labor, vitally important to the family,

was needed elsewhere in the slaves' home economy, rather than from any notion of a "weaker sex." See Jones, *Labor of Love.* Jane Arrington recalled: "My brothers caught possums, coons, and sich things an' we [the female children and their mother] cooked 'em in our house." Rawick, *American Slave,* vol. 16, pt.1, 47. North Carolina slave Emma Blaylock remembered: "At Christmas time de men hunted and caught plenty game. We barbecued it before de fire. I 'members seein' mother an' grandmother swinging rabbits 'fore de fire to cook 'em." Rawick, *American Slave,* vol. 16, pt.1, 105.

43. As Blassingame has argued, the level of status achieved by a slave depended upon his or her service to the slave community. Skilled slaves who used their talents to benefit the community, who displayed physical prowess, or who proved willing and able to provide for their families were accorded a high degree of esteem and respect. See *Slave Community,* especially chap. 4.

44. According to King, slave parents, whenever they could, "whether together or alone, taught their youngsters how to tolerate inhumane acts and degradation, to maintain their humanity, and to keep their spirits intact." See "'Rais Your Children,'" 144.

45. Henderson quoted in Rawick, *American Slave,* vol. 16, pt. 2, 7; Ford quoted in Rawick, *American Slave,* vol. 2, pt. 2, 44.

46. Loguen, *Reverend J. W. Loguen,* 26.

47. Wood, *Women's Work,* 179.

48. Courlander, *Treasury,* 432.

49. Botkin, *Lay My Burden Down,* 90.

50. Ososfky, *Puttin' On Ole Massa,* 189.

51. John Andrew Jackson, *The Experience of a Slave in South Carolina* (London: Passmore & Alabaster, 1862), 30. DASC, http://docsouth.unc.edu/jackson/jackson.html.

52. Rawick, *American Slave,* vol. 16, 25.

53. Bontemps, *Five Black Lives,* 152.

54. Rawick, *American Slave,* vol. 12, pt. 1, 93.

55. Ibid., vol. 15, pt. 2, 222.

56. Charles Alexander, *Battles and Victories of Allen Allensworth, A.M., Ph.D., Lieutenant-Colonel, Retired, U.S. Army* (Boston: Sherman, French & Company, 1914), 171. DASC, http://docsouth.unc.edu/neh/alexander/alexander.html.

57. Ibid., 131.

58. Mrs. Kate E. R. Pickard, *The Kidnapped and the Ransomed. Being the Personal Recollections of Peter Still and his Wife "Vina," After Forty Years of Slavery* (Syracuse: William T. Hamilton, 1856), 160–61. DASC, http://docsouth.unc.edu/pickard/pickard.html.

59. Rawick, *American Slave,* vol. 2, pt. 2, 44.

60. Andrew Jackson, *Narrative and Writings of Andrew Jackson of Kentucky: Containing An Account of his Birth, and Twenty-Six Years of His Life While a Slave; His Escape, Five Years of Freedom, Together with Anecdotes Relating to Slavery; Journal of One Year's Travels, Sketches, Etc.* (Miami: Mnemosyne Publishing Co., 1969), 28. DASC, http://docsouth.unc.edu/neh/jacksona/jacksona.html.

61. Social Science Institute, *Unwritten History,* 166.

62. Botkin, *Lay My Burden Down,* 3.

63. Smedes, *Memorials,* 115.

64. Harry Smith, *Fifty Years of Slavery in the United States of America* (Grand Rapids: West Michigan Printing Co., 1891), 17–19. DASC, http://docsouth.unc.edu/neh/smithhar/smithhar.html.

65. Edward J. Thomas, *Memoirs of a Southerner* (Savannah, GA: 1923), 14. DASC, http://docsouth.unc.edu/thomas/title.html.

66. Blassingame, *Slave Testimony,* 280–81.

67. Rawick, *American Slave,* vol. 16, pt. 4, 76.

68. Botkin, *Lay My Burden Down,* 198.

Chapter 4: Rural African American Women, Gardening, and Progressive Reform in the South

1. Campbell, *Movable School,* 86.

2. In *This Land, This South,* Cowdrey correctly points to the importance of the lucrative row-crop system as vital to an understanding of the environmental history of rural African Americans who labored in the fields, and invites environmental historians to draw on his broad interpretation to develop case studies of particular places and peoples in the South. In *"What Nature Suffers,"* Stewart emphasizes the relationship between labor and landscape and argues that historians must look closely at the practices of everyday life in the nineteenth-century South to identify their significant contours. In *Breaking the Land,* Daniel looks at the three crop monocultures and how African Americans functioned within them as these monocultures changed and resisted or lurched toward modernization after emancipation.

3. Norwood, *Made from This Earth,* 136.

4. Vlach, *Back of the Big House,* 166.

5. Gilmore, *Gender and Jim Crow,* 44.

6. Gottlieb, *Forcing the Spring,* 24.

7. As early as 1906 and prior to the Smith-Lever Act, African Americans had limited access to cooperative demonstration work. See Scott, *Reluctant Farmer,* 232; and Rasmussen, "Smith Lever Act," 1384.

8. Jones, *Labor of Love,* 38–39.

9. Campbell, *Movable School,* 86.

10. Jean S. McKimmon, *North Carolina Home Demonstration Work Annual Report.* Jane S. McKimmon Papers, 1910–1945, 1928. PC 234.3, North Carolina State Archives.

11. Hurston, "The Gilded Six Bits," 1011; Effie Graham, "The Passing On Party" (Chicago: McClurg, 1912), 24–25, quoted in Gundaker, *Keep Your Head,* 19; McKimmon, *North Carolina Home;* Vlach, *Back of the Big House,* 14.

12. Westmacott, "Yards and Gardens," 54, 55.

13. McKimmon, North Carolina State Archives; Jones, *Labor of Love,* 86; Westmacott, *African-American Gardens and Yards,* 83.

14. Westmacott, "Yards and Gardens," 54–55; McKimmon, *North Carolina Home.*

15. Lemaistre, "In Search of a Garden," 43; Lemke-Santangelo, *Abiding Courage,* 139–40; Westmacott, "Yards and Gardens," 54.

16. McKimmon, *North Carolina Home.*

17. Ibid.

18. DuBois, *Souls of Black Folk,* 99.

19. "Rural Education Courses in the Elizabeth City State Normal Summer School, 1936." Summer School Reports, NC 236.4. General Education Board (GEB), Rockefeller Archive Center (RAC).

20. "Division of Agriculture." Hampton Institute Pamphlets, VA 38 and "Tuskegee Normal and Industrial School, Agricultural Department, Part I, Organization and Courses of Study," Hampton Institute Pamphlets, VA 38; Hampton Institute, GEB, RAC.

21. Ibid.

22. Walker, *In Search of,* 241.

Chapter 5: Turpentine Negro

1. Recent empirical work comparing wilderness values for African Americans, Hispanics, Asians, and whites showed minority groups were significantly less likely than whites to visit federally designated wilderness areas. However, the research showed fewer race/ethnic differences with respect to appreciation for off-site wilderness benefits such as "wilderness as a contributor to clean air and water" or as a "habitat for plant and animal species." See Johnson, Bowker, Bergstrom, and Cordell, "Wilderness Values." Research shows that participation in wildland activities by Hispanics and Asians typically falls between the white and black extremes—e.g., Gramann, *Ethnicity, Race.*

2. The ethnicity perspective attributes differences in recreation behavior to value differences based on subcultural norms. The theory postulates that subcultures or ethnic minorities possess unique cultural value systems that influence their recreation behavior. Marginality is viewed as the theory that most sharply contrasts with the ethnicity explanation. Marginality attributes minority (particularly black) differences in recreation behavior to social structural barriers such as lack of discretionary funds, transportation, and information about facilities. Proponents of this view argue that historical discrimination, poverty, and ignorance have largely shaped the way black Americans respond to social and political activities. Floyd, "Getting Beyond."

3. Wildland areas are not necessarily federally designated wilderness but may include these lands.

4. Blum, "Power, Danger, and Control"; Stewart, "*What Nature Suffers,*" 193–96; Glave, "'Garden so Brilliant'"; Westmacott, *African-American Gardens.*

5. Berwanger, *Frontier against Slavery,* 4.

6. Tegeder, *Prisoners of the Pines,* 41. At the turn of the twentieth century, European immigrants were also recruited by industry agents, but the exploitative nature of the work caused many to abandon the camps. Abuse of foreign white workers also prompted federal investigations into industry operations. See Shofner, "Forced Labor"; Chiang, Burrows, Howard, and Woodard, *Study of the Problems,* 82.

7. Schultz, "Original Slash Pine Forest," 36.

8. The acid application was very dangerous, and many of the workers interviewed said that it often got into their eyes and on their skin. One chipper said that when he was drafted to go to Vietnam, he went for his physical, and medical examiners found that he did not have any fingerprints because the acid had worn them away. The draft board had him investigated to make sure that he was not a wanted criminal.

9. Flynt, *Poor But Proud*. The Florida legislature legalized the leasing of state convicts to turpentine operators. See Drobney, "Where Palm and Pine."

10. Jahoda, *Other Florida*, 231.

11. Turner, *Frontier in American History*.

12. Shofner, "Forced Labor," 21.

13. Arthur F. Raper, *The Tragedy of Lynching* (Chapel Hill: University of North Carolina Press, 1933), 56, quoted in Tegeder, *Prisoners of the Pines*, 161.

14. Besides labor problems, woods production was also hurt by the discovery that similar products could be extracted as a by-product of the pulping process for papermaking. See Hodges, "History of Naval Stores."

15. Chiang, Burrows, Howard, and Woodard, *Study of the Problems*, 73–84.

16. Two significant technological changes were introduced into the industry in the period 1900 to 1940. The first was a change in the gum receptacle. The Herty Box, named for University of Georgia chemist Charles Herty, was a clay cup that replaced the wooden boxes. Second, sulfuric acid was applied to trees to increase gum flow. See Lauriault, "From Can't to Can't."

17. *American Memory: Florida Folklife from the WPA Collections, 1937–1942*, http://memory.loc.gov/ammem/flwpahtml/flwpahome.html. See the following song titles: "I'm Going to Georgia," "All you Rounders Better Lie Down," "Captain's Mule," and "I Heard a Mighty Rumblin' at the Water Trough."

18. Cleaver, *Post-Prison Writings*, 58.

19. Jahoda, *Other Florida*, 239.

20. Leander Showers, interview by Josh McDaniel, Walnut Hill, FL, October 30, 2003.

21. Bliss and Flick, "With a Saw," 87.

22. Jahoda, *Other Florida*, 238.

Chapter 6: African Americans, Outdoor Recreation, and the 1919 Chicago Race Riot

This chapter draws upon numerous feature articles and columns, such as "YMCA News" and "Boy Scout Notes," from the *Chicago Defender* (hereafter cited as *CD*) from 1912 to 1935. Only those articles quoted or referenced directly have been cited in full here, but interested readers will find a wealth of additional information and context in *CD* issues from this period.

1. Taylor, "Unnatural Inequalities," 7.

2. Almost all of the environmental history literature on Americans and the move back to nature for leisure centers on middle- and upper-class European Americans. See, for instance, Nash, *Wilderness*; Schmitt, *Back to Nature*. Environmental historians who criticize wilderness leisure for perpetuating a false and environmentally troubling

distinction between nature and culture also tend to paint outdoor recreation as white and bourgeois. See, for instance, Cronon, "Trouble," 79; Richard White, "'Are You an Environmentalist," 171–85. There are a number of excellent environmental histories that address working-class and ethnic hunting, although this literature tends to view hunting as market- or subsistence-oriented. See, for example, Jacoby, *Crimes*. Unlike environmental historians, cultural and social historians have been far more attuned to ethnic and working-class leisure in nature. These historians, though, generally fail to give nature any agency and view park landscapes as an empty stage where social relations are played out. For an excellent cultural/social history on working-class use of a park, see Rosenzweig and Blackmar, *Park and the People*. On the hierarchy of needs argument, see Mohai, "Dispelling Old Myths."

3. For the details of the riot, see Tuttle, *Race Riot*, 3–10, 32–66; Chicago Commission on Race Relations, *The Negro in Chicago* (Chicago: The University of Chicago Press, 1922); 1–52.

4. For this argument, see Tuttle, *Race Riot*; Barrett, *Work and Community in the Jungle*, 202–24; Philpott, *Slum and the Ghetto*, 162–80; Spear, *Black Chicago*, 129–229. Spear is the only historian of the riot to seriously address tension in the parks, but he ultimately prioritizes "jobs and homes and . . . politics." See *Black Chicago*, 201.

5. See Cronon, *Nature's Metropolis*, especially 5–19.

6. On the forest preserves, see Forest Preserve District of Cook County in the State of Illinois, *The Forest Preserves of Cook County* (Chicago: Clohesey and Company, 1918); quote on "Indian Paradise" is on page 27.

7. "Race Girls Brutally Assaulted by Whites in Washington Park," *CD*, June 8, 1918; Chicago Commission on Race Relations, *Negro in Chicago*, 288–95.

8. For quote on Lake Michigan waters, see Bowen, *Colored People of Chicago*, 274. On projectiles, see Chicago Commission on Race Relations, *Negro in Chicago*, 286–88. On polluting the water, see "Color Line Drawn at Bathing Beach," *CD*, August 28, 1915. On white ruffians, see "Aldermen Have Protection Placed to Preserve Order at Beaches," *CD*, July 27, 1918.

9. Chicago Commission on Race Relations, *Negro in Chicago*, 277.

10. For quote on Beutner, see ibid., 277. On attendance, see ibid., 275, fig. XVII. On dunking, see "Color Line Drawn at Bathing Beach," *CD*, August 28, 1915. For quote from aldermen, see "Aldermen Have Protection Placed to Preserve Order at Beaches," *CD*, July 27, 1918. For police, see Chicago Commission on Race Relations, *Negro in Chicago*, 277–78. For attempted rape, see "Race Girls."

11. Philpott, *Slum and the Ghetto*, 307.

12. For quote on nature, see A. Wilberforce Williams, "Dr. A. Wilberforce Williams Talks on Preventative Measures, First Aid Remedies, Hygienic and Sanitation," *CD*, July 25, 1914. On conserved health and energy, see Williams's column of the same name, *CD*, May 27, 1916. Over the years, Williams frequently used his column to address the health-giving and regenerative power of leisure in nature.

13. "Vacation Time," *CD*, May 3, 1913. On the West Michigan Resort, see Foster, "In the Face of Jim Crow."

14. "Keep Healthy," *CD*, August 2, 1913; "Spring," *CD*, May 16, 1914.

15. Attwell, "Playgrounds," 223. On the black middle-class reaction to vice and commercialized amusement, see James R. Grossman, *Land of Hope,* 123–60.

16. On the Sunday School League, see Washington Intercollegiate Club of Chicago, *The Negro in Chicago, 1779–1929* (Chicago: Washington Intercollegiate Club, 1929). On settlements and recreation, see Knupfer, *Toward a Tenderer Humanity,* 98–100; Spear, *Black Chicago,* 102–6; Hendricks, *Gender, Race, and Politics,* 57–58. On the Urban League and outdoor recreation, see Strickland, *History of the Chicago Urban League,* 17, 39. On recreation and the YMCA and YWCA, see Chicago Commission on Race Relations, *Negro in Chicago,* 147–48.

17. According to the Chicago Commission on Race Relations, the combined average daily attendance (during vacation time) of the one beach and the five playgrounds that saw predominantly black visitation was 4,050. See *Negro in Chicago,* 275, fig. XVII.

18. "Ruffianism in the Parks," *CD,* July 12, 1919. On the tension in Washington Park and Carter Playground, see Chicago Commission on Race Relations, *Negro in Chicago,* 289–90, 283.

19. On carrying weapons in picnic baskets during the Fourth of July, see Graham Taylor, "Chicago in the Nation's Race Strife," *Survey* 42 (August 9, 1919): 695. On the melee, see Tuttle, *Race Riot,* 5–6.

20. Chicago Commission on Race Relations, *Negro in Chicago,* 640–51.

21. Travis, *Autobiography,* 26.

22. Quotes from the director of Fuller Park and from Officer Callahan both appear in Chicago Commission on Race Relations, *Negro in Chicago,* 295. On Armour Square, see ibid.

23. On Spencer Castle, see "Chicago 'Lily-Whites' Open Fight on Oakwood Bathing Beach Site," *CD,* May 6, 1933; and "Hyde Park Astir Over Race Mixing at Beach," *CD,* May 20, 1933. For Artman quote, see "On Guard White Voters," flyer, Charles E. Merriam Papers, Box 103, Folder II, University of Chicago, quoted in Guglielmo, *White on Arrival,* 101. On the fence, see St. Clair Drake and Clayton, *Black Metropolis,* 103–6. For police quote, see "Police Object to Mixing of Race on Beach, Arrest 18," *CD,* July 14, 1934.

24. On Wells's efforts to get a park, see "Playground, Park Assured South Side," *CD,* May 23, 1925. The health survey results are reported in Charles S. Johnson, *Negro in American Civilization,* 306. For quote on sunshine, see "A Park for South Side," *CD,* February 5, 1927. For quote on moving colored life, see Bond, "Chicago Board," 211.

25. Harry Solomon, "An Adventure I Remember," Idlewild, Michigan History Division, Department of State, Lansing, Michigan, quoted in Wilson, "Idlewild," 37; W. E. B. DuBois, "Hopkinsville, Chicago, and Idlewild," *Crisis* 22, no. 4 (August 1921): 177, quoted in Foster, "In the Face of 'Jim Crow,'" 138.

26. For quote on hike to dunes, see "Boy Scout News," *CD,* November 7, 1925. On trip to Sturgeon Bay, see "YMCA News," *CD,* July 10, 1920. For quote on Hammond, Indiana, see "YWCA," *CD,* August 7, 1920. For quote on trip to Benton Harbor, see "Defender Newsboys to Get Free Vacation Trip," *CD,* July 7, 1934. According to the *Defender,* there were three hundred Camp Fire Girls in the Second Ward in 1934. See "Camp Fire Girls Set Big Event," *CD,* June 2, 1934. For more on the statistics on boys'

and girls' organizations, see Arthur J. Todd, William F. Byron, and Howard L. Vierow, *Chicago Recreation Survey,* vol. 3 (Chicago: Chicago Recreation Commission and Northwestern University, 1938), 77.

27. On this subject, numerous documents of the Chicago Area Project Papers, Research Center, Chicago Historical Society, Box 98, are useful. See, for example, "Forbid Them Not a Fair Chance in Life," file 1; C. H. Keller, "Southside Community Committee Sponsors Summer Camp Program," file 1; and Golden Darby, "1942 Summer Activities Report of Citizens Betterment League Sponsored by Southside Community Council," file 1.

28. On Farrell's work and the Irish American exodus, see Fanning and Skerrett, "James T. Farrell," 8, 80–91. For a photograph of Duke Ellington playing at the picnic in 1933, see Chicago Public Library, Harsh Research Collection, *Black History Month, 1930s,* at http://www.chipublib.org/002branches/woodson/afamhistmonth/1930s.html.

29. Drake and Clayton, *Black Metropolis,* 603.

Chapter 7: Women, Environmental Rationale, and Activism during the Progressive Era

Throughout the notes to this chapter, the abbreviation NACW will be used for Lillian Serece Williams, consulting editor, *Records of the National Association of Colored Women's Clubs, 1895–1992* (Bethesda, Maryland: University Publications of America, 1993), microform. Similarly, the abbreviation *NAN* will be used for *National Association Notes,* the newsletter of the NACW, found in the same collection.

1. Melosi, *Sanitary City,* 107.

2. Historians have argued over the nature and effect of the type of maternalist language used by women during this time period. See, for example, Merchant, "Women of the Progressive Conservation Movement"; Hoy, "'Municipal Housekeeping.'" Merchant sees Progressive women's involvement as primarily conservative in nature since the women failed to question their gender roles in society, but many women in the early conservation and preservation movement adopted decidedly radical tactics through their maternalism. While Hoy states that many women approached urban pollution reform as an extension of their domestic duties, some of the groups ventured farther and farther afield from initial municipal housekeeping responsibilities.

3. Certainly, the appellations for many of these stereotypes are recent constructions; but African Americans faced these images with or without the nomenclature, of course. See, for example, Blassingame, *Slave Community.* Blassingame's work was partially a response to Elkin, *Slavery.* Elkin asserted that the horrors of slavery reduced slaves to complete submissiveness.

4. Jezebel, the earlier of the two images, described black women as inherently sexual beings. The Mammy image, developed in the South partially as an antidote to the sexual image of Jezebel, justified the continuation of slavery. The Mammy was the large, motherly slave woman, who cared for white and black children alike with great generosity and kindness. See White, *Ar'n't I a Woman?* 27–61. Several other scholars have linked African American women's Progressive Era activism with efforts to

improve or destroy stereotypes. See, for example, Giddings, *When and Where I Enter;* Shaw, "Black Club Women."

5. "Names of the Clubs of the National Association of Colored Women," *NAN,* April 1890, 1.

6. C. M. Wells and M. L. Lenard, "Report of the Women's Uplifting Club of Eufala, Alabama," Minutes of the 1896 National Convention, NACW, 108.

7. Rosetta E. Lawson, "Colored Women in the Reform Movement," *NAN,* January 1899, 3; Giddings, *When and Where I Enter,* 95. Other sources cite different numbers. Richard Wormser, writing for "The Rise and Fall of Jim Crow" Web site about the NAACW at http://www.pbs.org/wnet/jimcrow/stories_org_nacw.html, states, "By 1916, the [NACW] had 300 clubs as members."

8. Rosetta Douglass-Sprague, "Opening Remarks," minutes of the 1895 NACW convention, NACW, 37.

9. Selina Butler, minutes of 1896 convention, NACW, 57.

10. Mrs. Overton Ellis, "The General Federation of Women's Clubs in Conservation Work," First Conservation Congress, 150, quoted in Merchant, "Women of the Progressive Conservation Movement," 74.

11. Lydia Adams-Williams, "Conservation—Women's Work," *Forestry and Irrigation* 14 (June 1908): 350–51, quoted in Merchant, "Women of the Progressive Conservation Movement," 65.

12. Addams, *Women and Public Housekeeping,* 1–2.

13. Wald, *House on Henry Street,* 165.

14. Mary Church Terrell, "The Bright Side," *NAN,* December 1899, 1–3.

15. NACW resolution, meeting minutes of 1895, NACW, 11.

16. Mary Church Terrell, "A Reply to Hannibal Thomas," *NAN,* May 1901, 3.

17. Rosetta E. Lawson, "Colored Women in the Reform Movement," *NAN,* January 1899, 3.

18. The NACW never referred to itself or its reforms as "environmentalist." I use the modern sense of the word here to specifically link and compare their activism to later reforms.

19. Interestingly, this reaction by black women during one of the darkest and most dangerous times of race relations seems similar to the attitude developed by whites during the late 1940s and 1950s, during the stressful times of the Cold War. See May, *Homeward Bound.*

20. "Home Influence Among the Colored People," *NAN,* May 15, 1897, 2.

21. Alice L. White, "Woman's Work—Where Does it Begin?" *NAN,* January 1900, 1.

22. M. S. Pearson, "The Home," *NAN,* January 1917, 11.

23. Resolutions, Minutes of the 1904 Convention, NACW, July 15, 1904, 25; White, "Woman's Work" 1.

24. "Do We Need Reformatories?" *NAN,* February 1900, 1.

25. "Chicago Women's Conference," Minutes of 1899 NACW Convention, NACW, 2.

26. "Do We Need Reformatories?" 1.

27. H. G. Miller, "Helpless Females—Traps Laid for them in the Great City Pointed Out," *NAN*, March 1899.

28. *The Jeffersonian Cyclopedia: A Comprehensive Collection of the Views of Thomas Jefferson*, s.v., "Botany—Value of." Entry 930. From a letter to Thomas Cooper. The University of Virginia Library, Thomas Jefferson Digital Archives, http://etext.lib .virginia.edu/etcbin/foleydate-browse?id=1814.

29. Jefferson, *Notes on the State of Virginia*, 965.

30. "Do We Need Reformatories?" 1.

31. Emerson, *Nature*, 1472.

32. Ibid., 1473.

33. Thoreau, *Walden*, 640.

34. "Lend-a-Hand Circle of King's Daughters and Sons of Boston Report," *NAN*, September 1898, 1.

35. Louise Early Hawkins, "Report of the Lucy Thurman Union," minutes of the 1896 convention, NACW, July 20, 1896, 76–77.

36. The Fresh Air Movement began in the late nineteenth century as a way to promote healthier living conditions for lower-class children.

37. Cummings, "Report of Colored E.S. and F.A. Circles," *NAN*, June 1913, 15–16. In June 1912, through dedicated work, the African American women completed payments on the debt on the farm, burning the mortgage. Cummings considered this act particularly significant because slaves had worked the plantation since the early 1800s.

38. Addams, *Spirit of Youth*, 95; Addams, *Twenty Years*, 327.

39. Mrs. John Walker, *Fourth Conservation Congress*, 255, quoted in Merchant, "Women of the Progressive Conservation Movement," 75.

40. Wald, *House on Henry Street*, 71–72. One young girl, Annie, benefited greatly in Wald's eyes by exposure to the country. After a couple of weeks on a nearby farm, Annie and her siblings returned to the city, where "their joyousness and bubbling spirits attracted the attention of the onlookers." The closer she got to home, and farther from the country, the more subdued Annie became, until she immediately slipped into washing dishes upon arrival at the tenement (74–76).

41. Pearson, "Home," 11.

42. Without specifically mentioning race, Martin Melosi discusses the popularity of cleanup days in cities across the country in the late nineteenth and early twentieth centuries. Melosi doubts the efficacy of such efforts, however, stating: "too often, however, the cleanup campaigns were merely cosmetic exercises with few benefits other than good publicity for better sanitation practices." *Sanitary City*, 185–86.

43. Mattie Sykes, "Women's Work and Worth," minutes of the 1896 convention, 98, NACW.

44. *NAN*, August 1899, 3.

45. Dr. Mary F. Waring, "Clean Up," *NAN*, July 1913, 17 (emphasis in original).

46. Margaret Murray Washington, convention minutes of 1914, NACW, August 6, 1914, 35.

47. "Notes," *NAN,* March–April 1915, 11.

48. Christine Smith, "The Larger Life for Women," *NAN,* May–June 1915, 6–8.

49. Dr. Mary F. Waring, "Sanitation," *NAN,* April–May 1917, 8.

50. Lenora L. [illegible], "Notes," *NAN,* March 1899, 2.

51. Minutes of the National Association of Colored Women, Howard Chapel Congregational Church, Nashville, TN, September 15–18, 1897, NACW.

52. Laura Oliver, "Notes," *NAN,* November 1911, 7. Examination of the records of the California NACW may reveal more details about the activities of the Forestry Department.

53. For additional information on early environmental interaction and activism by women, see, for example, Norwood, *Made From This Earth;* Riley, *Women and Nature;* Kaufman, *National Parks;* Gottlieb, *Forcing the Spring;* Dunlap, *Saving American Wildlife.*

54. For examples of these attitudes and the quotations cited here, see Smith, "The Larger Life for Women"; Smith, "Home Influences Among the Colored People," *NAN,* May 15, 1897, 2; Miller, "Helpless Females"; Douglass-Sprague, "Opening Remarks"; Resolutions, minutes of the 1896 convention, NACW, 47; Wells and Lenard, "Report of the Women's Uplifting Club of Eufaula, Alabama"; "Report of the Department of Music," minutes of the 1904 convention, NACW, 12.

55. Golden Rule Club Report, minutes of the 1896 convention, NACW, 93.

56. Addams, *Twenty Years,* 99; 99–100; 281, 283.

Chapter 8: Nature and Blackness in Suburban Passage

1. All quotations in this chapter from Eugene and Bernice Burnett come from two interviews conducted by the author in the Burnetts' home in Wyandanch, NY: Eugene Burnett, March 19, 1999; and Eugene and Bernice Burnett, January 7, 2004. The following people were also interviewed by the author; their statements throughout the chapter come from these interviews: Mary Leftenant, March 30, 1999, North Amityville, NY; James Merrick, December 8, 1998, Central Islip, NY, interview by phone; McKinley Banks and Charles Ballenger, April 28, 1999, North Amityville, NY; Eugene Reed, May 17, 2003, Babylon, NY; Harold and Jane Kopchinsky, December 11, 1998, Wheatley Heights, NY; William Larrequi, July 27, 1999, North Amityville, NY.

2. See Hays, *Beauty, Health, and Permanence* and *Explorations in Environmental History.*

3. Wiese, "Other Suburbanites"; see also Clark, *Blacks in Suburbs;* and Schnore and Sharp, "Black Suburbanization, 1930–70."

4. As Richard White and others have shown, oral history enables many questions about the cultural making of experience into memory, which too resolutely "materialist" an environmental history often neglects. See White, *Remembering Ahanagran.*

5. For a critique of this inclination, see Sellers, "Thoreau's Body."

6. For a sketch of contemporary "antiracist" scientific notions of race, see Luca and Cavalli-Sforza, *Great Human Diasporas.* My relational approach to the notion of blackness has been shaped by "whiteness" scholarship such as that reviewed in Fishkin, "Interrogating Whiteness"; and Kolchin, "Whiteness Studies."

7. "Where the Goat Is King," *New York Times,* July 13, 1890, 14. For differing accounts of Harlem's "blackening," see Osofsky, *Harlem;* McKay, *Harlem;* and Frazier, "Negro Harlem."

8. Cited in City-Wide Citizens' Committee on Harlem, "Report of the Sub-Committee on Housing,"1942, Schomburg Center for Research in Black Culture, New York, NY.

9. McKay, *Harlem,* 132.

10. City-Wide Citizens Committee on Housing, "Report of the Sub-Committee on Housing," 3.

11. See Collins and Morgo, "Race and Homeownership."

12. See Wiese, "Other Suburbanites."

13. On the Romano firm, see "Ronek Park Group Adding 200 Homes," *New York Times,* October 14, 1951, 242.

14. "'Non-Racial' Colony of Houses at $7000 Will Open Tomorrow at North Amityville," *New York Times,* January 27, 1950, 48.

15. "140 Dwellings Sold," *New York Times,* January 31, 1950, 45; advertising flyer for Ronek Park, Burnett family papers, Wheatley Heights, NY.

16. On black difficulties with lenders, see: "Thirty Acres Sold in Hicksville, L.I. For Housing Group," *New York Times,* March 19, 1952, R1; "Non-White Housing," *House and Home,* April 1953, in part 5, reel 10, NAACP papers, Schomburg Center for Research in Black Culture, New York, NY.

17. Advertising flyer for Ronek Park.

18. "Town Urged to Clear Out Shanty Area," *Amityville Record,* May 21, 1953, 1.

19. "Statement of William J. Larrequi, Amityville, Long Island," in "Housing Constructed under VA and FHA Programs," *Hearings before the Subcommittee on Housing of the Committee on Banking and Currency; Housing of Representatives, 82nd Congress, Second Session* (Washington DC: GPO, 1952), 357–59.

20. By 1960, when the earliest figures are available but when oral testimony suggests many had left the area, only 5 percent of nonwhite male employees in the North Amityville tract had professional, technical, or managerial jobs, and only another 6 percent did clerical or sales work; almost all the rest held blue-collar positions. In the same year, 46 percent of nonwhite women over the age of fourteen in the North Amityville census tract held full-time jobs. See 1960 U.S. Census of Population and Housing, *Census Tracts: New York, N.Y.; Part 2, Outside New York City* (Washington DC: GPO, 1961), 201.

21. "Farmhouse Deeded to Civic Group," *Amityville Record,* August 27, 1953.

22. See Mary Ross, "Albany Avenue Notes," a column published regularly in the *Amityville Record* through the early 1950s.

23. "Amityville, NY Branch," part 26, reel 8, series B, "The Northeast, 1940–55"; also "Membership Drive NAACP Central Long Island Branch Progress Report (May 1957), "Central Long Island" folder, group 3, branch files, 1956–65, all in NAACP papers.

24. On Strachan's activities, see for instance, Strachan to Jones, August 11, 1955, part 5, reel 10, NAACP papers; Strachan to Jones, March 4, 1957, part 5A, reel 10,

NAACP papers. On other branch activities, see "Central Long Island" branch folders, in branch files, 1956–65, NAACP papers; Charles Howlett, "The Long Island Civil Rights Movement in the 1960's, Part Two: Schools and Housing," *Long Island Historical Journal* 9 (1997): 25–46; "School Board Hears 3 Tell Fears of Segregation Here," *Amityville Record,* May 20, 1954; "New School Plans Are Hit by NAACP," *Amityville Record,* April 22, 1954.

25. For instance, letter of Herbert Hill, February 11, 1958, reel 18; statement of Herbert Hill, September 4, 1957, reel 19, both in part 22, legal department administrative files, NAACP papers.

26. Town of Babylon, *Master Plan Summary* (Massapequa: Sanders and Thomas, 1970), 38–40.

27. White, *Remembering Ahanagran,* 4.

Chapter 9: Environmental Justice, Ecoracism, and Environmental History

Portions of this essay were derived from some of my earlier studies, including *Coping with Abundance,* 296–97; "Public History and the Environment," 11–13; "Equity, Eco-Racism," 47–75. See also Melosi, "Environmental Justice, Political Agenda Setting," 238–62, 307–13; Foreman and Melosi, "Environmental Justice: Policy Challenges," 227–50.

1. Szasz, *Ecopopulism,* 5. The 1987 Women in Toxics Organizing conference, held in Arlington, Virginia, played an important part in promoting the central role of women in the antitoxics efforts. See Szasz, 90, 150–53; Gottlieb, *Forcing the Spring,* 203, 207–12.

2. Gibbs, "Celebrating Ten Years," 2.

3. Bullard, *Confronting Environmental Racism,* 9.

4. Hamilton, "Coping," 63.

5. Bullard, *Dumping in Dixie,* xiii.

6. Bryant and Mohai, *Race and the Incidence,* 1–2.

7. Gottlieb, "Reconstructing Environmentalism," 16–17. A good example of the attempt to relate environmental justice issues with the work environment—in this case recycling—is Pellow, *Garbage Wars.*

8. Quoted in Grossman, "People of Color," 272.

9. The "Group of Ten" refers to the Sierra Club, National Wildlife Federation, Audubon Society, Environmental Defense Fund, Environmental Policy Institute/ Friends of the Earth, Greenpeace, and so forth.

10. Bryant and Mohai, *Race and the Incidence,* 6.

11. Quoted in Grossman, "Environmental Racism," 15.

12. Alston, *We Speak for Ourselves,* 3.

13. Davis, "Environmental Voting Record"; Bryant and Mohai, *Race and the Incidence,* 55–63; Truax, "Beyond White Environmentalism," 19, 27; "Do Environmentalists Care," 52.

14. Taylor, "Can the Environmental Movement," 38.

15. Taylor, "Blacks and the Environment," 175–98. Such indicators as monetary (e.g., donations to environmental causes), political (e.g., attendance at meetings),

legal (e.g., participating in litigation), educational (e.g., attending courses, workshops), nature (e.g., visits to national parks), wildlife (e.g., hunting or fishing), membership affiliation, and so forth may not unveil levels of black interest in environmental issues.

16. Lynch, "Garden and the Sea," 108–18.

17. Definitions vary to some degree, but generally "environmental racism" is regarded as an extension of traditional racism, can be intentional or unintentional, and suggests discrimination in policy making, enforcement of laws, and in targeting certain communities for polluting industries and waste-disposal sites. "Environmental equity" incorporates the idea of equal treatment and protection for all people under statutes, regulations, and practices without variation in the impacts relative to the majority population. "Environmental justice," broader in scope, emphasizes the *right* to safe and healthy living and working spaces for all people, and defines "environment" to include social, political, economic, and physical features.

18. The CRJ was founded in 1963 after the assassination of black activist Medgar Evers, church bombings in Birmingham, Alabama, and other anti–civil rights activities. Also note that prior to Chavis, others, such as Robert Bullard, had been exploring the issue of environmental racism since the late 1970s.

19. Quoted in Bullard, *Confronting Environmental Racism*, 3.

20. Bullard, *Unequal Protection*, xvi.

21. United States Environmental Protection Agency, *Environmental Justice Initiatives.*

22. Among others, Christopher Foreman has taken a hard look at the environmental justice movement, and while sympathetic, has questioned some of its premises and strategies. See Foreman, *Promise and Peril*. Vicki Been, associate professor of Law at New York University, has been most critical of the blanket claim of race as the key variable in siting toxic facilities. She has argued that studies showing a disproportionate number of waste facilities being sited in minority and poor communities tend to be based on the current socioeconomic makeup of those neighborhoods. This leaves open the possibility that "market forces drove down property values in these communities *after* the waste facilities were sited here, thereby attracting the poor and minorities, who are relegated to less desirable neighborhoods through housing discrimination and economic restraints." See Been, "Market Forces," 1386, 1406.

23. Schnaiberg, "Redistributive Goals," 214.

24. Gottlieb, *Forcing the Spring*, 235–40.

25. Koppes, "Efficiency, Equity, Esthetics," 251. 1 have argued elsewhere that "wise use" was not a tool for equity but a "happy compromise" for government officials who began to realize that they faced a potential contradiction in promoting economic growth, on one hand, and providing stewardship over the public lands, on the other. The wise use concept provided a middle ground to support sustained economic growth. In either case, however, efficiency, not equity or esthetics, dominated Progressive Era America and beyond. See Melosi, "Energy and Environment."

26. Hurley, *Environmental Inequalities*, xiii–iv.

27. Johnston, *Who Pays the Price?* 234–35.

Chapter 10: Identity Politics and Multiracial Coalitions in the Environmental Justice Movement

Throughout the notes to this chapter, the abbreviation WC will be used to stand for Warren County File, North Carolina Department of Environment and Natural Resources, Division of Waste Management, Solid Waste File Room, Raleigh, North Carolina. The following individuals were interviewed by the author, and their statements should be attributed to these interviews unless otherwise indicated: Mike Kelly, December 17, 2002; Patricia Backus, February 6, 2003; Massenburg Kearney, February 2, 2003; Deborah Ferruccio, February 6, 2003; Jim Warren, February 3, 2003.

1. Tesh and Williams, "Identity Politics," 286.

2. Merchant, "Shades of Darkness"; Taylor, "Blacks and the Environment."

3. Taylor, "Can the Environmental Movement," 44.

4. For a historical analysis of the initial phase, see McGurty, "From NIMBY to Civil Rights."

5. Stuart Leavenworth, "State Planning to Drain Water from Toxic Landfill," *Raleigh News & Observer,* May 15, 1993: A6.

6. Ken Ferruccio to Jonathan Howes, May 17, 1993, author's personal file.

7. Jonathan Howes to Ken Ferruccio, May 21, 1993, author's personal file.

8. Ibid.

9. John Humphrey, statement on status of PCB landfill, March 1994, WC, 2.

10. "Hunt to Citizens of Warren County," *Warren Record,* October 20, 1982, 1, 14.

11. Jonathan Howes, statement to Working Group, January 20, 1995, WC.

12. Sharron Rogers to Henry Lancaster, January 27, 1994, WC.

13. Eva Clayton to Jonathan Howes, April 6, 1995, WC.

14. Joel Hirschhorn to technical committee of the Joint Working Group, August 15, 1996, WC, 2.

15. Warren County Citizen Advisory Board Files, Warrenton, NC, 2-2.

16. Ibid., 2-3; 4-9.

17. Ibid., 4-12; 4-13

18. Patrick A. Barnes and Joel Hirschhorn, *PCB Landfill Site Investigation Report,* BFA Associates, Tallahassee, FL, September 1997, E1.

19. "The BCD process utilized non-incineration chemical reactions to detoxify the PCBs and dioxins/furans in the contaminated materials. Chlorine atoms are chemically removed from the PCB and dioxin/furan molecules and replaced with hydrogen, rendering them non-hazardous. Detoxified soils will be replaced on-site, covered and revegetated." Michael Kelly, "Status of PCB Landfill Detoxification Warren County, NC," May 26, 1998, WC.

20. "Governor Requests $15 Million to Detoxify PCB Landfill," North Carolina Department of Environment and Natural Resources, April 27, 1998, WC.

21. Ken Ferruccio to Working Group members, July 2, 1997, WC.

22. Mike Kelly to Deborah and Ken Ferruccio, February 5, 1999, WC.

23. Ken Ferruccio to Wayne McDevitt, June 15, 1999, WC, 2–3.

24. Ibid., 3.

25. Jim Warren to citizen members and science advisors of the Working Group, November 16, 1996, WC.

26. Patrick Barnes to Dollie Burwell, September 29, 1995, PCB Citizen Advisory Board files, Warrenton, NC.

27. Ken Ferruccio to Dollie Burwell, December 5, 1995, WC.

28. Ken Ferruccio to Working Group, December 26, 1995, WC.

29. Warren to citizen members and science advisors of the Working Group.

30. Kelly, interview.

31. Backus, interview.

32. Dollie Burwell and Henry Lancaster to Joel Hirschhorn, March 25, 1998, WC.

33. "Job Training Updates," *Community News Wire,* 1 (August 2002): 3.

34. Joel Hirschhorn to PCB Working Group, February 6, 1997, WC.

Chapter 11: Religion and African American Environmental Activism

Thanks to my colleagues Alwyn Barr and Benjamin Newcomb for reading and commenting on an early version of this essay. Thanks, too, to Dianne Glave for her eternal enthusiasm for this book, and to the audience and participants in the two panels where I presented earlier versions of this essay, "The African Diaspora and the Environment," (American Society for Environmental History, annual meeting, Tacoma, WA, March 15–19, 2000); and "Roundtable: *To Love the Wind and the Rain:* African American Environmental History" (American Society for Environmental History, annual meeting, Victoria, British Columbia, April 3, 2004).

1. Quoted in Gottlieb, *Forcing the Spring,* 5; Obituary, Dana Ann Alston, Public Welfare Foundation, http://www.ejrc.cau.edu/(s)heros.html.

2. Roszak, "Ecopsychology," 265, 273; Carl Anthony, "The Civil Rights Movement, and Expanding the Boundaries of Environmental Justice in the San Francisco Bay Area, 1960–1999," oral history conducted in 1999 by Carl Wilmsen, Regional Oral History Office, Bancroft Library, University of California, Berkeley, 2003, 59–63.

3. David Harvey has some thoughts on this point. See *Justice,* 117.

4. James Noel Smith, *Environmental Quality,* 37, 39.

5. Declaration of the United Nations Conference on the Human Environment, http://www.unep.org/Documents/Default.asp?DocumentID=97&ArticleID=1503. Thanks to Cecilia Wygant for bringing the declaration to my attention.

6. Quoted in Krauss, "Women of Color," 266.

7. A superb survey of the literature of this issue is in Taylor, "Blacks and the Environment." See also Mohai, "Black Environmentalism"; Baugh, "African Americans and the Environment"; Davis, "Environmental Voting Record."

8. "Benjamin F. Chavis," in Judith Graham, ed. *Current Biography Yearbook, 1994* (New York: H. W. Wilson, 1994), 101–4; Garland, "'Good Noise'"; Oliver, "Living on a Superfund Site," 109. A sociological study suggests that membership and activity in churches positively correlate with black environmentalism, but not with white environmentalism: Arp and Boeckelman, "Religiosity," 255–67.

9. Frederick Harris, *Something Within,* 40, 65–70.

10. Fowler quoted in Baer and Singer, *African American Religion,* x; Tucker quoted in Gibson, "Cora Tucker," 13; analysis quoted in Baer and Singer, 42; poll statistics in Beverly Hall Lawrence, *Reviving the Spirit,* 173.

11. DuBois, *Souls of Black Folk,* 144, quoted in Levine, *Black Culture,* 58. Michael A. Gomez investigates DuBois's "preacher-king" thesis in "Preacher Kings."

12. Paris, *Spirituality of African Peoples,* 58–60; Long, "Perspectives for a Study," 24–25; Lincoln and Mamiya, *Black Church,* 2–7; Baer and Singer, *African American Religion,* 56; Levine, *Black Culture,* 47; Blassingame, *Slave Community,* 131; Creel, *"Peculiar People,"* chap. 2 and part 4. For a good general source on African American religion, see Raboteau, *Fire in the Bones.* On African-Christian syncretism among black Baptists, see Sobel, *Trabelin' On.*

13. Paris, *Spirituality of African Peoples,* 34, 41; Levine, *Black Culture,* 38, 141; Creel, *"Peculiar People,"* 261, 298–302; Sanders, *Saints in Exile,* 11–12.

14. Paris, *Social Teaching,* xi; George, "Widening the Circle"; Lincoln and Mamiya, *Black Church,* 43–58, 121, 202–3, 210–11, 231; Baer and Singer, *African American Religion,* 30, 58–64; Carson, "Martin Luther King, Jr."; Hopkins, *Introducing Black Theology,* introduction; Harris, *Something Within,* 66; Powell, "Outspoken Activist Takes the National Stage," *Washington Post,* June 29, 2003, A1.

15. Swift, *Black Prophets;* Paris, *Black Pentecostalism,* chap. 6; Harris, *Something Within,* 182; Walsh, Warland, and Smith, *Don't Burn It Here,* 164.

16. Paris, *Spirituality of African Peoples,* 44–45, 57, 101, 111, 120–24; Raboteau, "African Americans, Exodus"; Raboteau, "Black Experience"; Long, "Perspectives for a Study," 29–30; Levine, *Black Culture,* 33, 50–51, 187–89; Blassingame, *Slave Community,* 33–34, 147–48.

17. Clifton Joseph Furness, "Communal Music Among Arabians and Negroes" *Musical Quarterly* 16 (1930): 49–51, quoted in Levine, *Black Culture,* 27, which contains other similar examples and more references. (The dialectical spellings are Furness's. I assume "sodger" is for "soldier.")

18. Blassingame, *Slave Community,* 133–47; Levine, *Black Culture,* 34–35, 38, 41–49.

19. Long, "Perspectives for a Study," 26; Sernett, *Bound for the Promised Land,* chap. 3.

20. Lee, "Toxic Waste and Race"; Pinn, *Black Church,* 85, 92; Garland, "'Good Noise'"; Oliver, "Living on a Superfund Site," 109; Cole and Foster, *From the Ground Up,* 49–50; Walsh, Warland, and Smith, *Don't Burn It Here,* 73.

21. Summit requests quoted in Pinn, *Black Church,* 86–88.

22. Ecologists Eugene and Howard T. Odum, raised Methodists in North Carolina, as well as biologist E. O. Wilson, a former Southern Baptist from Alabama, are notable exceptions. Interestingly in this context, the Odums' father, Howard W. Odum, was a sociologist opposed to segregation and racial injustice, whose 1909 dissertation was entitled, "Religious Folk-Songs of the Southern Negroes." On the Odums, see Craige, *Eugene Odum.* On Wilson, see Mark Stoll, "Edward O. Wilson." One should also note the presence of numerous small, local environmental groups focused on issues like strip mining, parks, and preservation, particularly in the Appalachian area and

Florida. While environmentalism is thus certainly not absent from the South, the region lags and has lagged behind the North and West.

23. See Stoll, *Protestantism, Capitalism, and Nature;* Stoll, "Green *versus* Green."

24. Fowler, *Greening of Protestant Thought,* 150–52.

25. Anthony, "Civil Rights Movement," 8–10. Anthony's mother is otherwise unusual: she came from the light-skinned elite of South Carolina ("high yellow" his family called them) and was Episcopalian.

Chapter 12: Politicized Memories in the Struggle for Miami's Virginia Key Beach

Throughout the notes to this chapter, the abbreviation ORL will be used for Special Collections, Otto Richter Library, University of Miami.

1. Kayden, *Privately Owned Public Space.* On civil rights for the homeless, see *Pottinger v. City of Miami,* No 88–2406-CIV, 1992. See also Kathy Glasgow, "Street Sweepers," *Miami New Times,* December 24, 1998.

2. See the op-ed piece by Elizabeth Plater-Zyberk and Gregory Bush, "Keep Bayfront for the Public," *Miami Herald,* November 4, 1996.

3. See, for example, "The Daily Aesthetic: Leisure and Recreation in a Southern City's Segregated Park System," University of Kentucky Geography Department. Available at http://www.uky.edu/Projects/TDA/welcome-tda.html.

4. Article 6 of the Miami-Dade Charter written by Dan Paul covers county and city parks for which the charter has been approved. This does not include parks in the city of Miami, which declined the referendum.

5. For highway impact in Overtown, see Mohl, "Race and Place," 100–58.

6. For contemporary articles on this tension, see: "White Chauffeurs Believed to Have Dynamited Hall," *Miami Daily Metropolis,* July 17, 1917, 1; "Rowdy Chauffeur Attacks Negro For Driving His Auto," *Weekly Miami Metropolis,* June 8, 1917, 1.

7. "What of That Park for Colored Town?" *Miami Metropolis,* August 1, 1919, 2.

8. "So-Called 'Blue Laws' Are Not Being Enforced," *Weekly Miami Metropolis,* May 10, 1920.

9. "Park Plan Held Up—No Funds," *Miami Herald,* December 27, 1956; Glenn Kirchhock, "Squabble Keeping Dixie Park Pool Dry," *Miami News,* June 16, 1957.

10. Enid Pinkney, oral history by Gregory Bush, Miami, Florida, June 24, 1999, ORL.

11. James Nimmo, oral history by Kip Vought, Miami, Florida, November 8, 1990, 199, ORL. On black police see Jacob Bernstein, "Black in Blue," *Miami New Times,* November 13, 1997.

12. Dade County Commission, *Resolution No 627, Book of Resolutions, Book 10,* pages 56–57, August 13, 1935.

13. Thomas Pancoast and Carl Fisher letters, Carl Fisher Collection, box 13, "Negroes" folder. Historical Museum of Southern Florida. Miami, Florida.

14. Juanita Greene, "Inter-Race Hotel, Hall Proposed," *Miami Herald,* February 25, 1961; John Connors, "Integrated Resort Rejected," *Miami Herald* February 28, 1961; "Private Projects in Key Opposed," *Miami Times,* April 20, 1962; City Manager Cesar

Odio, letter to Diana Gonzalez (director of the Department of Development), December 14, 1989.

15. For example, Susan Markley, letter to Jack Luft, December 5, 1994 (in author's possession); John Renfrow, letter to Nancy Brown, president, Friends of the Everglades, February 10, 1995, (in author's possession).

16. Carl Hiaasen, "'Revitalization' a Threat to Virginia Key," in *Kickass: Selected Columns of Carl Hiaasen* (Gainesville: University of Florida Press, 1999), 376–77.

17. "Public/Private Development Projects on City Land: An Estimated Timetable," City of Miami's Five Year Plan of Recovery, 1997, 25, 26; Donald Warshaw, letter to Guillermo Olmedillo, September 3, 1998; Merrit Stierheim, letter to Donald Warshaw, October 19, 1998.

18. Jacob Bernstein, "Who's Afraid of Virginia Key?" *Miami New Times,* March 4, 1999, 9.

19. Athalie Range, oral history by author, Miami, Florida, 1999, ORL.

20. Enid Pinkney quoted in Kirk Nielsen "A Historic Dip: Witnesses to the Segregated History of Virginia Beach Tell a Sorry but Inspiring Tale," *Miami New Times,* April 8, 1999.

21. Gayle Pollard, "Blacks Say They Always Braved Beach," *Miami Herald,* February 19, 1975, 4B.

22. Bea Hines, "A Deserted 'Old World' Beach," *Miami Herald,* February 22, 1975; Nielsen, "Historic Dip."

23. See also Shaila K. Dewan, "Civil Rights Battlegrounds Enter World of Tourism," *New York Times,* August 10, 2004, 1.

24. Dinizulu Gene Tinnie, oral history by Channell Rose, Miami, Florida, ORL.

25. Pinkney quoted in Nielsen, "A Historic Dip."

26. Dinizulu Gene Tinnie, "Virginia Key in Jeopardy," *Miami Times,* March 4, 1999, 1. Bernstein, "Who's Afraid of Virginia Key?"

27. UEL Resolution. "Future Enhancement of Virginia Key Park," February 22, 1999.

28. Jim Mullin, "Saviors of Virginia Key," *Miami New Times,* April 1, 1999.

29. Nielsen, "Historic Dip"; Teresa Mears, "Black Pearl," *San Francisco Chronicle,* September 6, 1999, A3; Rick Bragg, "Alliance Fights a Plan to Develop a Florida Getaway Born of Racism," *New York Times,* March 28, 1999.

30. Range, oral history.

31. "Park It on Virginia Key," *Miami Herald,* July 7, 1999, B1.

Chapter 13: Black Environmental Liberation Theology

1. For the foundations of black liberation theology, see: Cone, *Black Theology of Liberation,* 12; Hopkins, *Introducing Black Theology of Liberation,* 41. Cummings, *Common Journey,* suggests that black liberation theology and Latin American liberation theology emerged discretely and simultaneously in the late 1960s.

2. All verses cited in this chapter are from the New King James Version (NKJV).

3. Cone, "Whose Earth?"

4. "National Black Church Environmental and Economic Justice Summit," National Council of Churches of Christ in the USA, Prophetic Justice Unit, Washington DC, December 1–2, 1993, 51.

5. Hopkins, *Introducing Black Theology*, 4.

6. Martin Luther King Jr. "Letter from a Birmingham Jail," April 16, 1963, http://www.stanford.edu/group/King/frequentdocs/birmingham.pdf.

7. Lynn White Jr., "The Historical Roots," 1287.

8. For Western interpretations of biblical dominion, see: Mark Stoll, *Protestantism, Capitalism, and Nature*, ix and 6–7; Nash, *Rights of Nature*, 88.

9. Cone, "Whose Earth?"

10. Gottlieb, *Forcing the Spring*, 262.

11. Bullard, *Unequal Protection*, 3–4.

12. Leroy Bonner quoted in Cornell Christion, "The Memphis Sanitation Strike: Blood and Strife Brought Dignity for City Workers," *Commercial Memphis*, February 28, 1993, http://commercialappeal.com.

13. Martin Luther King Jr., "I've Been to the Mountaintop," April 3, 1968, http://www.stanford.edu/group/King/publications/speeches/I've_been_to_the_mountaintop.pdf.

14. Dixon, *Ride Out the Wilderness*, 1.

15. "National Black Church Environmental and Economic Justice Summit," 14.

16. Ibid., 15.

17. United Church of Christ, *Toxic Wastes*, x.

18. Buck Jones quoted in Martha Kendrick Cobb, "The Legacy of a Trio of Justice Seekers," United Church of Christ, *Witness for Justice*, May 20, 2002, http://www.ucc.org/justice/witness/wfj052002.htm.

19. "'Toxic Tour' Marks 15th Anniversary," *United Church News*, June 2002, http://www.ucc.org/ucnews/jun02/toxic.htm.

20. "National Black Church Environmental and Economic Justice Summit," 3.

21. "African American Denominational Leaders Pledge Their Support to the Struggle Against Environmental Racism," *AME Christian Recorder*, May 18, 1998, 11.

22. Taylor, "Can the Environmental Movement," 40.

23. Alexander Crummell, "Incidents of Hope for the Negro Race in America: A Thanksgiving Sermon, November 26th, 1895," Library of Congress, http://memory.loc.gov.

24. Davis, *Spearheads for Reform*.

SELECTED BIBLIOGRAPHY

This bibliography includes books and journal articles cited in the text, as well as titles that may be useful to interested readers as background information or extended scholarship on the issues contained in this volume. It is not meant to be an exhaustive list of titles in this field. Newspaper articles, interviews, and government and archival documents are not listed here but are cited in full in the chapter notes.

Adamson, Joni, Mei Mei Evans, and Rachel Stein, eds. *The Environmental Justice Reader: Politics, Poetics, and Pedagogy*. Tucson: University of Arizona Press, 2002.

Addams, Jane. *The Spirit of Youth and the City Streets*. New York: MacMillan Company, 1923.

———. *Twenty Years at Hull House*. New York: The Macmillan Company, 1911.

———. *Women and Public Housekeeping*. New York: National Woman Suffrage Publishing Company, n.d.

Aiken, Charles S. *The Cotton Plantation South Since the Civil War*. Baltimore: The Johns Hopkins University Press, 1998.

Anthony, Carl. "Why Blacks Should be Environmentalists." In Erickson, *Call to Action*, 199–213.

Aptheker, Herbert. "Maroons Within the Present Limits of the United States." *Journal of Negro History* 24 (1939): 167–84. Reprint, in *Maroon Societies: Rebel Slave Communities in the Americas*, ed. Richard Price, 151–67. Baltimore: The Johns Hopkins University Press, 1996.

Arp, William III, and Keith Boeckelman. "Religiosity: A Source of Black Environmentalism and Empowerment?" *Journal of Black Studies* 28, no. 2 (1997): 255–67.

Attwell, Ernest T. "Playgrounds for Colored America." *Park International* 1, no. 3 (November 1920): 223.

Avirett, James Battle. "Turpentining with Slaves in the 30's and 40's." In *Naval Stores: History, Production, Distribution and Consumption*, ed. Thomas Gamble, 25–27. Savannah: Review Publishing & Printing Company, 1921.

Baer, Hans A., and Merrill Singer. *African American Religion in the Twentieth Century: Varieties of Protest and Accommodation*. Knoxville: University of Tennessee Press, 1992.

Bailey, David Thomas. "A Divided Prism: Two Sources of Black Testimony on Slavery." *Journal of Southern History* 46, no. 3 (1980): 381–404.

Baker, Lindsay, and Julie P. Baker, eds. *The WPA Oklahoma Slave Narratives*. Norman: University of Oklahoma Press, 1996.

Barrett, James R. *Work and Community in the Jungle: Chicago's Packinghouse Workers, 1894–1922*. Urbana: University of Illinois Press, 1990.

Baugh, Joyce A. "African Americans and the Environment: A Review Essay." *Policy Studies Journal* 19, no. 2 (Spring 1991): 182–91.

Baxandall, Rosalyn, and Elizabeth Ewen. *Picture Windows: How the Suburbs Happened*. New York: Basic Books, 2000.

Been, Vicki. "Locally Undesirable Land Uses in Minority Neighborhoods: Disproportionate Siting or Marketing Dynamics?" *Yale Law Journal* (April 1994): 1386, 1406.

———. "Market Forces, Not Racist Practices, May Affect the Siting of Locally Undesirable Land Uses." In *Environmental Justice*, ed. Jonathan S. Petrikin, 38. San Diego: Greenhaven Press, 1995.

Bennett, Jennifer. *Lilies of the Hearth: The Relationship Between Women and Plants*. Camden East, Ontario: Camden House Publishers, 1991.

Berlin, Ira. *Generations of Captivity: A History of African-American Slaves*. Cambridge, MA: Harvard University Press, 2003.

Bernal, Martin. "Race in History." In *Global Convulsions: Race, Ethnicity, and Nationalism at the End of the Twentieth Century*, ed. Winston A. Van Horne, 75–92. New York: State University of New York Press, 1997.

Berry, Thomas. *The Dream of the Earth*. San Francisco: Sierra Club Books, 1990.

Berwanger, Eugene H. *The Frontier against Slavery: Western Anti-Negro Prejudice and the Slavery Extension Controversy*. Urbana: University of Illinois Press, 1967.

Blake, Nelson. *Land into Water, Water into Land: A History of Water Management in Florida*. Tallahassee: University Presses of Florida, 1980.

Blassingame, John W. *The Slave Community: Plantation Life in the Antebellum South*. New York: Oxford University Press, 1972.

———, ed. *Slave Testimony: Two Centuries of Letters, Speeches, Interviews, and Autobiographies*. Baton Rouge: Louisiana State University Press, 1977.

———. "Using the Testimony of Ex-Slaves: Approaches and Problems." *Journal of Southern History* 4, no. 5 (1975): 473–92.

Bliss, John C. and Warren A. Flick. "With a Saw and a Truck: Alabama Pulpwood Producers." *Forest and Conservation History* 38 (1994): 79–89.

Blum, Elizabeth D. "Pink and Green: A Comparative Study of Black and White Women's Environmental Activism in the Twentieth Century." PhD diss., University of Houston, 2000.

———. "Power, Danger, and Control: Slave Women's Perceptions of Wilderness in the Nineteenth Century." *Women's Studies* 31 (2002): 247–67.

Bond, Maxwell H. "The Chicago Board of Education, Playgrounds, and the Colored Child." *Playground* 20 (July 1926): 211.

Bontemps, Arna. *Five Black Lives: The Autobiographies of Venture Smith, James Mars, William Grimes, The Rev. G.W. Offley, and James L. Smith.* Middletown, CT: Wesleyan University Press, 1971.

Botkin, B. A., ed. *Lay My Burden Down: A Folk History of Slavery.* Athens: University of Georgia Press, 1989.

Bowen, Louise DeKoven. *The Colored People of Chicago: An Investigation Made for the Juvenile Protective Association.* Chicago: Press of Rogers and Hall, Co., 1913.

Bryant, Bunyan, ed. *Environmental Justice: Issues, Policies, and Solutions.* Washington DC: Island Press, 1995.

Bryant, Bunyan, and Paul Mohai, eds. *Race and the Incidence of Environmental Hazards: A Time for Discourse.* Boulder, CO: Westview Press, 1992.

Bryant, Pat. "Toxics and Racial Justice." *Social Policy* 20 (Summer 1989): 51.

Bullard, Robert D., ed. *Confronting Environmental Racism: Voices from the Grassroots.* Boston: South End Press, 1993.

———. *Dumping in Dixie: Race, Class, and Environmental Quality.* Boulder, CO: Westview Press, 1994.

———. "The Quest for Environmental Equity: Mobilizing the African-American Community for Social Change." *Society and Natural Resources* 3 (1990): 301–11.

———. "Race and Environmental Justice in the United States. *Yale Journal of International Law* 18 (1993): 325.

———, ed. *Unequal Protection : Environmental Justice and Communities of Color.* San Francisco: Sierra Club Books, 1994.

Butler, Carroll B. *Treasures of the Longleaf Pine: Naval Stores.* Shalimar, FL: Tarkel Publishing, 1998.

Buttel, Frederick H. and William L. Flinn. "Social Class and Mass Environmental Beliefs: A Reconsideration." *Environment and Behavior* 10 (1978): 433–50.

Camacho, David E., ed. *Environmental Injustices, Political Struggles: Race, Class, and the Environment.* Durham, NC: Duke University Press, 1998.

Camp, Stephanie M. H. "'I Could Not Stay There': Enslaved Women, Truancy and the Geography of Everyday Forms of Resistance in the Antebellum Plantation South." *Slavery and Abolition* 23 (December 2002): 1–20.

———. *Closer to Freedom: Enslaved Women and Everyday Resistance in the Plantation South.* Chapel Hill: University of North Carolina Press, 2004.

Campbell, John. "'My Constant Companion': Slaves and Their Dogs in the Antebellum South." In Hudson, *Working Toward Freedom.*

Campbell, Marie. *Folks Do Get Born.* 1946. Reprint, New York: Garland Publishers, 1984.

Campbell, Thomas Monroe. *The Movable School Goes to the Negro Farmer.* Tuskegee, AL: Tuskegee Institute Press, 1936.

Capek, Stella M. "The 'Environmental Justice' Frame: A Conceptual Discussion and an Application." *Social Problems* 40 (1993): 8.

Carney, Judith H. *Black Rice: The African Origins of Rice Cultivation in the Americas.* Cambridge, MA: Harvard University Press, 2001.

Caron, Judi Anne. "Environmental Perspectives of Blacks: Acceptance of the 'New Environmental Paradigm.'" *Journal of Environmental Education* 20, no. 3 (1989): 21–26.

Carson, Clayborne. "Martin Luther King, Jr., and the African-American Social Gospel." In Johnson, *African-American Christianity,* 159–77.

Carter, Luther. *The Florida Experience: Land and Water Policy in a Growth State.* Baltimore: Johns Hopkins University Press, 1974.

Cashin, Joan E. "Landscape and Memory in Antebellum Virginia." *Virginia Magazine of History and Biography* 102 (October 1994): 483.

Chiang, Tze I., W. H. Burrows, William C. Howard, and G. D. Woodard Jr. *A Study of the Problems and Potentials of the Gum Naval Stores Industry.* Atlanta: Georgia Institute of Technology, 1971.

Childs, Arney R. *Rice Planter and Sportsman: The Recollections of J. Motte Alston, 1821–1909.* Columbia: University of South Carolina Press, 1953.

Clark, Thomas. *Blacks in Suburbs; A National Perspective.* New Brunswick: Rutgers Center for Urban Policy Research, 1979.

Cleaver, Eldridge. *Eldridge Cleaver: Post-Prison Writings and Speeches.* New York: Random House, 1969.

Cole, Luke W., and Sheila R. Foster. *From the Ground Up: Environmental Racism and the Rise of the Environmental Justice Movement.* New York: New York University Press, 2001.

Collins, William J., and Robert A. Margo. "Race and Home-ownership: A Century-Long View." *Explorations in Economic History* 38 (2001): 68–92.

Cone, James H. *A Black Theology of Liberation.* Philadelphia: J. B. Lippincott Co., 1970.

———. "Whose Earth Is It Anyway?" *CrossCurrents* 50, no.1–2 (Spring/Summer 2000). http://www.crosscurrents.org/cone.htm.

Courlander, Harold. *A Treasury of Afro-American Folklore: The Oral Literature, Traditions, Recollections, Legends, Tales, Songs, Religious Beliefs, Customs, Sayings, and Humor of Peoples of African Descent in the Americas.* New York: Marlowe, 1996.

Cowdrey, Albert E. *This Land, This South: An Environmental History.* Lexington: University Press of Kentucky, 1983.

Craige, Betty Jean. *Eugene Odum: Ecosystem Ecologist & Environmentalist.* Athens: University of Georgia Press, 2001.

Creel, Margaret Washington. *"A Peculiar People": Slave Religion and Community-Culture Among the Gullahs.* New York: New York University Press, 1988.

Croker, Thomas C., Jr. "The Longleaf Pine Story." *Southern Lumberman* 239 (December 1979): 69–74.

Cronon, William. *Changes in the Land: Indians, Colonists, and the Ecology of New England.* New York: Hill and Wang, 2003.

———. "Modes of Prophecy and Production: Placing Nature in History." *Journal of American History* 76 (March 1990): 1128–29.

———. Nature's Metropolis: Chicago and the Great West. New York: W. W. Norton, 1991.

———. "The Trouble with Wilderness or, Getting Back to the Wrong Nature." In Cronon, *Uncommon Ground*, 69–90.

———, ed. *Uncommon Ground: Toward Reinventing Nature*. New York: W. W. Norton, 1995.

Crosby, Alfred. *Ecological Imperialism: The Biological Expansion of Europe, 900–1900*. New York: Cambridge University Press, 1986.

Cummings, George C. L. *A Common Journey: Black Theology (USA) and Latin American Liberation Theology*. Maryknoll, NY: Orbis Books, 1993.

Daniel, Pete. *Breaking the Land: The Transformation of Cotton, Tobacco, and Rice Cultures Since 1880*. Urbana: University of Illinois Press, 1985.

Davis, Allen Freeman. *Spearheads for Reform: The Social Settlements and the Progressive Movement, 1890–1914*. New York: Oxford University Press, 1967.

Davis, Henry Vance. "The Environmental Voting Record of the Congressional Black Caucus." In Bryant and Mohai, *Race and the Incidence*, 55–63.

Davis, Jack E. "'Conservation is Now a Dead Word': Marjorie Stoneman Douglas and the Transformation of American Environmentalism." *Environmental History* 8 (January 2003): 53–76.

DiChiro, Giovanna. "Nature as Community: The Convergence of Environmental and Social Justice." In Cronon, *Uncommon Ground*, 303.

Din, Gilbert C. *Spaniards, Planters, and Slaves: The Spanish Regulation of Slavery in Louisiana, 1763–1803*. College Station: Texas A&M University Press, 1999.

Dixon, Melvin. *Ride Out the Wilderness: Geography and Identity in Afro-American Literature*. Urbana: University of Illinois Press, 1987.

"Do Environmentalists Care about Poor People?" *U.S. News and World Report* 96 (April 2, 1984): 52.

Dobson, Andrew. *Justice and the Environment: Conceptions of Environmental Sustainability and Theories of Distributive Justice*. New York: Oxford University Press, 1998.

Drake, St. Clair, and Horace Clayton. *Black Metropolis: A Study of Negro Life in a Northern City*. New York: Harcourt, Brace and Company, 1945.

Drew, Benjamin. *A North Side View of Slavery*. New York: Negro Universities Press, 1968.

Drobney, Jeffrey A. "Where Palm and Pine are Blowing: Convict Labor in the North Florida Turpentine Industry, 1877–1923." *Florida Historical Quarterly* 72 (1994): 411–34.

DuBois, W. E. B. *The Souls of Black Folk*. New York: Bantam Books, 1989.

Dunbar, Barrington. "Factors in Cultural Backgrounds of the British West Indian Negro." Master's thesis, Columbia University, 1936.

Dunlap, Thomas. *Saving America's Wildlife: Ecology and the American Mind, 1850–1990*. Princeton: Princeton University Press, 1988.

Dunn, Marvin. *Black Miami in the Twentieth Century*. Gainesville: University of Florida Press, 1998.

Elkin, Stanley. *Slavery: A Problem in American Institutional and Intellectual Life*, rev. 3rd ed. Chicago: University of Chicago Press, 1976.

Elliott, William. *Carolina Sports By Land and Water: Including Incidents of Devil-Fishing, Wild-Cat, Deer and Bear Hunting, etc.* New York: Derby and Jackson, 1859.

Emerson, Ralph Waldo. *Nature.* In *The Heath Anthology of American Literature.* Vol. 1, ed. Paul Lauter. Lexington, MA: D. C. Heath and Company, 1990.

"End of an Era: Georgia's Turpentine Industry Fades into History." *Georgia Forestry* (Spring 2003): 4–7.

Erickson, Brad, ed. *Call to Action: Handbook for Ecology, Peace and Justice.* San Francisco: Sierra Club Books, 1990.

Fanning, Charles, and Ellen Skerrett. "James T. Farrell and Washington Park: The Novel as Social History." *Chicago History* 8, no 2 (1979): 80–91.

Faust, Drew Gilpin. "Culture, Conflict, and Community: The Meaning of Power on an Ante-Bellum Plantation." *Journal of Social History* 14 (Fall 1980): 93–94.

Fett, Sharla M. *Working Cures: Healing, Health, and Power on Southern Slave Plantations.* Chapel Hill: University of North Carolina Press, 2002.

Fields, Dorothy Jenkins. "Tracing Overtown's Vernacular Architecture." *The Journal of Propaganda and Decorative Art* 23 (1998): 323–32.

Findlay, James F. Jr. *Church People in the Struggle: The National Council of Churches and Black Freedom Movement, 1950–1970.* New York: Oxford University Press, 1993.

Fisher, Robert Colin. "Frontiers of Leisure: Nature, Memory, and Nationalism in American Parks, 1850–1930." PhD diss., University of California, Irvine, 1999.

Fishkin, Shelley Fisher. "Interrogating Whiteness, Complicating Blackness: Remapping American Culture." *American Quarterly* 47 (1995): 428–56.

Flanagan, Maureen A. "The City Profitable, the City Livable: Environmental Policy, Gender, and Power in Chicago in the 1910s." *Journal of Urban History* 22, no. 2 (January 1996):163–90.

———. "Gender and Urban Political Reform: The City Club and the Woman's City Club of Chicago in the Progressive Era." *American Historical Review* 95, no. 4 (October 1990): 1032–50.

Floyd, Myron F. "Getting Beyond Marginality and Ethnicity: The Challenge for Race and Ethnic Studies in Leisure Research." *Journal of Leisure Research* 30 (1998): 3–22.

Flynt, Wayne J. *Poor But Proud: Alabama's Poor Whites.* Tuscaloosa: University of Alabama Press, 1989.

Fogel, Robert William. *Without Consent or Contract: The Rise and Fall of American Slavery.* New York: W. W. Norton, 1989.

Foreman, Christopher H. *The Promise and Peril of Environmental Justice.* Washington DC: Brookings Institution Press, 1998.

———. "A Skeptic Scrutinizes Environmental Justice." *Brookings* 8 (Winter 1998): 5.

Foreman, Christopher H., and Martin V. Melosi. "Environmental Justice: Policy Challenges and Public History." In *Public History and the Environment,* ed. Martin V. Melosi and Philip V. Scarpino, 227–50. Malabar, FL: Krieger Pub. Co., 2004.

Foster, Mark S. "In the Face of 'Jim Crow': Prosperous Blacks and Vacations, Travel, and Outdoor Leisure, 1890–1945." *Journal of Negro History* 84, no. 2 (1999): 138–39.

Fowler, Robert Booth. *The Greening of Protestant Thought.* Chapel Hill: University of North Carolina Press, 1995.

Franklin, John Hope, and Loren Schweninger. *Runaway Slaves: Rebels on the Plantation.* New York: Oxford University Press, 1999.

Frazier, E. Franklin. "Negro Harlem: An Ecological Study." *American Journal of Sociology* (1936): 72–88.

Fulop, Timothy, and Albert J. Raboteau, eds. *African-American Religion: Interpretive Essays in History and Culture.* New York: Routledge, 1997.

Gandy, Matthew. *Concrete and Clay: Reworking Nature in New York City.* Cambridge, MA: MIT Press, 2002.

George, Carol V. R. "Widening the Circle: The Black Church and the Abolitionist Crusade, 1830–1860." In Fulop and Raboteau, *African-American Religion,* 153–73.

Georgia Writers' Project, Works Projects Administration. *Drums and Shadows: Survival Studies Among the Georgia Coastal Negroes.* Athens: University of Georgia Press, 1986.

Gibbs, Lois Marie. "Celebrating Ten Years of Triumph." *Everyone's Backyard* 11 (February 1993): 2.

Gibbs, Tyson, Kathleen Cargill, Leslie Sue Lieberman, and Elizabeth Reitz. "Nutrition in a Slave Plantation: An Anthropological Examination." *Medical Anthropology* 4 (Spring 1980): 175–262.

Gibson, W. E. "Cora Tucker: Organizing for a Better America." *Egg* 18, no. 2 (Summer 1988): 13.

Giddings, Paula. *When and Where I Enter: The Impact of Black Women on Sex and Race in America.* New York: William Morrow, 1984.

Gill, Joan Blank. *Key Biscayne.* Sarasota: Pineapple Press, 1996.

Gilmore, Glenda Elizabeth. *Gender and Jim Crow: Women and the Politics of White Supremacy in North Carolina, 1896–1920.* North Carolina: University of North Carolina Press, 1996.

Glave, Dianne D. "The African American Cooperative Extension Service: A Folk Tradition in Conservation and Nature Appreciation in the Early Twentieth Century." *International Journal of Africana Studies* 6, no. 1 (Fall 2000): 85–100.

———. "Fields and Gardens: An Environmental History of African American Farmers in the Progressive South." PhD diss., State University of New York at Stony Brook, 1998.

———. "'A Garden So Brilliant with Colors, So Original in its Design': Rural African American Women Gardening, Progressive Reform, and the Foundation of an African American Environmental Perspective." *Environmental History* 8, no. 3, (July 2003): 395–411.

———. "The Theological and Historical Roots of Environmental Justice Activism by the African American Church." *Griot: The Journal of Black Heritage* 25, no. 2 (Fall 2004).

Gomez, Michael A. "The Preacher Kings: W. E. B. DuBois Revisited." In *African Americans and the Bible: Sacred Texts and Social Textures,* ed. Vincent L. Wimbush, 501–13. New York: Continuum, 2000.

Gosse, Philip Henry. "Possum Hunting in Alabama." In *Hunting in the Old South: Original Narratives of the Hunters*, ed. Clarence Gohdes, 88. Baton Rouge: Louisiana State University Press, 1967.

Gottlieb, Robert. *Forcing the Spring: The Transformation of the American Environmental Movement*. Washington DC: Island Press, 1993.

———. "Reconstructing Environmentalism: Complex Movements, Diverse Roots." *Environmental History Review* 17 (Winter 1993): 16–17.

Gramann, James H. *Ethnicity, Race, and Outdoor Recreation: A Review of Trends, Policy, and Research*. Miscellaneous Paper R-96-1. Washington DC: U.S. Army Corps of Engineers, March 1996.

"The Grassroots Movement for Environmental Justice." *Everyone's Backyard* 11 (February 1993): 3.

Greensfelder, Claire, and Mike Roselle. "Grassroots Organizing for Everyone." In Erickson, *Call to Action*, 12–18.

Gregory, Steven. *Black Corona; Race and the Politics of Place in an Urban Community*. Princeton: Princeton University Press, 1998.

Grime, William. *Ethnobotany of the Black Americans*. Algmac, MI: Reference Publications, 1979.

Grossman, James R. *Land of Hope: Chicago, Black Southerners, and the Great Migration*. Chicago: University of Chicago Press, 1989.

Grossman, Karl. "Environmental Racism." *Crisis* 98 (April 1991): 15.

———. "From Toxic Racism to Environmental Justice." *E: The Environmental Magazine* 3 (May/June 1992): 30–32.

———. "The People of Color Environmental Summit." In Bullard, *Unequal Protection*, 272.

Grossman, Richard. "Creating Cultures of Resistance." In Erickson, *Call to Action*, 9.

Guglielmo, Thomas A. *White on Arrival: Italians, Race, Color, and Power in Chicago, 1890–1945*. New York: Oxford University Press, 2003.

Gugliotta, Angela. "Class, Gender, and Coal Smoke: Gender Ideology and Environmental Injustice in Pittsburgh, 1868–1914." *Environmental History* 5, no. 2 (April 2000): 165–93.

Gundaker, Grey. "African-American History, Cosmology, and the Moral Universe of Edward Houston's Yard." *Journal of Garden History* 14 (1994): 179–205.

———, ed. *Keep Your Head to the Sky: Interpreting African American Home Ground*. Charlottesville: University Press of Virginia, 1998.

Gundaker, Grey, and Judith McWillie. *No Hidden Space: The Spirit of African American Yard Work*. Knoxville: University of Tennessee Press, 2005.

Guthrie, Patricia. "Catching Sense: the Meaning of Plantation Membership Among Blacks on St. Helena Island, South Carolina." PhD diss., University of Rochester, 1977.

Gutman, Herbert G. *The Black Family in Slavery and Freedom, 1750–1925*. New York: Pantheon Books, 1976.

Hadsell, Heidi. "Eco-Justice and Liberation Theology: The Priority of Human Well-Being." In *After Nature's Revolt: Eco-Justice and Theology*, ed. Dieter T. Hessel, 79–88. Minneapolis: Fortress Press, 1992.

Hahn, Steven. "Hunting, Fishing and Foraging: Common Rights and Class Relations in the Postbellum South." *Radical History Review* 26 (October 1982): 36–64.

———. *A Nation Under Our Feet: Black Political Struggles in the Rural South from Slavery to the Great Migration.* Cambridge, MA: Harvard University Press, 2003.

Hall, Gwendolyn Midlo. *Africans in Colonial Louisiana: The Development of Afro-Creole Culture in the Eighteenth Century.* Baton Rouge: Louisiana State University Press, 1992.

Hamilton, Cynthia. "Coping with Industrial Exploitation." In Bullard, *Confronting Environmental Racism*, 63–75.

Harding, Sandra. *The "Racial" Economy of Science: Toward a Democratic Future.* Bloomington: Indiana University Press, 1993.

Harris, Frederick. *Something Within: Religion in African American Political Activism.* New York: Oxford University Press, 1999.

Harvey, David. *Justice, Nature & the Geography of Difference.* Cambridge, MA: Blackwell, 1996.

Hatley, Tom. "Tending Our Gardens." *Southern Changes* 6, no. 5 (July/August 1984): 18–24.

Hayden, Dolores. *The Power of Place: Urban Landscapes as Public History.* Cambridge, MA: MIT Press, 1995.

Hays, Samuel P. *Beauty, Health, and Permanence: Environmental Politics in the United States, 1955–1985.* New York: Cambridge University Press, 1987.

———. *Conservation and the Gospel of Efficiency.* New York: Cambridge University Press, 1959.

———, ed. *Explorations in Environmental History.* Pittsburgh: University of Pittsburgh Press, 1998.

Hendricks, Wanda. *Gender, Race, and Politics in the Midwest: Black Club Women in Illinois, Blacks in the Diaspora.* Bloomington: Indiana University Press, 1998.

Henry, H. M. *The Police Control of the Slave in South Carolina.* New York: Negro Universities Press, 1914.

Herman, Daniel Justin. *Hunting and the American Imagination.* Washington DC: Smithsonian Institution Press, 2001.

Hershey, Marjorie Randon, and David B. Hill. "Is Pollution 'A White Thing'?: Racial Differences in Preadults' Attitudes." *Public Opinion Quarterly* 41 (1978): 439–58.

Hiaasen, Carl. "'Revitalization' a Threat to Virginia Key." In *Kickass: Selected Columns of Carl Hiaasen*, ed. Diane Stevenson, 376–77. Gainesville: University Press of Florida, 1999.

Hinds, C., et al. "From the Front Lines of the Movement for Environmental Justice." *Social Policy* 22 (Spring 1992): 12.

Hird, John A. "Environmental Policy and Equity: The Case of Superfund." *Journal of Policy Analysis and Management* 12 (1993): 323–35.

Hodges, Allen W. "The History of Naval Stores: Bridge Between Settlement and Sustainability." Presentation for the 34th Annual SAF/SFRC Spring Symposium (April 2003).

Hopkins, Dwight N. *Introducing Black Theology of Liberation.* Maryknoll, NY: Orbis, 1999.

Hoy, Susan. "'Municipal Housekeeping:' The Role of Women in Improving Urban Sanitation Practices, 1880–1917." In *Pollution and Reform in American Cities, 1870–1930,* ed. Martin V. Melosi, 61. Austin: University of Texas Press, 1980.

Hudson, Larry E., Jr., ed. *Working Toward Freedom: Slave Society and Domestic Economy in the American South.* Rochester: University of Rochester Press, 1994.

Hurley, Andrew. *Environmental Inequalities: Class, Race, and Industrial Pollution in Gary, Indiana, 1945–1980.* Chapel Hill: University of North Carolina Press, 1995.

Hurston, Zora Neale. "The Gilded Six Bits." In *The Norton Anthology: African American Literature,* ed. Henry Louis Gates, Jr. and Nellie Y. McKay, 1011–19 New York: W. W. Norton, 1997.

Irvine, F. R. *West African Crops.* New York: Oxford University Press, 1969.

Jablonsky, Thomas. *Pride in the Jungle: Community and Everyday Life in Back of the Yards Chicago.* Baltimore: The Johns Hopkins University Press, 1993.

Jacoby, Karl. *Crimes Against Nature: Squatters, Poachers, Thieves and the Hidden History of American Conservation.* Berkeley: University of California Press, 2001.

———. "Slaves by Nature? Domestic Animals and Human Slaves." *Slavery and Abolition* 15 (April 1994): 89–99.

Jahoda, Gloria. *The Other Florida.* New York: Charles Scribner's Sons, 1967.

Jefferson, Thomas. *Notes on the State of Virginia.* In *The Heath Anthology of American Literature.* Vol. 1, ed. Paul Lauter, 965. Lexington, MA: D. C. Heath and Company, 1990.

Jenkins, Virginia. *The Lawn; A History of an American Obsession.* Washington DC: Smithsonian Press, 1994.

Jennings, Francis. *The Ambiguous Iroquois Empire: The Covenant Chain Confederation of Indian Tribes with English Colonies from Its Beginnings to the Lancaster Treaty of 1744.* New York : W. W. Norton, 1984.

Johnson, Cassandra, J. M. Bowker, John Bergstrom, and H. Ken Cordell. "Wilderness Values in America: Does Immigrant Status or Ethnicity Matter?" *Society and Natural Resources* 17 (2004): 611–28.

Johnson, Cassandra, Patrick M. Horan, and William Pepper. "Race, Rural Residence, and Wildland Visitation: Examining the Influence of Sociocultural Meaning." *Rural Sociology* 62 (1997): 89–110.

Johnson, Charles S. *The Negro in American Civilization: A Study of Negro Life and Race Relations in the Light of Social Research.* New York: Henry Holt and Company, 1930.

Johnson, James H., Jr., and Melvin L. Oliver. "Blacks and the Toxic Crisis." *The Western Journal of Black Studies* 13, no. 2 (Summer 1989): 72–78.

Johnson, Paul E. *African-American Christianity: Essays in History.* Berkeley: University of California Press, 1994.

Johnston, Barbara Rose, ed. *Who Pays the Price? The Sociocultural Context of Environmental Crisis*. Washington DC: Island Press, 1994.

Jones, Charles C., Jr. *Negro Myths from the Georgia Coast Told in the Vernacular*. New York: Houghton, Mifflin & Co., 1888.

Jones, Jacqueline. *Labor of Love, Labor of Sorrow : Black Women, Work, and the Family from Slavery to the Present*. New York: Basic Books, 1985.

Jones, Robert. "Black Concern for the Environment: Myth versus Reality." *Society and Natural Resources* 1, no. 3 (April–May 1998): 209–28.

Jones-Jackson, Patricia. *When Roots Die: Endangered Traditions on the Sea Islands*. Athens: University of Georgia Press, 1987.

Joyner, Charles W. "Soul Food and the Sambo Stereotype: Foodlore from the Slave Narrative Collection." *Keystone Folklore Quarterly* 16 (1971): 171–78.

Kaufman, Polly Welts. *National Parks and the Woman's Voice: A History*. Albuquerque: University of New Mexico Press, 1996.

Kayden, Gerald. *Privately Owned Public Space: The New York City Experience*. New York: John Wiley, 2000.

King, Wilma. "'Rais Your Children Up Rite': Parental Guidance and Child-Rearing Practices Among Slaves in the Nineteenth-Century South." In Hudson, *Working Toward Freedom*, 143–62.

Kiple, Kenneth F., and Virginia Himmelsteib King. *Another Dimension to the Black Diaspora: Diet, Disease, and Racism*. New York: Cambridge University Press, 1981.

Kirby, Jack Temple. *Poquosin: A Study of Rural Landscape and Society*. Chapel Hill: University of North Carolina Press, 1995.

Knupfer, Anne Meis. *Toward a Tenderer Humanity and A Nobler Womanhood: African-American Women's Clubs in Turn of the Century Chicago*. New York: New York University Press, 1996.

Kolchin, Peter. "Whiteness Studies: The New History of Race in America." *Journal of American History* 89 (2002):154–73.

Krauss, Celene. "Women of Color on the Front Line," In Bullard, *Confronting Environmental Racism*, 256–71.

Kreger, Janet. "Ecology and Black Student Opinion," *Journal of Environmental Education* 4 (Spring 1973): 30–34.

Kulik, Gary. "Dams, Fish and Farmers: Defense of Public Rights in Eighteenth Century Rhode Island." In *The Countryside in the Age of Capitalist Transformation: Essays in the Social History of Rural America*, ed. Steven Hahn and Johnathan Prude, 25–50. Chapel Hill: University of North Carolina Press, 1985.

Lauriault, Robert N. "From Can't to Can't: The North Florida Turpentine Camp, 1900–1950." *Florida Historical Quarterly* (1989): 310–28.

Lawrence, Beverly Hall. *Reviving the Spirit: A Generation of African Americans Goes Home to Church*. New York: Grove Press, 1996.

Lee, Charles. "Toxic Waste and Race in the United States." In Bryant and Mohai, *Race and the Incidence*, 10–27.

Leibhardt, Barbara. "Interpretation and Causal Analysis: Theories in Environmental History." *Environmental Review* 12 (Spring 1988): 23–24.

Lemaistre, Elise Eugenia. "In Search of a Garden: African Americans and the Land in Piedmont Georgia." AB thesis, Princeton University, 1981.

Lemke-Santangelo, Gretchen. *Abiding Courage: African American Migrant Women and the East Bay Community*. Chapel Hill: University of North Carolina Press, 1996.

Lester, James P., David W. Allen, and Kelly M. Hill. *Environmental Injustice in the United States: Myths and Realities*. Boulder, CO: Westview Press, 2000.

Levine, Lawrence W. *Black Culture and Black Consciousness: Afro-American Folk Thought from Slavery to Freedom*. New York: Oxford University Press, 1977.

Leynes, Jennifer Brown, and David Cullison. *Biscayne National Park: Historic Resource Study*. Atlanta, GA: National Park Service, 1998.

Lincoln, C. Eric, and Lawrence H. Mamiya. *The Black Church in the African American Experience*. Durham, NC: Duke University Press, 1990.

Lippard, Lucy. *The Lure of the Local: Senses of Place in a Multicentered Society*. New York: New Press, 1997.

Liu, Feng. *Environmental Justice Analysis: Theories, Methods, and Practice*. Boca Raton, LA: Lewis Publishers, 2001.

Loguen, J. W. *The Reverend J. W. Loguen, as a Slave and as a Freeman: A Narrative of Real Life*. New York: Negro Universities Press, 1968.

Long, Charles J. "Perspectives for a Study of African-American Religion in the United States." 1971. Reprinted in Fulop and Raboteau, *African-American Religion*, 24–25.

Luca, Luigi, and Francesco Cavalli-Sforza. *The Great Human Diasporas: The History of Diversity and Evolution*. Translated by Sarah Thorne. Reading: Addison Wesley, 1995.

Lynch, Barbara Deutsch. "The Garden and the Sea: U.S. Latino Environmental Discourse and Mainstream Environmentalism." *Social Problems* 40 (February 1993): 108–18.

Margolick, David. *Strange Fruit: the Biography of a Song*. New York: Ecco Press, 2001.

Marks, Stuart A. *Southern Hunting in Black and White: Nature, History, and Ritual in a Carolina Community*. Princeton: Princeton University Press, 1991.

May, Elaine Tyler. *Homeward Bound: American Families in the Cold War Era*. New York: Basic Books, 1988.

Mayor, Archer H. *Southern Timberman*. Athens: The University of Georgia Press, 1988.

McCarthy, Michael P. "Politics and the Parks: Chicago Businessmen and the Recreation Movement." *Journal of the Illinois State Historical Society* 65 (Summer 1972): 158–72.

McDaniel, Josh, and Vanessa Casanova. "Pines in Lines: Tree Planting, H2B Guest Workers, and Rural Poverty in Alabama." *Southern Rural Sociology*. Forthcoming.

McDonald, Roderick. The Economy and Material Culture of Slaves: Goods and Chattels on the Sugar Plantations of Jamaica and Louisiana. Baton Rouge: Louisiana State University Press, 1993.

McGurty, Eileen Maura. "From NIMBY to Civil Rights: The Origins of the Environmental Justice Movement." *Environmental History* 2, no. 3 (July 1997): 301–23.

McKay, Claude. *Harlem: Negro Metropolis*. New York: E. P. Dutton, 1940.

Mealy, Rosemari. "Charles Lee on Environmental Racism." In Alston, *We Speak for Ourselves*, 8.

Meeker, Joseph W. "Red, White, and Black in the National Parks." In *On Interpretation: Sociology for Interpreters of Natural Resource and Cultural History*, ed. Gary E. Machlis and Donald R. Field, 195–205. Corvallis, Oregon State University Press, 1992.

Melosi, Martin V. "Battling Pollution in the Progressive Era." *Landscape* 26 (1982): 36–37.

———. *Coping with Abundance. Energy and Environment in Industrial America.* New York: Knopf, 1985.

———. "Energy and Environment in the United States: The Era of Fossil Fuels." *Environmental Review* 11 (Fall 1987): 167–68.

———. "Environmental Justice, Political Agenda Setting, and the Myths of History." In *Effluent America: Cities, Industry, Energy, and the Environment*, ed. Martin V. Melosi, 238–62. Pittsburgh: University of Pittsburgh Press, 2001.

———. "Equity, Eco-Racism and Environmental History." *Environmental History Review* 19, no. 3 (Fall 1995): 1–16.

———. "The Place of the City in Environmental History." *Environmental History Review* 17 (Spring 1993): 1–23.

———. "Public History and the Environment." *Public Historian* 15 (Fall 1993): 11–13.

———. *The Sanitary City : Urban Infrastructure in America from Colonial Times to the Present.* Baltimore, MD: The Johns Hopkins University Press, 2000.

Merchant, Carolyn, ed. *The Columbia Guide to American Environmental History.* New York: Columbia University Press, 2002.

———. "Shades of Darkness: Race and Environmental History." *Environmental History* 8, no. 3 (2003): 380–94.

———. "The Theoretical Structure of Ecological Revolutions." *Environmental History Review* 11 (1987): 265–84.

———. "Women of the Progressive Conservation Movement: 1900–1916." *Environmental Review* 8 (Spring 1984): 57–85.

Mohai, Paul. "Black Environmentalism." *Social Science Quarterly* 71 (1990): 744–65.

———. "Dispelling Old Myths: African American Concern for the Environment." *Environment* 45 (June 2003): 11–26.

Mohai, Paul, and Bunyan Bryant. "Environmental Racism: Reviewing the Evidence." In Bryant and Mohai, *Race and the Incidence* 163–76.

———. "Is There a 'Race' Effect on Concern for Environmental Quality?" *The Public Opinion Quarterly* 62 (1998): 475–75.

Mohl, Raymond. "Race and Place in the Modern City: Interstate 95 and the Black Community in Miami." In *Urban Policy in Twentieth Century America*, ed. Arnold Hirsch and Raymond Mohl, 100–158. New Brunswick: Rutgers University Press, 1993.

Moore, Stacy Gibbons. "'Established and Well Cultivated': Afro-American Foodways in Early Virginia." *Virginia Cavalcade* 39 (1989): 70–83.

Morgan, Philip. *Slave Counterpoint: Black Culture in the Eighteenth-Century Chesapeake and Lowcountry.* Chapel Hill: University of North Carolina Press, 1998.

Morrison, Toni. *Beloved.* NY: Plume, 1988.

———. *Love.* New York: Alfred A. Knopf, 2003.

Mowrey, Marc, and Tim Redmond. *Not in Our Backyard: The People and Events That Shaped America's Modern Environmental Movement.* New York: William Morrow and Co., 1993.

Myers, Robert Manson, ed. *The Children of Pride: Selected Letters of the Family of the Rev. Dr. Charles Colcock Jones from the Years 1860–1868.* New Haven: Yale University Press, 1984.

Nash, Roderick. *The Rights of Nature: A History of Environmental Ethics.* Madison: University of Wisconsin Press, 1989.

———. *Wilderness and the American Mind.* New Haven: Yale University Press, 1967.

Newton, David E. *Environmental Justice: A Reference Handbook.* Santa Barbara, CA: ABC-Clio, 1996.

Nijkamp, Peter. "Equity and Efficiency in Environmental Policy Analysis: Separability Versus Inseparability." In *Distributional Conflicts in Environmental-Resource Policy,* ed. Allan Schnaiberg, et al., 61–73. New York: St. Martin's Press, 1986.

Northup, Solomon. *Twelve Years a Slave.* Edited by Sue Eakin and Joseph Logsdon. Baton Rouge: Louisiana State University Press, 1968.

Norwood, Vera. *Made From This Earth: American Women and Nature.* Chapel Hill: University of North Carolina Press, 1993.

Oliver, Patsy Ruth. "Living on a Superfund Site in Texarkana." In Bullard, *Dumping in Dixie,* 77–91.

Olmsted, Frederick Law. *The Cotton Kingdom.* New York, Mason Brothers, 1861.

Opie, John. "Environmental History: Pitfalls and Opportunities." *Environmental Review* 7 (1983): 10.

———. *Nature's Nation: An Environmental History of the United States.* Fort Worth: Harcourt Brace College Publishing, 1998.

Orser, Charles E., Jr. *The Material Basis of the Postbellum Tenant Plantation: Historical Archaeology in the South Carolina Piedmont.* Athens: University of Georgia Press, 1988.

Osofsky, Gilbert. *Harlem; the Making of a Ghetto; Negro New York, 1890–1930.* New York: Harper & Row, 1966.

———, ed. *Puttin' On Ole Massa: The Slave Narratives of Henry Bibb, William Wells Brown, and Solomon Northup.* New York: Harper & Row, 1969.

Otto, John Solomon, and Augustus Marion Burns III. "Black Folks and Poor Buckras: Archeological Evidence of Slave and Overseer Living Conditions on an Antebellum Plantation." *Journal of Black Studies* 14, no. 2 (1983): 185–200.

Ownby, Ted. *Subduing Satan: Religion, Recreation and Manhood in the Rural South 1865–1920.* Chapel Hill: University of North Carolina Press, 1990.

Paehlke, Robert. *Environmentalism and the Future of Progressive Politics.* New Haven: Yale University Press, 1989.

Paris, Arthur E. *Black Pentecostalism: Southern Religion in an Urban World.* Amherst: University of Massachusetts Press, 1982.

Paris, Peter J. *The Social Teaching of the Black Churches.* Philadelphia: Fortress Press, 1985.

———. *The Spirituality of African Peoples: The Search for a Common Moral Discourse.* Minneapolis: Fortress Press, 1995.

Parker, Julia D., and Maureen H. McDonough. "Environmentalism of African Americans: An Analysis of the Subculture and Barriers Theories." *Environment and Behavior* 31 (1999): 155–77.

Pellow, David Naguib. *Garbage Wars: The Struggle for Environmental Justice in Chicago.* Cambridge, MA: MIT Press, 2002.

Penningroth, Dylan C. *The Claims of Kinfolk: African American Property and Community in the Nineteenth-Century South.* Chapel Hill: University of North Carolina Press, 2003.

Philpott, Thomas Lee. *The Slum and the Ghetto: Neighborhood Deterioration and Middle-Class Reform, Chicago, 1880–1930.* New York: Oxford University Press, 1978.

Pinn, Anthony B. *The Black Church in the Post-Civil Rights Era.* Maryknoll, NY: Orbis Books, 2002.

Porcher, Francis Peyre. *Resources of Southern Fields and Forests.* Charleston: Evans and Cogswell, 1863; repr. New York: Arno Press, 1970.

Proctor, Nicholas W. *Bathed in Blood: Hunting and Mastery in the Old South.* Charlottesville: University of Virginia Press, 2002.

Raboteau, Albert J. "African Americans, Exodus, and the American Israel." In Johnson, *African-American Christianity,* 1–17.

———. "The Black Experience in American Evangelicalism: The Meaning of Slavery." In Fulop and Raboteau, *African-American Religion,* 89–106.

———. *A Fire in the Bones: Reflections on African-American Religious History.* Boston: Beacon Press, 1995.

Rakestraw, Lawrence. "Conservation History: An Assessment." *Pacific Historical Review* 41 (1972): 276.

Rasmussen, Wayne D., ed. "Smith Lever Act, 1914." *Agriculture in the United States: A Documentary History,* vol. 1, 1384. New York: Random House, 1975.

Rawick, George P., ed. *The American Slave: A Composite Autobiography.* 12 vols. Westport, CT: Greenwood Press, 1972.

———. *From Sundown to Sunup: The Making of the Black Community.* Westport, CT: Greenwood Press, 1972.

Rhodes, Edwardo Lao. *Environmental Justice in America: A New Paradigm.* Bloomington: Indiana University Press, 2003.

Richter, Daniel K. *The Ordeal of the Longhouse: The Peoples of the Iroquois League in the Era of European Colonization.* Chapel Hill: University of North Carolina Press, 1992, Published for the Institute of Early American History and Culture, Williamsburg, VA.

Riley, Glenda. *Women and Nature: Saving the "Wild" West*. Lincoln: University of Nebraska Press, 1999.

Rivers, Jacob F. *Cultural Values in the Southern Sporting Narrative*. Columbia: University of South Carolina Press, 2002.

Romaine, Eldon Van. "Naval Stores, 1919–1939." *Naval Stores Review* 100 (1990): 6–16.

Roosevelt, Theodore. "The American Wilderness." In *The Great New Wilderness Debate*, ed. J. Baird Callicott and Michael P. Nelson, 63–74. Athens: University of Georgia Press, 1998.

———. *Wilderness Writings*. Ed. Paul Schullery. Salt Lake City: Peregrine Smith Books, 1986.

Rosenzweig, Roy, and Elizabeth Blackmar. *The Park and the People: A History of Central Park*. New York: Henry Holt and Company, 1992.

Roszak, Theodore. "Ecopsychology and the Deconstruction of Whiteness: An Interview with Carl Anthony." In *Ecopsychology: Restoring the Earth, Healing the Mind*, ed. Roszak et al. San Francisco: Sierra Club Books, 1995.

Rubin, Charles T. *The Green Crusade: Rethinking the Roots of Environmentalism*. New York: Free Press, 1994.

Russell, Dick. "Environmental Racism." *Amicus Journal* 11 (Spring 1989): 22–25.

Sanders, Cheryl J. *Saints in Exile: The Holiness-Pentecostal Experience in African American Religion and Culture*. New York: Oxford University Press, 1996.

Schelhas, John. "Race, Ethnicity, and Natural Resources in the United States: A Review." *Natural Resources Journal* 42 (2002): 723–63.

Schlosberg, David. *Environmental Justice and the New Pluralism: The Challenge of Difference for Environmentalism*. New York: Oxford University Press, 1999.

Schmitt, Peter J. *Back to Nature: The Arcadian Myth in Urban America*. Baltimore: The Johns Hopkins University Press, 1969.

Schnaiberg, Allan. "Redistributive Goals versus Distributive Politics: Social Equity Limits in Environmental and Appropriate Technology Movements." *Sociological Inquiry* 53 (Spring 1983): 214.

Schnore, Leo, Carolyn Andre, and Harry Sharp. "Black Suburbanization, 1930–70." In *The Changing Face of the Suburbs*, ed. Barry Schwartz, 69–94. Chicago: University of Chicago Press, 1976.

Schultz, Robert P. "The Original Slash Pine Forest—An Historical View." In *The Managed Slash Pine Ecosystem: Proceedings of a Symposium Held at the University of Florida, June 9–11, 1981*, ed. E. L. Stone, 24–47. Gainesville: School of Forest Resources and Conservation, University of Florida, 1983.

Scott, Roy V. *The Reluctant Farmer: The Rise of Agricultural Extension to 1914*. Urbana: University of Illinois Press, 1970.

Sellers, Christopher. "Thoreau's Body: Towards an Embodied Environmental History." *Environmental History* 4 (1999): 486–514.

Semmes, Clovis E. *Racism, Health, and Post-Industrialism: A Theory of African American Health*. Westport: CT: Praeger Publishers, 1996.

Sernett, Milton C. *Bound for the Promised Land: African American Religion and the Great Migration*. Durham, NC: Duke University Press, 1997.

Shackel, Paul A. *Memory in Black and White: Race, Commemoration, and the Post-Bellum Landscape*. Walnut Creek, CA: Rowman and Littlefield, 2003.

Shaw, Stephanie J. "Black Club Women and the Creation of the National Association of Colored Women." In *"We Specialize in the Wholly Impossible": A Reader in Black Women's History*, ed. Darlene Clark Hine, Wilma King, and Linda Reed, 433–42. Brooklyn, NY: Carlson Publishing, Inc., 1995.

Shofner, Jerrell H. "Forced Labor in the Florida Forests: 1880–1950." *Journal of Forest History* 25 (1981): 14–25.

Simmons, Charles. "Don't Dump on Us: The Environmental Justice Movement." In *Race and Resistance: African Americans in the Twenty-First Century*, ed. Herb Boyd, 43–52. Cambridge, MA: South End Press, 2002.

Sinclair, Upton. *The Jungle*. 1905. Reprint, New York: The New American Library of World Literature, Inc., 1980.

Singer, Brent A. "An Extension of Rawls' Theory of Justice to Environmental Ethics." *Environmental Ethics* 10 (Fall 1988): 217–31.

Singleton, Theresa A., ed. *The Archaeology of Slavery and Plantation Life*. Orlando, FL: Academic Press, 1985.

Smith, James Noel, ed. *Environmental Quality and Social Justice in Urban America*. Washington DC: The Conservation Foundation, 1974.

Smith, Susan L. *Sick and Tired of Being Sick and Tired: Black Women's Health Activism in America, 1890–1950*. Philadelphia: University of Pennsylvania Press, 1995.

Sobel, Mechal. *Trabelin' On: The Slave Journey to an Afro-Baptist Faith*. Westport, CT: Greenwood Press, 1979.

Social Science Institute, Fisk University. *Unwritten History of Slavery: Autobiographical Accounts of Negro Ex-Slaves*. Washington DC: Microcard Editions, 1968.

Spear, Allan H. *Black Chicago: The Making of a Negro Ghetto, 1890–1920*. Chicago: The University of Chicago Press, 1967.

Stein, Rachel. *New Perspectives on Environmental Justice: Gender, Sexuality, and Activism*. New Brunswick: Rutgers University Press, 2004.

Stewart, Mart A. *"What Nature Suffers to Groe": Life, Labor, and Landscape on the Georgia Coast, 1680–1920*. Athens: University of Georgia Press, 1996.

Stoll, Mark. "Edward O. Wilson: The Science of Religion and the Religion of Science." Paper presented, Science and Religion: The Religious Beliefs and Practices of Scientists: 20th Century, University of Göttingen, Germany, May 29, 2002.

———. "Green *versus* Green: Religions, Ethics, and the Bookchin-Foreman Debate." *Environmental History* 6 (July 2001): 412–27.

———. *Protestantism, Capitalism, and Nature in America*. Albuquerque: University of New Mexico Press, 1997.

Stoll, Steven. *Larding the Lean Earth: Soil and Society in Nineteenth-Century America*. New York: Hill and Wang, 2002.

Stradling, David. *Smokestacks and Progressives: Environmentalists, Engineers, and Air Quality in America, 1881–1951*. Baltimore: The Johns Hopkins University Press, 1999.

Strickland, Arvarh. *History of the Chicago Urban League*. Urbana: University of Illinois Press, 1966.

Stroud, Ellen. "Troubled Waters in Ecotopia: Environmental Racism in Portland, Oregon." *Radical History Review* 74 (1999): 65–95.

Swift, David E. *Black Prophets of Justice: Activist Clergy Before the Civil War.* Baton Rouge: Louisiana State University Press, 1989.

Szasz, Andrew. *Ecopopulism: Toxic Waste and the Movement for Environmental Justice.* Minneapolis: University of Minnesota Press, 1994.

Tarr, Joel A. "Urban History and Environmental History in the United States: Complementary and Overlapping Fields." In *Environmental Problems in European Cities in the 19th and 20th Century*, ed. Christoph Bernhardt, 25–39. Munich: Waxman, 2001.

Taylor, Alan. "Unnatural Inequalities: Social and Environmental Histories." *Environmental History* 1 (October 1996): 7.

Taylor, Dorceta E. "Blacks and the Environment: Toward an Explanation of the Concern and Action Gap Between Blacks and Whites." *Environment and Behavior* 21 (March 1989): 175–98.

———. "Can the Environmental Movement Attract and Maintain the Support of Minorities?" In Bryant and Mohai, *Race and the Incidence,* 28–54.

———. "Women of Color, Environmental Justice, and Ecofeminism." In *Ecofeminism: Women, Culture, Nature*, ed. Karen J. Warren, 38–58. Bloomington: Indiana University Press, 1997.

Tegeder, Michael David. *Prisoners of the Pines: Debt Peonage in the Southern Turpentine Industry.* PhD diss., University of Florida, 1996.

Tesh, Sylvia N., and Bruce A. Williams. "Identity Politics, Disinterested Politics and Environmental Justice." *Polity* 18, no. 3 (1996): 286.

Thoreau, Henry David. *Walden.* In *The Harper American Literature*, Compact Edition, ed. Donald McQuade, 640. New York: Harper & Row, 1987.

Tippens, William W., and Julia Sniderman. "The Planning and Design of Chicago's Neighborhood Parks." In *A Breath of Fresh Air: Chicago's Neighborhood Parks of the Progressive Reform Era, 1909–1925*, ed. Special Collections Department, Chicago Public Library, 21–28. Chicago: Chicago Public Library, 1989.

Tolany, Stewart, Kyle Crowder, and Robert Adelman. "'Narrow and Filthy Alleys of the City'?: The Residential Patterns of Black Southern Migrants to the North." *Social Forces* 78 (2000): 989–1015.

Tomes, Nancy. *The Gospel of Germs: Men, Women, and the Microbe in American Life.* Cambridge, MA: Harvard University Press, 1998.

Travis, Dempsey J. *An Autobiography of Black Chicago.* Chicago: Urban Research Press, 1981.

Trotter, Joe. "African Americans in the City: The Industrial Era, 1900–1960." *Journal of Urban History* 21 (1995): 438–57.

Truax, Hawley. "Beyond White Environmentalism: Minorities and the Environment." *Environmental Action* 21 (1990):19–31.

Turner, Frederick Jackson. *The Frontier in American History.* New York: Henry Holt and Company, 1953.

Tuttle, William M., Jr. *Race Riot: Chicago in the Red Summer of 1919.* New York: Atheneum, 1984.

United Church of Christ. *Toxic Wastes and Race in the United States: A National Report on the Racial and Socio-Economic Characteristics of Communities with Hazardous Waste Sites*. New York: Public Data Access, 1987.

United States Environmental Protection Agency. *Environmental Justice Initiatives, 1993*. Washington DC: EPA, February 1994.

Visgilio, Gerald R., and Diana M. Whitelaw. *Our Backyard: A Quest for Environmental Justice*. Lanham: Rowen and Littlefield Publishers, Inc., 2003.

Vlach, John Michael. *The Back of the Big House: The Architecture of Plantation Slavery*. Chapel Hill: University of North Carolina Press, 1993.

Wald, Lillian D. *The House on Henry Street*. New York: Henry Holt and Company, 1915.

Walker, Alice. *In Search of Our Mothers' Gardens: Womanist Prose*. San Diego: Harcourt Brace Jovanovich, 1983.

Walker, Thomas Calhoun. *The Honey-Pod Tree: The Life Story of Thomas Calhoun Walker*. New York: The John Day Co., 1958.

Walsh, Edward J., Rex Warland, and D. Clayton Smith. *Don't Burn It Here: Grassroots Challenges to Trash Incinerators*. University Park: Pennsylvania State University Press, 1997.

Washburne, Randel F. "Black Underpartcipation in Wildland Recreation: Alternative Explanations." *Leisure Sciences* 1 (1978): 175–89.

Washington, Sylvia Hood. *Packing Them In: An Archaeology of Environmental Racism in Chicago, 1865–1954*. Lanham: Lexington Books, 2005.

Watson, Harry L. "'The Common Rights of Mankind': Subsistence, Shad and Commerce in the Early Republican South." *Journal of American History* 83 (1996): 13–43.

Wenz, Peter S. *Environmental Justice*. Albany: State University of New York Press, 1988.

Westmacott, Richard. *African-American Gardens and Yards in the Rural South*. Knoxville: University of Tennessee Press, 1992.

———. "Pattern and Practice in Traditional African American Gardens in Rural Georgia." *Landscape Journal* 10 (Fall 1991): 86–104.

———. "Yards and Gardens of Rural African Americans as Vernacular Art." *Southern Quarterly* 32 (Summer 1994): 45–63.

White, Deborah Gray. *Ar'n't I a Woman: Female Slaves in the Plantation South*. New York: W. W. Norton, 1999.

White, Lynn, Jr. "The Historical Roots of Our Ecological Crisis." *Science* 155, no. 3767 (March 1967): 1287.

White, Richard. "'Are You an Environmentalist or Do You Work for a Living?': Work and Nature." In Cronon, *Uncommon Ground*, 171–85.

———. *Remembering Ahanagran; A History of Stories*. New York: Hill and Wang, 1999.

———. *The Roots of Dependency: Subsistence, Environment, and Social Change among the Choctaws, Pawnees and Navajos*. Lincoln: University of Nebraska Press, 1983.

Wiese, Andrew. "The Other Suburbanites: African American Suburbanization in the North before 1950." *Journal of American History* 85 (1999): 1495–524.

Wilson, Benjamin C. "Idlewild: A Black Eden in Michigan." *Michigan History* 65, no. 5 (1981): 37.

Wood, Betty. *Women's Work, Men's Work: The Informal Slave Economies of Lowcountry Georgia.* Athens: University of Georgia Press, 1995.

Worster, Donald. "Doing Environmental History." In *The Ends of the Earth,* ed. Donald Worster, 290–91. New York: Cambridge University Press, 1988.

———. *Nature's Economy: A History of Ecological Ideas.* 2nd edition. New York: Cambridge University Press, 1994.

———. *Rivers of Empire: Water, Aridity, and the Growth of the American West.* New York: Pantheon Books, 1985.

Worster, Donald, et al. "A Roundtable: Environmental History." *Journal of American History* 74, no. 4 (March 1990): 1087–147.

Wright, Gavin. *Old South, New South: Revolutions in the Southern Economy Since the Civil War.* New York: Basic Books, Inc., 1986.

Wright, Gay Goodman. *Turpentining: An Ethnohistorical Study of a Southern Industry and Way of Life.* Master's thesis, University of Georgia, 1979.

Yetman, Norman R., ed. *Voices from Slavery.* New York: Holt, Rinehart and Winston, 1970.

CONTRIBUTORS

CARL ANTHONY has recently been appointed acting director of the Community and Resource Development Unit at the Ford Foundation. At the same time, he continues to direct the foundation's Sustainable Metropolitan Communities Initiative and the Regional Equity Demonstration Initiative. Prior to joining the foundation he was a convenor and cochair of the Bay Area Alliance for Sustainable Development (BAASD). He founded and was, for twelve years, executive director of Urban Habitat. From 1991 through 1997, Anthony served as president of Earth Island Institute, and Congressman Ron Dellums appointed him chair and principal administrative officer of the East Bay Conversion and Reinvestment Commission in 1993. He has taught at the Columbia University Graduate School of Architecture and Planning and the University of California Colleges of Environmental Design and Natural Resources, and has been an advisor to the Stanford University Law School on issues of environmental justice. Anthony has a professional degree in architecture from Columbia University. In 1996, he was appointed fellow at the Institute of Politics, John F. Kennedy School of Government, Harvard University.

ELIZABETH D. BLUM received her PhD in American history at University of Houston; her dissertation was entitled "Pink and Green: A Comparative Study of Black and White Women's Environmental Activism in the Twentieth Century." Blum is assistant professor at Troy University. She has several publications, including an article in *Women's Studies*. Her book, *God, Gold and Family,* a gendered examination of activism at Love Canal, is currently under contract for publication.

GREGORY BUSH is the director of the Institute for Public History at the University of Miami. He is the author of the *Lord of Attention: Gerald Stanley Lee and the Crowd Metaphor in Industrializing America* (1991) and the coauthor of the award winning *Miami: The American Crossroad* (1991). He served as president of the Urban Environment League of Miami, started the city's park advisory board, and has initiated the Florida Public Space Project, which involves students studying and redesigning public parks in South Florida.

COLIN FISHER is assistant professor of history at the University of San Diego. He is currently working on a book that addresses the ways that European immigrants, African Americans, and industrial workers appropriated nature in and around early twentieth-century Chicago.

SCOTT GILTNER is an instructor at the University of Pittsburgh, where he teaches courses in United States history, the history of sports, and the history of the American South. His research interests include African American history, emancipation and Reconstruction, and southern environmental history. His dissertation is entitled "African American Hunting and Fishing in the Post-Emancipation South, 1865–1920."

DIANNE D. GLAVE is an Aron Senior Environmental Fellow with the Center for Bioenvironmental Research, Tulane University and Xavier University, in New Orleans, Louisiana. Glave has published in *Calaloo, African American Review, The Griot: The Journal of Black Heritage, Environmental History* and *The International Journal of Africana Studies*. A new book, *Fields, Gardens, and Woods: An Environmental History of Rural African American in the South, 1890–1930* is forthcoming.

CASSANDRA Y. JOHNSON is a research social scientist in recreation, wilderness, urban forest, and demographic trends research, United States Department of Agriculture–Forest Service in Athens, Georgia. Her current research is ethnic perceptions of natural environments; outdoor recreation behavior and preferences for minority groups, and her collaborative research is environmental justice and environmental sociology. Johnson has published a number of articles; the most recent appeared in *Environmental Ethics.*

JOSH MCDANIEL is assistant professor in the School of Forestry and Wildlife Sciences at Auburn University. He received his PhD in anthropology from the University of Florida. His research interests include cultural issues in natural resource management and historical ecology. McDaniel is currently working on book on the turpentine industry that explores labor organization, cultural history, race and ethnicity, and environmental impacts.

EILEEN M. MCGURTY is associate chair of the environmental sciences and policy graduate program at Johns Hopkins University. Her research focuses on environmental justice activism and waste-related policies. She has published widely on topics related to the connections between social disparity and environmental risk. McGurty is currently working on a book about Warren County and the development of the environmental justice movement in the United States.

MARTIN V. MELOSI, Distinguished University Professor of History and director of the Center for Public History at the University of Houston, is the author of ten influential books in urban history, environmental history, and diplomatic history. He is an international authority on pollution and urban technology, and has been a visiting professor at the University of Southern Denmark, the University of Paris, and the University of Helsinki. His books include *Effluent America* (2001), *Thomas A. Edison and the Modernization of America* (1990), *Coping with Abundance* (1985), *Garbage in the Cities* (1981, 2005), and *Pollution and Reform in American Cities* (1980). The National Endowment for the Humanities awarded him a major grant resulting in the award-winning book entitled *The Sanitary City* (2000).

CAROLYN MERCHANT is the Chancellor's Professor of Environmental History, Philosophy, and Ethics in the Department of Environmental Science, Policy, and Management at the University of California, Berkeley. She is the author of *The Death of Nature: Women, Ecology, and the Scientific Revolution* (1980); *Ecological Revolutions: Nature, Gender, and Science in New England* (1989); *Radical Ecology: The Search for a Livable World* (1992); *Earthcare: Women and the Environment* (1996); *The Columbia Guide to American Environmental History* (2002); and *Reinventing Eden: The Fate of Nature in Western Culture* (2003).

CHRISTOPHER SELLERS is associate professor of history at Stony Brook University. In 1992, he received a PhD in American studies from Yale, and an MD from the Medical School at the University of North Carolina at Chapel Hill. He is the author of *Hazards of the Job; From Industrial Disease to Environmental Health Science* (1997). He has written numerous articles and edited collections on environmental, medical, and general American history, and has received grants and awards from National Science Foundation, the National Library of Medicine, the Mellon Foundation, and the National Endowment for the Humanities among others. He is currently completing an "eco-cultural" history of post–World War II suburbanization in the United States.

MART A. STEWART is professor of history and affiliate professor at Huxley College of the Environment at Western Washington University and author of *"What Nature Suffers to Groe": Life, Labor, and Landscape on the Georgia Coast, 1680–1920* (1996; paperback 2003). He is currently working on a cultural history of climate in America.

MARK STOLL is associate professor in the history department and director of environmental studies at Texas Tech University. He is the author of *Protestantism, Capitalism, and Nature in America* (1997) and the editor of the World Environmental History series of seventeen books to be published beginning 2005.

INDEX

Adams, Louisa, 25
Adams-Williams, Lydia, 80
Addams, Jane, 80, 85–86, 90, 91
Africa, 44, 131, 155–56, 159–60
African American studies, 7–8
African Methodist Episcopal Church, 4,
    156, 196
African Methodist Episcopal Zion
    Church, 196
Agassiz, Louis, 173
agriculture: education in, 48–49;
    Progressivism and, 3, 37; slavery and,
    6, 10–11, 17–18. *See also* plants
Alexander, Charles, 33
Allensworth, Allen, 33
Alston, Dana A., 125, 150–51
Alston, J. Motte, 28
Alvord, J. W., 16–17
American Baptist Church, 162
American Society for Environmental
    History, 121, 131, 151
animals: prevention of cruelty to, 89;
    slave relations with, 13. *See also*
    hunting and fishing
Anthony, Carl, 151, 163
anthropocentrism, 123, 131
Artman, Joseph M., 73
Asian Pacific Environmental Network
    (APEN), 208
Askew, Reuben, 167
Association of Bay Area Governments,
    208
Attwell, Ernest, 70

Audubon Society. *See* National Audubon
    Society; Tropical Audubon Society
Avirett, James Battle, 23
Azusa Christian Community, 191

BAASC. *See* Bay Area Alliance for
    Sustainable Communities
Ball, Charles, 27, 28
Ballance, Frank, 142, 145
Banneker, Benjamin, 112
Baptist Church, 4, 157, 159
Barnes Ferland and Associates (BFA),
    145–46
Barnes, Patrick, x, 139, 141–42, 145–48
Bay Area Alliance for Sustainable
    Communities (BAASC), 208
Bay Area, California, 200–201, 206–8
Bay Area Council, 208
Bay Area Footprint Planning Process, 208
Bay Area Social Equity Caucus, 208
*Bean v. Southwestern Waste Management
    Corp.* (1979), 126
Berkeley, California, 200–201, 206–7
Berry, Thomas, 203, 209
Berwanger, Eugene, 52
Bethune, Mary McCleod, 157
Bibb, Henry, 25
Bill Sadowski Critical Wildlife Area, 174
Biscayne National Park, 186
Bizzell, Mrs. Bryan, 46
Black Archives Research and Study
    Center, Miami, 172

Hurston, Zora Neale, 44, 58, 61
hygiene. *See* health

identity politics: African American
    religion and, 159–60; environmental
    justice and, 133–35, 143–49
Idlewild, Michigan, 74
"In the Pines" (folksong), 51
insects, and disease, 87–88
interdisciplinary studies, 7–8

Jacks, John, 81
Jackson, Jesse, 154, 156
Jackson, John Andrew, 32
Jefferson, Thomas, 83–84
Jerzavitz, Benjamin, 99
Jesus People Against Pollution (JPAP),
    195
Johns Committee, 172
Johnson, Diane, 177
Johnson, Mrs. Roscoe, 46
Johnston, Barbara Rose, 131
Jones, Buck, 195–96
Jones, George, 30
Jones, Jacqueline, 39, 40, 45
Jones, William A., Jr., 157
Judson, Clyde, 185

Kayden, Gerald, 166
Kearney, Massenburg, 139, 148
Kelly, Mike, 142, 144
Kennedy, Stetson, 171
King, Martin Luther, Jr., 154, 157, 158,
    163, 164, 189, 192–94
King's Daughters and Sons, Boston, 85
Kopchinsky, Harold, 112–13, 116
Kopchinsky, Jane, 110
Koppes, Clayton, 130
Krupp, Frederick D., 124
Ku Klux Klan, 169, 171, 172

labor, in relation to land, 51–62
Ladson, Augustus, 34
Lancaster, Henry, 143–44, 146–47
Latinos, environmental concerns of, 125–
    26
Lawrence, Jacob, 7–8

Lee, Mary, 46
Lee, Nancy, 177, 178, 180, 183–85
Leftenant, Jimmy, 110
Lenard, M. L., 79
Lend-a-Hand Circle, King's Daughters
    and Sons, Boston, 85
Levitt and Sons, 100, 102–3, 110
Levitt, William, 103
Levittown, Long Island, New York, 100,
    103, 105–8
Lewis, J. Vance, 26
Loeb, Henry, 193
Logan, Onnie Lee, 46
Loguen, J. W., 30
Long Island, New York, 100–119
Louis, Joe, 76
Love Canal, 122–23
Lowery, Joseph, 126, 160, 194
Lucy Thurman Union, 85
Luft, Jack, 174
Lutheran churches, 162
Luzner, Jim, 174
Lynch, Barbara Deutsch, 125–26
lynching, 1

marginality theory, 220n2
marronage, 16
Marshall, Thurgood, 112
Mast Academy, 174
maternalism, 77–81, 88, 92, 224n2
McMaster, Jim, 177
Mears, Teresa, 184
medicine, 14–15
Meek, Carrie, 186
Meeropol, Abel (Lewis Allan), 1
memory. *See* collective memory
Memphis sanitation workers strike, 189,
    193–94
Merrick, James, 107, 109
Mesa, Blanca, 184
Methodists, 156–57
methodology: of African American
    studies, 7–8; applicable to environ-
    mental historiography, 7–8, 131;
    feminist, 4; use of WPA narratives,
    215n17

Vaux, Calvert, 67
Vesey revolt, 157
Vincent, Mrs. Clarence, 47
Virgin Islands, 96–98
Virginia Emergency Relief Administration, 1–2
Virginia Key, Florida, 164–67, 172–87
Virginia Key Park Beach Trust, 185–87
Voices from the Community (BAASC), 208
Voting Rights Act (1965), 191

Wald, Lillian, 80–81, 86
Walker, Alice, 4–5, 37, 50
Walker, Thomas Calhoun, 1–2
Ward Transformer Company, 194
Waring, Mary F., 87–89
Warner, Mrs. George, 90
Warren County, North Carolina, 126, 133–49, 160, 194
Warren, Jim, 145, 149
Warshaw, Donald, 175, 185
Washington, Booker T., 42, 81–82, 154, 157
Washington, Margaret Murray, 42, 81–82, 88
wastes. *See* toxic wastes
Weinreb, Bob, 168, 177, 180, 185
Weldon, Elsie, 145
Wells, C. M., 79
Wells-Barnett, Ida B., 4, 5, 73
West Africa, 10, 12
West Michigan Resort, 70
White, Alice, 82

White, Leon, 160
whites: and gardening, 2, 39; Protestant churches and environmentalism, 161–62; white supremacy, 205; women and Progressivism, 78–80, 81, 85–86, 90
Whitney, Eli, 10
Wiese, Andrew, 93, 102
Wilkins, Roy, 112
Williams, A. Wilberforce, 69
Williams, Charley, 24
Williams, Eugene, x, 64
womanism, 4–5
women: and conservation, 80–81; in environmental justice movement, 122; as gardeners, 37–50; and Progressive movement, 77–92. *See also* feminism; gender
Women's Uplifting Club, 79
Wood, Betty, 31
woods: African American experience of, 51–53; NACW and forestry work, 89–90; pulp and paper industry, 60–61; transcendentalist view of, 84–85; turpentine camps, 56–57; turpentiners' relationship to, 58–60
Woods, Alex, 23
Woods, Wes, 32
Works Progress Administration, 7, 171

Yad Vashem, Israel, 180
YMCA, 69, 71
Young, Annie, 34
YWCA, 69